Film Fatales

Independent Women Directors

Judith M. Redding and Victoria A. Brownworth

Seal Press

Seattle

Seal Press
3131 Western Avenue, Suite 410
Seattle, Washington 98121
sealprss@scn.org
www.sealpress.com

Library of Congress Cataloging-in-Publication Data
Redding, Judith M.
Film fatales : independent women directors / Judith M. Redding and Victoria A. Brownworth. Filmography: p. 281 Includes bibliographical references.
1. Women motion picture producers and directors. 2. Women motion picture producers and directors—Interviews. I. Brownworth, Victoria A. II. Title
PN1998.2.R43   1997   791.43'0233'082—dc21   97-29205
ISBN 1-878067-97-4

Printed in the United States of America
First printing, December 1997
10 9 8 7 6 5 4 3 2 1

Acknowledgments: Portions of some of these profiles have appeared in the following newspapers, magazines and periodicals: the *Philadelphia Inquirer,* the *Philadelphia Gay News,* the *Philadelphia City Paper, Philadelphia Magazine, Curve, The Advocate,* the *Front Page, Metroline, LN, Outweek, QW, Windy City Times* and *San Francisco Bay Times.*

Distributed to the trade by Publishers Group West
In Canada: Publishers Group West Canada, Toronto, Canada
In Europe and the U.K.: Airlift Book Company, London, England
In Australia: Banyan Tree Book Distributors, Kent Town, South Australia

Cover design by Patrick Barber
Cover photograph by Dennis Wise. Styling by Christine Foye. Model: Lindsay Heider.
Text design by Rebecca Engrav
Text composition by Rebecca Engrav and Laura Gronewold

For
Constance Stanley Kaminsky
and
Edmund L. Kaminsky

true patrons of the arts
who have supported our artistic
endeavors on both sides of the Atlantic
with love and patience

Acknowledgments

A small but essential group of people were invaluable in researching and completing this book. Our thanks go to Linda Blackaby, executive director of the Neighborhood Film/Video Project in Philadelphia and executive director of the Philadelphia Festival of World Cinema; Gretjen Clausing, media director of the Philadelphia Festival of World Cinema; Debra Zimmerman, executive director of Women Make Movies; Erika Vogt and the entire staff of Women Make Movies for their help in locating women directors and obtaining photographs and stills; Ada Gay Griffin, executive director of Third World Newsreel; Barbara Grier, publisher of Naiad Press, for her help in accessing filmmakers and videos; Constance Kaminsky and other staff at the Chester County Public Library in Exton, Pennsylvania; Zélie Polon and Rebecca Alber, editors at *Curve* magazine; Patti Tihey, editor of the *Philadelphia Gay News;* Diane DeKelb-Rittenhouse and Jennifer Goldenberg for typing transcripts; Elizabeth M. Brownworth for transcribing interviews; Midge Stocker, publisher of Third Side Press, Loralee MacPike, editor of *Lesbian Review of Books,* and Lee Boojamra and Alice Friel, publishers of Rising Tide Press, for offering us computers or parts of computers when ours crashed—this book could not have been completed without their generous help; James Baird, whose computer expertise makes the impossible possible; Art Carduner who transmitted his boundless love and incredible knowledge of film to Victoria in endless discussions at the Bandbox Cinema and in the film festival work he and Victoria did together; David Haas, coordinator of the Philadelphia Independent Film and Video Association, for arranging access to visiting filmmakers; Amalia Pistilli for film research in the United Kingdom; Tee A. Corinne for her fabulous photographs; Brenda L. Reed of the American Film Institute for research; Julie Dash for her theory on the role of minority characters in film and TV—what we have come to refer to in criticism and conversation as "the Dash theory"; Roberta L. Hacker and her annual search for quality film and video work by women, which led us to Allie Light; Shilpa Mehta for insights into Indian cinema and Indian women filmmakers; Jenni Olsen, the consummate film archivist; Ray Murray, the encyclopedic archivist; Lizzie Borden and Barbara Hammer, who have consistently supported our work on and in film and repeatedly encouraged us to do this book; Joan Poole for her generous support of this project; Dr. Beverly Shapiro, Dr. Tish Favens and Dr. Jonathon Gomberg; and to Ruthann Robson, Mabel Maney, Terri de la Peña, Judith Katz, Susan Raffo, Nikki Baker, Kathleen DeBold, Grace Caputo, Tina Rebane, Diane Pontius, Brenda L. Reed, Amalia Pistilli and Dina Jacobsen for their supportive friendship and discussions about film and the state of publishing.

We especially want to thank each of the directors who took the time to talk to us and be interviewed, sometimes several times, for this project. Their work and lives are inspirational—at a time lacking in inspiration. We also want to thank them for providing stills of their work and, when necessary, videotapes. Working with these women was always an interesting experience. Obviously, this book could not have been done without their generous spirits and thought-provoking work.

And finally, our deep thanks to our editors, Holly Morris and Jennie Goode, and our publisher, Faith Conlon, for agreeing to do this book and for their patience when computer disaster struck and deadlines were missed. Jennie was particularly helpful in the eleventh hour of this project when we most needed editorial assistance. Our thanks to our copyeditor, Cathy Johnson, and Ingrid Emerick, Rebecca Engrav, and the entire staff of Seal Press for their support of and encouragement for this project. We have enjoyed this, our second project with the Seals, and are terribly gratified by the press's commitment to women's work and ideas and to feminist publishing at a time when it remains far easier to capitulate to a more restrictive view of the world than to try to expand our knowledge of women's lives. These women provide books of invaluable import to women everywhere.

Contents

Introduction   3   The Female Lens

Ida Lupino   23   Hard, Fast and Beautiful

Documentary Film

Allie Light   37   Learning About Metaphors

Pratibha Parmar   45   Warrior Marks

Michelle Parkerson   58   I Just Do My Work

Catherine Saalfield   66   Art and Activism

Experimental Film

Barbara Hammer   73   Filling the Blank Screens

Su Friedrich   88   Damned If You Do

Trinh T. Minh-ha   94   Surname Viet Given Name Nam

Frances Negrón-Muntaner   99   The Politics of Identity, Part One

Michelle Mohabeer   103   The Politics of Identity, Part Two

Margaret Tait   109   Blue Black Permanent

Yvonne Welbon   112   Memory

Ayoka Chenzira   117   I Really Wanted It to Move

Sadie Benning   123   Teen with a Toy Camera

Narrative Film

Lizzie Borden   129   Let's Talk About Sex

Susan Seidelman   145   Independent Box Office

Mira Nair   158   Exiles, Expatriates, and Life on the Margins

Marleen Gorris   173   Uncompromisingly Feminist

Jane Campion   179   A Girl's Own Story

Allison Anders   185   Woman Alone

Julie Dash   190   Someone Always Says No

Patricia Rozema   203   I've Heard the Mermaids Singing

Lourdes Portillo   212   You Can Only Make a Good Film If You Look Inward

Zeinabu irene Davis   219   A Powerful Thang

Donna Deitch   225   Desert Hearts and Beyond

Radha Bharadwaj   231   Coming Out of Closet Land

Jan Oxenberg   239   Scowling Jan

Vijaya Mehta   245   Women, Work and Parallel Cinema

Marta Balletbò-Coll   253   Costa Brava

Beyond the Director's Chair

Debra Zimmerman   261   Women Make Movies

Christine Vachon   266   Poison, Swoon, Safe

Ada Gay Griffin   271   Third World Newsreel

Barbara Grier   276   Mail-Order Movie Mogul

Selected Filmography   281

Bibliography   291

About the Authors   293

Film Fatales

Introduction: The Female Lens

For lovers of visual imagery, film captivates in a way no other cultural medium can. Film expands and encapsulates experience, captures real life and explores the interiors of the mind. Film presents a vision, a perspective, a vantage point that only the director sees, but the audience is invited to engage that vision, to enter into a dialogue with the film (and, hence, the director) and offer, in response, their own corresponding vision of what they have seen on screen. Film proffers that ripple effect—the initial image that broadens into a multiplicity of images.

And those images are amazingly diverse—from the phantasmagoric nightmare presented in a surrealist classic like Luis Buñuel and Salvador Dali's *Un Chien Andalou* (who could forget the razor slicing across the eye?) to the emotional wrench of the one remembered love object, Rosebud, in the final frames of Orson Welles's *Citizen Kane* to the sensually sybaritic romping of Anita Ekberg in the Trevi Fountain in Federico Fellini's *La Dolce Vita* to the bleak despair of the owner of the stolen vehicle in Vittorio De Sica's *The Bicycle Thief* to the hideous scrambling for the exits to the gas chambers in Steven Spielberg's *Schindler's List*—these are all incomparable cinematic images, not merely memorable but culturally archetypal, visions imparted by directors with a pivotal story to tell, a tale they could not help but tell, but which, in the telling, sears our memories as indelibly as their own.

When we watch films, we experience the director's story as our own; we become the players, their tales—tragic, comic, desperate, revivifying, horrifying, hopeful—become, inextricably, our own. The power of the darkened theater is almost primeval; it lures us just as fire drew our ancestors. Within those velvet recesses are scenes we need to see, *must* see; when we enter a theater we are entering a cave in which all experience is transmogrified, in which we are drawn inexorably into the director's vision and incorporated, like Mia Farrow in Woody Allen's *The Purple Rose of Cairo*, into the film itself. In the best filmmaking, we are not passive viewers but complicitous actors; the film requires our involvement and engagement, the director demands we be magnetized by the images he or she presents.

That is the power of film. Those of us who love books, who constantly wonder at the complexities of language and ideas, know how fundamentally compelling words can be, how a complement of images can stick in the mind. The lines of a poem recited again and again; the couplet from a Shakespearean drama; the lyrics to a song; the description of a person or place from a novel—these words and the images they create resonate with us. But, alas for the writer, words can blur and dim with time, memory rends, the consanguinity of language falters; we are, undeniably, more overtly visual as humans, and our experience of written language is, fundamentally, interior. Words represent our interior selves (some would say our souls), but the visual encompasses interior *and* exterior, the text and the subtext of who we are and how we view the world—quite literally. We must draw on a great deal more of ourselves to register language and interpret it as part of our experience than we do to register a visual image; anyone with sight can call to mind the memory of a sunset or a blooming flower or a crying child, but far fewer of us can call to mind intepretations of those images in language.

So when we see a movie, the initial experience may be passive, as passive as the viewing of that sunset or flower or child. What the director does is take that image—the familiar image of a child's sled, the fearful image of a razor slicing across a woman's eye, or the terrifying image of people we have come to associate as ourselves and our families being herded into what we know is not a shower but a death chamber—and present it to us in a context that is the director's own but which, because of the tremendous power the visual has for us as humans, warps into our own context, our own experience. Why else would we want to run from a theater, our hearts pounding, from the fear engendered by what is high on the screen above us in any thriller from Alfred Hitchcock's *Psycho* to Wes Craven's *Scream*? Why else would our eyes fill with tears from the wrenching emotion drawn from the images in a romance or drama, from Victor Fleming's *Gone with the Wind* to David Lean's *Doctor Zhivago* to Anthony Minghella's *The English Patient*? Why else would we be infused with rage at the injustice we see in *Schindler's List*, suffused with laughter during Penny Marshall's *Big*, sickened by fascism and gore in Pier Paolo Pasolini's *Salo*, made hungry by the repast laid out by Stephane Audran in Gabriel Axel's *Babette's Feast?*

Emily Dickinson noted that "a book is like a frigate/to take us miles away"; a film can take us miles away or deep into our selves. When we see a film like *Schindler's List*, for example, or Pratibha Parmar's *Warrior Marks* or Lourdes Portillo's *Las Madres: The Mothers of Plaza de Mayo* or Radha Bharadwaj's *Closet Land* or Mira Nair's *Salaam Bombay!*, we ache for justice as if it were ourselves on that screen, even though we may not be, like the characters in those films, Jewish, African, Chilean or Indian; even though we may never have experienced violence or torture or even known someone who has. In searing the images of those experiences into our visual memory, the directors have inextricably connected us to their vision: We become those characters, those people; their experience and our own meld in the darkened theater, becoming a universal experience.

Filmmaking then is, inevitably, intensely political, a tool with which the director presents a vision so complete that the viewer is immersed. John Frankenheimer's *The Manchurian Candidate* and Stanley Kubrick's *A Clockwork Orange* present scenes in which film becomes a literal brainwashing technique. Leni Riefenstahl's *Olympia* and *Triumph of the Will* express, alternately, the beauty and physical perfection of the Aryan ideal fostered by Adolf Hitler and the implacable and monolithic power of the Third Reich. Her films explain how dynamic the visual image can be; Riefenstahl as filmmaker was a dangerous propagandist for Nazism. We view her films today through the revisionist scrim of historical context and with the antidote of other powerful films about the Nazi reign of terror like *Schindler's List*, Sidney Lumet's *The Pawnbroker*, Liliana Cavani's *The Night Porter* and *The Berlin Affair*, Claude Lanzmann's *Shoah* and Marcel Ophuls's *The Sorrow and the Pity*. We *know* about Nazism through history, but we can only imagine the impact Riefenstahl's vision of Hitler and the Third Reich had on audiences of the time, because her films are compelling, mesmerizing—even knowing what we now know about the Nazis. Film has such intense and provocative power, its visual impact manipulates our emotions so dramatically, we can be led to believe the truth of the film, rather than the truth itself. Riefenstahl was not the first filmmaker to prove that, and she won't be the last.

Film can also skew perspective while maintaining the essence of historical truth. Thus Richard Attenborough's *Cry Freedom*, ostensibly about

Introduction

5

apartheid in South Africa, focuses primarily on journalist Donald Woods and the white liberal experience and only tangentially on Steven Biko and the effects of apartheid on black South Africans. Alan Parker's *Mississippi Burning* portrays the black civil rights movement in America from an almost wholly white perspective, redefining the role of the FBI as one of savior, rather than subversive subterfuge undercutting the very goals of the movement. The essential historical truths are all there, but the perspective is vastly different because of the vantage point taken by the directors. Similar material in the hands of black filmmakers—Julie Dash's *Illusions*, Tim Reid's *Once Upon a Time . . . When We Were Colored* and John Singleton's *Rosewood*—has a very different emphasis, with black characters at the center of what remain, essentially, black historical events and experience.

Just as films by black directors redefine the cinematic perspective on black experience, in the United States and abroad, films by women definingly alter the cinematic vantage point we, as audience, are familiar with. Seeing the world through a female lens may make the film inalterably and obviously female in vantage point or may only subtly influence the film as a whole. Thus a movie like Penny Marshall's *Big* appears to have no specific features that define it as female; we can only presume that few men would focus on the issues and conflicts the film engages, that the male protagonist might get a far different reading from a male director. The films of Penelope Spheeris run the gamut, from films about women, like *Prison Stories: Women on the Inside*, to films about modern society, like *The Decline of Western Civilization* and *Suburbia*, which incorporate male and female protagonists, to films about teenage boys, like *Dudes* and *Wayne's World*. Critics can argue that her films, or films by action-filmmaker Kathryn Bigelow (*Blue Steel*, *Point Break*), aren't qualitatively different from similar films by men, that their lens has no distinctively female components.

But other films by women directors present a wholly and succinctly female vantage point, not only using female protagonists, as in Patricia Rozema's *I've Heard the Mermaids Singing*, in which men are utterly peripheral and barely appear in either the film or the consciousness of the film or its characters, but also addressing intensely female subjects, such as domestic violence in Lee Grant's groundbreaking film *Battered*.

The female lens can view cinematic ground previously seen as traditionally male from a perspective that alters the subject matter entirely. Lizzie Borden's *Working Girls* and Marleen Gorris's *Broken Mirrors* address a topic regularly presented by male directors—prostitution. These women directors open the lens onto a different element of this experience than has traditionally been made commonplace in the movies. Hence we see the tedious dailiness of the job in Borden's film and how that tedium wears away at the humanity of the women involved, or how, in the Gorris film, it might lead inexorably to violence. These images of women prostitutes are fictional, but in both narratives we see the life of the prostitute from *her* vantage point. What we *don't* see in these representations is the male gaze, the various permutations—often glamorized and romanticized by male fantasy—that have come to represent the reality of women's lives, even though they are fictional images. The image of the "whore with the heart of gold" that is the essence of films like Jules Dassin's classic *Never on Sunday* or Colin Higgins's *The Best Little Whorehouse in Texas* has come to represent prostitution; in male films prostitution is either a happy-go-lucky career choice, as it is in these films with singing prostitutes, or a dangerous job controlled by bad men—pimps—from which the otherwise "good" girl prostitute must be reclaimed in a Prince Charming–style denouement.

There is, then, an extraordinary difference between Louise Smith in Borden's *Working Girls* and Jane Fonda in Alan Pakula's *Klute*. Both women give finely rendered performances (Fonda won an Oscar for Best Actress for her role as the beleaguered prostitute), and each portrays the underlying vulnerability of the prostitute, but the significant difference in these representations lies in the way the viewer perceives the characters. Fonda's character is what men make her—she has no independence, no sense of self; she's a woman who cannot function without a man, whether that man is her pimp, her john or her savior in the form of detective Donald Sutherland; she is the quintessential (and utterly fictional) good girl gone bad, a male fantasy woman, the call girl redeemed by the love of a good man.

Smith's character is transgressive, but in an almost mundane way; a lesbian who lives with her African-American lover and their child, she is an artist who makes money as a call girl. She experiences different things with different johns, some of whom she actually likes or feels pity for, but she doesn't need them, she isn't dependent on them for her identity because she has an identity outside the claustrophobic space of the brothel. In *Klute* the call girl cannot escape what prostitution has brought to her life; her choices nearly kill her when she tries to leave. In *Working Girls* the call girl protagonist chooses to leave rather than lose her sense of self, even briefly; prostitution is her job, not her way of life.

The action in these films is decidedly different. *Working Girls* shows the unglamorous world of beds being stripped and sheets and towels being washed, sending a courier out for more condoms and lubricant, cleaning up between tricks in the bathroom. The set is interior, claustrophobic, like the job itself; the protagonist is outside only when she is going to or leaving her job—then and only then do we see her bright and sunny apartment, see her riding through the streets of New York on her bicycle, a bunch of flowers for her lover under her arm. *Klute* moves from interior to exterior shots, from the "gritty" world of heroin addicts, call girls and murder to the comfort and security of the detective's small apartment. Fonda's character always seems caged, despite her milieu, while Smith's character seems like any other worker watching the clock, waiting for the day to end, upset at the prospect of unwanted overtime, eager to get home to her family and "real" life. This succinctness of vantage point delineates what differentiates the work of women directors from that of men.

Why do women become independent directors? That question is answered in various ways by the women profiled in *Film Fatales*. But the pivotal reasons ultimately have to do with Hollywood, studio systems and the role women have played in cinema historically. As these profiles explain, often the issue isn't that women have chosen to be independent filmmakers so much as it is that their choices are limited by their gender, disallowing them access to studio systems and the financial support for filmmaking that those systems offer. How many women directors are there in Hollywood, Bombay, London, Rome, Berlin or any other city with a significant studio system? Few, very few. Some of the most important women filmmakers of the last three decades have been unable to make films within the studio systems of their own countries simply because of gender. Mira Nair, India's best-known director since Satyajit Ray, is but one example: Nair said she had to leave India in order to make her films because she had no access to funding for her films. The great German director Margarethe von Trotta (*Rosa Luxemburg*, *Sheer Madness*), one of the *auteurs* of the German New Wave in cinema, struggled for recognition separate from her husband, director Volker Schlörndorff (*The Tin Drum*), with whom she made her directorial debut, co-directing the award-winning *The Lost Honor of Katarina Blum*. Von Trotta, despite more than two decades of provocative and award-winning films made within the German studio system, has yet to achieve the same recognition as her male counterparts—Wim Wenders, Werner Herzog and Rainer Fassbinder.

Other examples of the double standard regarding women in the film industry include Lizzie Borden, whose film *Working Girls* won monumental acclaim as an independent smash at the Sundance, Berlin and other major film festivals three years prior to Steven Soderbergh's *sex, lies and videotape*, which was declared the "first" independent breakthrough film. Or Susan Seidelman, whose *Smithereens* was the first independent American feature to win at the Cannes International Film Festival—a feat also attributed to Soderbergh seven years later. The complication of being a female director is immense; one often begins as an independent because there is no entrée for women in the studios, but even major success as an independent can go unrecognized, making it more difficult to make films, even as an independent, let alone be granted access to the studio system and the big money that attaches to filmmaking there.

Women's films remain the uncredited cameos of international cinema. When women directors *do* achieve success, film critics and historians often neglect to mention it. That same invisibility does not obtain, however, when women directors fail. One of the only women to sustain a directorial career in Britain, Muriel Box, was never able to direct a film again after her film *Rattle of a Simple Man* bombed in 1964; yet Box had been working in the film industry and as a director since the late 1920s, and was the only woman director to achieve success in the British film industry. Dorothy Arzner, the only woman to direct in the heyday of Hollywood in the 1930s and 1940s, also "chose to retire" at the age of thirty-seven when her last film lagged at the box office and she complained that studio interference had caused the film to fail.

When a man makes a bad film or a box-office bomb, it's simply a bad movie; that failure doesn't translate into a conception that all men are bad directors. In fact, in Hollywood and other systems, one bomb doesn't even necessarily mean that particular male director is considered bad; invariably, he will get the opportunity to direct another film. But when a woman makes a movie that doesn't do well, then *all* women are suspect; it becomes more difficult for the next woman to get a shot at directing. One director claimed a virtual moratorium on studio contracts for women was imposed after Elaine May's disastrous multimillion dollar box-office dud, *Ishtar;* studio heads wouldn't even look at *treatments* by women. Yet a few years earlier, Michael Cimino's *Heaven's Gate* became the biggest box-office bomb in history; *books* were written about the debacle, yet Cimino continued to make movies in Hollywood. Less than a decade later Kevin Costner outbombed Cimino with *Waterworld,* the most expensive movie (and box-office bomb) ever made; he too continues to direct.

Quite simply, the rules for women directors differ vastly from those for men. As the profiles in *Film Fatales* indicate, women have a much tougher battle to get funding, garner a good distribution deal or achieve bankable (or historical) status as a director. Although women now enter film schools at a rate almost equal with men, they remain far less likely to get jobs in the industry or to be able to make movies, whether within the studio system or independently. In fact, despite a plethora of media coverage of women filmmakers in recent years, despite the resurgence of women making films in Hollywood in the last two decades, the golden age of women directors has long passed and a renaissance of women's filmmaking has yet to be achieved. More women directed (and produced, and were screenwriters and cinematographers) in Hollywood in 1915 than in 1995. That trend continues.

One answer *not* given by any of the women filmmakers in this book to the question of why women become independent filmmakers is as complex as it is elemental: *History.* Cinema began in the United States and France with women at the forefront of the brand-new art form. Yet, with nary a splice mark, the vast and significant contributions of women filmmakers have been edited almost completely out of cinematic history.

How many people know, for example, that it was a *woman,* Alice Guy-Blaché, who directed the first narrative film in 1896? How many people know that the most prolific and highest paid director in the United States in the days of silent films was not D. W. Griffith or Cecil B. DeMille, but Lois Weber, who had made over a hundred films by 1920? The first surrealist film was not made by Salvador Dali and Luis Buñuel, as most students of film imagine (or are taught); it was made by a woman, Germaine Dulac (who also portrayed shocking violence). Maya Deren pioneered avant-garde cinema in the United States in the 1940s. (Dulac and Deren also pioneered film theory, writing extensively about surrealist and avant-garde cinema and the role of the cinematic gaze.)

These women filmmakers are so pivotal to moviemaking as we know it today, it astonishes that their work has been so marginalized. In France, Guy-Blaché worked for Gaumont studios in the 1890s, where she became the first woman director in the world. When she moved to the United States, she founded (some would say invented) independent cinema with her small company, Solax. Guy-Blaché worked in every avenue of film—writing, directing, producing, editing and even doing wardrobe for her films. She experimented with sound as early as 1906. Between 1896 and 1907 she made over four hundred films, in France and the United States. Throughout her career, she wrote, produced and directed over seven hundred films, yet when she died in 1968 at ninety-five, she was virtually unknown. Many of her surviving films had been incorrectly credited to her male assistants, particularly in France. For years Guy-Blaché tried to have her name restored to

Alice Guy-Blaché documented in Marquise Lepage's *The Lost Garden: The Life and Cinema of Alice Guy-Blaché* (photo from Collection Roberta Blaché; still courtesy of Women Make Movies)

her original work but was mostly unsuccessful. In 1995 Canadian director Marquise Lepage detailed Guy-Blaché's life and work in a documentary, *The Lost Garden: The Life and Cinema of Alice Guy-Blaché*, but Guy-Blaché's groundbreaking contributions to cinema remain largely unrecorded and unrecognized.

In the early days of Hollywood, women also broke ground. It was Weber, not Griffith (*The Birth of a Nation, Intolerance*), who pioneered the use of narrative film as a means to promote a political idea; her films focused on social issues—the death penalty, child abuse, child labor, abortion and temperance, among others. But she was a moneymaker for the studios; her films were always big box office because she knew, as critics of the day wrote, "how to tell a good story." Weber also knew how to tell a story from a female vantage point; her films are the first American movies to view the action from the perspective of the female protagonist. In 1916, at the peak

Introduction

of the silent era, Weber was the highest paid director in Hollywood, making close to four hundred films. By 1920, she was making films for $50,000 each—an extraordinary sum at that time. However, like Guy-Blaché, she suffered a reversal of fortune with the advent of sound, changing tastes among moviegoers and the rise of male moguls running the studio system. By 1930 her directing career had ended and she died penniless and unknown in 1939.

Dulac and Deren fared marginally better in life and history. Germaine Dulac's first foray into surrealist and avant-garde filmmaking predates Buñuel and Dali's *Un Chien Andalou* by eleven years, but she is rarely credited for her innovations. Her pivotal surrealist film, *The Seashell and the Clergyman*, scripted by and starring surrealist playwright and theorist Antonin Artaud, was so controversial for its feminist perspective (Dulac is always credited as being the first feminist filmmaker) that it was rarely shown after its 1927 premiere. Dulac continued to write film theory and work in various aspects of film, but she never repeated her early successes; she was head of Gaumont newsreels until her death in 1942.

Maya Deren in *Meshes of the Afternoon.* Deren directed and appeared in the film. (courtesy of Women Make Movies)

Deren, *the* avant-garde director of the forties and fifties, also became increasingly marginalized, as much for her involvement in politics and interest in voodoo (she wrote a compelling anthropological treatise on voodoo in Haiti in 1953, *Divine Horsemen: The Living Gods of Haiti*) as for her innovative film style. Deren was officially the first woman to direct since Dorothy Arzner was forced out of Hollywood in 1943. She won the first Guggenheim grant ever given for filmmaking. Like Dulac, she was a groundbreaking avant-garde experimentalist, credited with being the first American woman director to make nonlinear films. As Buñuel had collaborated with Dali, Deren collaborated with Marcel Duchamp; as Dulac had collaborated with Artaud, Deren collaborated with black choreographer and anthropologist Katheryn Dunham and novelist and diarist Anaïs Nin. A maverick theorist as well as director, Deren was among the very first directors to take her films on the road, touring and lecturing with her work around the United States and abroad. She organized screenings and symposia on experimental and avant-garde film and she established the Creative Film Foundation in 1954. Deren died prematurely at forty-four of a brain aneurysm.

The history of cinema is over a hundred years old, but the history of women in cinema has yet to truly be written. At the end of the first century of filmmaking there are still only a handful of books—nearly all written by feminist historians and film theorists—detailing the role women have played in cinematic history in an attempt to splice women back into the historical picture.

It's a difficult task. There has been a conscious manipulation of historical fact in an effort to excise women from the cinematic picture, just as they have been edited out of so much other history. And leaving women out of the history of filmmaking contributes to the problems women directors continue to have in achieving their filmmaking goals, making it that much easier to restrict women's roles in filmmaking today: If no precedent exists for women's place in the directorial (or cinematographic, producing, management, et cetera) *oeuvre*, then each new female director (cinematographer, producer, studio head, et cetera) looks like the *only* one—she stands out not for her accomplishments, but for her difference. She becomes her gender and nothing else.

The history of women filmmakers is a rich one. Women—directors, producers, editors and cinematographers—were among the guiding forces in the early days of Hollywood. The opportunities offered by the new and exciting development of moviemaking at the end of the nineteenth century brought women to Hollywood (and Paris) to work in every aspect of moviemaking. The Gish sisters, Lillian and Dorothy, were made famous in the silent films of D. W. Griffith and others, but both women directed as well. Mary Pickford, "America's Sweetheart" and the preeminent actress of the silent era, also directed films and established United Artists production company. Numerous other famous actresses of the silent era, among them Mabel Normand, also directed and established their own production companies. Women like Anita Loos were prominent among screenwriters. Weber, the most extraordinarily prolific talent of the silent era, directed more films than any other director (though some conflicting evidence grants Guy-Blaché top directing honors).

Yet with the dawn of talking pictures came the demise of women in leading roles behind the camera and as producers in Hollywood. By 1929

Dorothy Arzner was the only woman making movies in Hollywood and would be until 1943, when she retired, forced out of Hollywood by her own frustration with the male-only studio system and leaving no one to take her place. (There would be no women producers other than Ida Lupino and Barbra Streisand until the 1980s.) Between 1940 and 1980, fewer than one-fifth of one percent of all the movies released by Hollywood studios were directed by women, as opposed to nearly fifty percent in 1920.

It could be said there has been a celluloid ceiling for women in Hollywood and other major studio systems around the world. At the end of the first century of filmmaking, women have only been directing in Hollywood again in the last twenty years, and their numbers remain pitifully few. Women still represent fewer than ten percent of directors *worldwide* and only about six percent in Hollywood. What began as an equal opportunity employment venture for women remains, as the millenium approaches, a male-dominated field in which women are still the exception where once they were the rule.

Laura Mulvey's pivotal semiotic essay "Visual Pleasure and Narrative Cinema," defining the female gaze, raised the question of how women view themselves through the lens. In presenting the work of independent women directors, we chose to focus specifically on this essential theme that has formed the foundation of much of the criticism, theory and semiotics of women and film in the last decade. In an interview about her pivotal experimental film *Jeanne Dielman*, Belgian filmmaker Chantal Akerman responded to criticism about the film's attention to what appear, on the surface, to be incidental moments in a woman's life. Akerman focuses on the details of the title character's (played by Delphine Seyrig) life: Thus we see Jeanne peeling potatoes, examining the dishes, going through the dailiness of a woman's ordinary routine. As Lizzie Borden later explored the dailiness (and drudgery) of prostitution in *Working Girls*, Akerman details the extraordinarily dreadful life Jeanne leads by training her narrative and her lens on the tedium of her character's definingly routinized life, which, in the film's pivotal scene, leads the character to murder.

Akerman noted that the film is feminist because she views the character and what she does, how she lives her life, in a unique and distinctly *female* way—through a *female gaze*. She said, "If you choose to show a woman's gestures so precisely, it's because you love them. In some way you recognize those gestures that have always been denied and ignored"—and, she added, never, ever ("*jamais, jamais*") shown from that vantage point.

Each filmmaker presented in *Film Fatales* has a definingly female gaze, made more explicit by her status as a director working outside mainstream studio systems either in Hollywood or abroad. We chose to interview and profile independent women directors because of the dearth of such material and our own eagerness to have that material accessible to a variety of audiences. With the notable exception of Canadian filmmakers Janis Cole and Holly Dale, who published *Calling the Shots: Profiles of Women Filmmakers* in 1993, culling their interviews of twenty directors from material they used in their documentary of the same name, no book exists that is solely a compendium of women directors discussing their own work. A vast array of criticism, theory and semiotics of film has been written in the last decade focusing on women and film as well as feminism and film, but these books have focused on message and metaphor in movies, rather than on the filmmakers themselves. And while these books provide a rich cache of critical information on women's filmmaking and on images of women in film generally, they do not give entrée into the mind of the director and how and why she works, nor are these books readily accessible to a diverse audience.

I have been a devoted student of film since adolescence, a film critic for over twenty years, had a radio program on film for many years and have taught college courses in film criticism and film history. Judith is a filmmaker, film and video editor of *Curve* magazine, frequently writes on and reviews film and teaches college courses in video, filmmaking and screenwriting. We have collaborated on several video projects together, she as director, producer and editor, I as screenwriter. Coming from these divergent yet complementary backgrounds, we were both intensely interested in the specifics of women's directing: how it might differ from filmmaking by men or might be more difficult to accomplish; why a woman might choose directing rather than the more traditionally female fields of editing or acting (fields in which some of these filmmakers were involved before they became directors); why a woman thought she could enter such a male-dominated field in which financing is both essential and extremely hard to get; how feminism did or did not influence her

Introduction

work; and how political—or nonpolitical—she felt her films should be.

We wanted the answers to these and other questions and knew a larger audience of movie buffs, students and filmmakers of both genders would also be interested in the answers. In addition, as women's work has become of greater interest to women themselves as well as to the general population, we knew there was an audience waiting to hear what these women had to say about their work. Since filmmaking remains a field from which women are still largely excluded, despite improvements (fewer than five percent of films were made by women in 1996), women discussing their struggles to do their work, have it distributed and get it recognized provides material for the larger dialogue on the mainstreaming of feminism and women in the workplace.

Our choices were made on the basis of what may seem somewhat biased criteria. First and foremost, we feel the work of the directors presented here is important cinematically and historically, regardless of the number of films a director may have made (some are extraordinarily prolific, like Pratibha Parmar and Barbara Hammer, while others, like Radha Bharadwaj, are not). We also fundamentally like the work of these directors overall, even where we may find some films uneven or where the work has received limited critical success, and think it should be seen because the directors have particular insights and/or styles that are exceptional and provocative.

We feel these filmmakers are representative of a range of women's work in the cinema. There were a number of directors beyond those profiled we would have liked to have included, but were unable to do so for a variety of reasons—primarily because they did not respond to our requests for interviews or simply do not do interviews. Regrettably we were also unable to interview several non-English-speaking directors because of language barriers and availability factors.

In addition to trying to present a range of directorial styles, from narrative to documentary to experimental, we have worked hard to represent other elements important to a filmmaker's vision. Though the majority of the filmmakers are American, there are also directors from Central America, Canada, the United Kingdom, Europe, the Caribbean, Asia, Australia and New Zealand. We strove for balances frequently lacking in writing about women directors, particularly race and sexual orientation. Thus we have women of color as well as white women; lesbians as well as heterosexuals; younger and older women in addition to the predominance of women at the peak of their filmmaking careers who are in their thirties and forties; women of various classes and economic access to filmmaking; and established directors as well as those new to the craft.

With only a few exceptions, we have personally interviewed all the living filmmakers in this book. Some were reinterviewed as the book came closer to completion in order to have the most up-to-date information on each woman and her work. Jane Campion, Marleen Gorris, Margaret Tait and Sadie Benning were unavailable for interview due to scheduling conflicts but sent us a vast array of personal material from which to cull our profiles. Ida Lupino was seriously ill and subsequently died before we were able to do a more in-depth interview with her beyond a short interview I had done several years ago.

Unlike Cole and Dale's book, we have not presented these profiles in a simple question and answer format. Rather we have integrated other material about the filmmakers, often provided by the filmmakers themselves, into the profiles, while letting the directors speak for themselves. The interviews vary in style, content and length. A few are collaborative, written by us both; most were done individually. My profiles tend to include more critical material on the films themselves, while Judith's tend to focus more directly on the technical, logistical and political aspects of moviemaking. However, although our styles differ, each of us brings the filmmaker and her work directly into focus.

Film Fatales, like many other books about film and filmmakers, is a labor of love. We both love cinema in all its grand (and *Grand Guignol*) aspects.

Movies, even bad movies, have always captivated me. I have loved the movies since I was a young child and cut my cinematic teeth on what were then called "art films"—the works of Fritz Lang, Carl Dreyer, Ingmar Bergman, Federico Fellini, Vittorio De Sica, Francois Truffaut, Luis Buñuel, Bernardo Bertolucci, Akira Kurosawa, Yasujiro Ozu, John Schlesinger and Martin Scorcese—as well as the classic Hollywood directors like Alfred Hitchcock, Eric von Stroheim, Ernst Lubitsch, Billy Wilder, Raoul Walsh, John Huston, Frank Capra and John Ford. I spent as much time as I could at the movies and was lucky enough to spend my adolescence living within walking distance of one of the best repertory cinemas on the East Coast in

Introduction

17

the sixties and seventies, Philadelphia's The Bandbox, second only to New York's St. Marks. There I learned a great deal about film and, as a consequence, about life, and saw without question (or hyperbole) many of the best films ever made.

Still, I was fifteen before I saw a film directed by a woman—before I knew films *could* be directed by women. That film was Riefenstahl's *Triumph of the Will*. An unfortunate first for me—had my parents known I was going to see it, they might have forbidden it. The experience left me both revulsed and awed, because regardless of the hideous nature of Riefenstahl's politics, she was a remarkable director who clearly understood the expansive properties of filmmaking.

My subsequent experiences were different—Liliana Cavani's *The Night Porter* and Lina Wertmuller's *Swept Away*—but not necessarily better, as the politics inherent in these films, too, are questionable. (I was later to write that both women directed not like men, but *as* men, often with more brutality toward women than men did.) But then came films by the incomparable Margarethe von Trotta and Agnes Varda; those filmmakers taught me what women could do with film (and leftist politics). In college I discovered Maya Deren and Chantal Akerman; *Meshes of the Afternoon* and *je tu il elle* remain among my favorite experimental films.

Over the course of nearly thirty years of studying film and viewing film, however, an amazingly small percentage of the movies I have seen have been made by women. And yet those films have fascinated me—which is why I wanted to do this book.

Judith's involvement in this project came a bit later. Long a film and video critic, she became more and more interested in filmmaking herself. She attended a highly technical film school in London, where she acquired good skills but few nuances. When she returned to the United States, I invited her to accompany me to interviews for this book. It was through those interviews, she says, that she "learned about the business of filmmaking, the business of low-budget filmmaking and the aesthetics of female filmmaking. It can be argued that if I had not become involved in this book, the film work I was trying to do might have amounted to nothing at all because I would have been frustrated by the costs and personnel involved. So these filmmakers were, necessarily, part of a feminist mentoring process for me. It was through studying the work of Barbara Hammer, Su Friedrich and Sadie Benning that I saw what a solo independent filmmaker could do."

Thus our respective relationships to the cinema are reflected in this book, as are our feminist politics. There *are* women filmmakers who disclaim associations with feminism; none, except Ida Lupino, are in this book. Each filmmaker here gives recognition to the facts of filmmaking for women—it *is* more difficult, as directors like Lizzie Borden, Susan Seidelman and Jan Oxenberg found when they made the transition from New York to Hollywood. Financing remains perilous and retaining final cut if one works with a studio is nearly impossible. Women directors continue to be marginalized, despite the awesome work of some women or even the box-office pull of directors like Barbra Streisand, Amy Heckerling (*Fast Times at Ridgemont High*, *Look Who's Talking*), Penny Marshall, Penelope Spheeris and Kathryn Bigelow.

But as any of those filmmakers might note, some with irony, others with bitterness, women directors have yet to be truly accepted within the Hollywood system. Streisand has been repeatedly snubbed for Best Director nominations at the Academy Awards even when her films, such as *The Prince of Tides* and *Yentl*, have received nominations. Randa Haines directed *Children of a Lesser God*, another nominee for Best Picture and for which deaf actress Marlee Matlin won an Oscar for Best Actress; Haines, like Streisand, was not nominated for Best Director. Nor was Jane Campion nominated for Best Director, even though her film *The Piano* was nominated for Best Picture, as well as a host of other awards, including Best Actor, Best Supporting Actor, Best Actress, Best Supporting Actress and Best Screenplay. Campion won for Best Original Screenplay, Holly Hunter for Best Actress and Anna Pacquin for Best Supporting Actress. Campion again missed the Best Director nod in 1997, despite a host of nominations for her film *Portrait of a Lady*.

Marshall didn't garner a nomination for Best Director for *Awakenings*, which was nominated for Best Picture and, like Streisand's *The Prince of Tides*, numerous other awards. In fact, *The Prince of Tides* was a nominee in the year designated by the Academy of Motion Picture Arts and Sciences as "The Year of the Woman." It was also the year two-time Best Actress Oscar–winner Jodie Foster debuted as a director with her feature *Little Man Tate*. But as quite a few well-known actresses over forty noted, it was a year in which, despite the Academy's noises, there *were* no women directors nominated, most notably, Streisand.

Of course Hollywood isn't the only arbiter of filmmaking, but it (and other studio systems) still retains a great deal of power over moviemaking, and as a consequence over the *content* of films. Mira Nair and Vijaya Mehta point out that India, the world's largest filmmaking center, suffers from a similar problem—Bombay studios don't make films by women. Mehta has made her films through the independent National Film Development Corporation while Nair has gone outside India for funding for her films. The impact of financing on filmmaking and particularly on the content of films cannot be minimized, and the more marginal a director or her ideas are perceived to be, the less likely she will be to achieve her filmmaking goals.

The directors in *Film Fatales* return to these financing and content questions again and again. A female director is far more likely to get repeat funding with box-office hits like Spheeris's *Wayne's World*, Marshall's *Big* or Bigelow's *Point Break* than with films like Martha Coolidge's award-winning *Rambling Rose* or Lizzie Borden's *Love Crimes*. And one can see where films like Marleen Gorris's *A Question of Silence*, Julie Dash's *Daughters of the Dust* or Jane Campion's early feature, *Sweetie*, have little mainstream box-office appeal and therefore would not be likely candidates for big studio funding. Actress Frances McDormand, Best Actress Oscar winner for her role in the 1996 independent feature *Fargo* (directed, co-written and co-produced by her husband Joel Coen) stated in her acceptance speech how vital it was to have independent features, where content wasn't governed by studio committee. McDormand noted that roles like hers in *Fargo* (she plays a pregnant North Dakota sheriff investigating a murder) gave women important and diverse opportunities as actors.

Who directs a film, as McDormand pointed out so succinctly, is what defines both story and actors. Every actress over forty in Hollywood hopes for roles where she does not, like Sally Field in 1994's Best Picture winner, *Forrest Gump*, play the mother of an actor only a few years younger than she. Women directors present opportunities for other women, as actors and in other key filmmaking roles, from producer to cinematographer to editor. They also, as McDormand suggested in her acceptance speech and as many women directors stated in their *Film Fatales* interviews, bring a totally different perspective to film—not just with the female gaze but with the female story. Hence rarely seen characters, like women of color who are not objects of sexual exoticism, or rarely seen storylines, like sexual taboos, are given voice in films by women.

Each director brings something personal to a film; but what women directors bring to a film rarely appears on any screen. Black women directors like Julie Dash, Michelle Parkerson and Zeinabu irene Davis put black women and their stories on screen. Frances Negrón-Muntaner and Lourdes Portillo address Latina issues from the inside, *as* Latina directors. Jan Oxenberg, Pratibha Parmar and Michelle Mohabeer tell lesbian stories from their vantage point *as* lesbians, and within their lesbian vantage point also extend their gaze to include their ethnic perspectives. Mehta's and Nair's films become antidotes for the plethora of *Jewel in the Crown* Raj-oriented films on Indian experience that exoticize or demean India and Indian characters from their British colonialist perspective. Susan Seidelman, Lizzie Borden, Patricia Rozema and Barbara Hammer all tackle women's identity and sexuality conflicts through a distinctly female lens but from different perspectives. Women directors bring women's lives to the screen in ways male directors, regardless of their levels of sensitivity, never could.

It does not follow, however, that a handful of well-known women filmmakers will make it easier for women in general to direct. For example, while films by black male directors have, in recent years, begun to garner studio support in Hollywood, there have been no films made by black *women*. In fact, the first feature by a black woman to get mainstream theatrical release was Martinique filmmaker Euzhan Palcy's 1989 *A Dry White Season*, a film about South African apartheid based on the Andre Brink novel. Like Attenborough's *Cry Freedom*, the film's perspective on apartheid is more white than black, making it, in studio parlance, more accessible to a wider (and whiter) audience. The film also stars major box-office draws like Oscar winners Marlon Brando and Susan Sarandon, as well as Donald Sutherland.

The failure to allow women entrée into the studio system explains why many women of color remain independent directors, even after they acquire, like Dash or Parkerson, considerable critical success for their independent films. Dash, like Seidelman after *Smithereens* and Borden after *Working Girls*, was invited to Hollywood after the critical success at the Sundance Festival of her first feature, *Daughters of the Dust*, but has not yet directed a studio feature. Allison Anders received critical acclaim for her feature *Mi Vida Loca* (*My Crazy Life*), about Chicana gang members, but Chicana filmmakers themselves have had little success breaking into

Hollywood. Jessica Lu was one of the few Asian Americans to have a film noticed by Hollywood; her 1996 documentary *Breathing Lessons: The Life and Work of Mark O'Brien* won an Academy Award. (When receiving her Oscar, Lu quipped that a documentary director knows she's in Hollywood when "your dress [for the Oscars] costs more than your film.")

Without didacticism, *Film Fatales* addresses the complexity of these issues, problems and conflicts for women directors. We hope this book will make more people aware of both how accomplished women directors are, and have been since filmmaking began over a century ago, and how many obstacles women still face. We also hope to open up a different, more accessible dialogue on women and film, and on women's directorial efforts, one that goes beyond the theoretical and critical texts currently available, by examining the concept of the female gaze and delineating the role of the female director at the end of a century of cinema.

Film Fatales is not a semiotic text nor a collection of film theory or criticism. Although we have incorporated some criticism into the profiles of these filmmakers as well as some of our own wealth of information on cinema, our primary goal was to present and contextualize the work of these women by allowing them to speak in their own words about their work, what it means and why they do it, as directors who have had to battle in various ways to get their work made, exhibited and distributed. Our work on this project was compelling and exciting, the group of filmmakers diverse and intriguing. We have striven to add a fresh document of historical value to the voluminous archive of extant cinematic writing because women's cinematic achievements have so often ended up on the cutting-room floor. *Film Fatales* is by no means definitive, but we hope like most "firsts" this book will spur others to research women and their cinematic work and to compile their own documents on women's films and filmmaking.

Victoria A. Brownworth
Philadelphia
June 1997

Ida Lupino

Hard, Fast and Beautiful

When Ida Lupino died in 1995 at age seventy-six, her death received none of the media attention accorded other film stars from her era. Nor was there any mention that Lupino had been one of only two women directing films in Hollywood between the 1930s and 1960s—a remarkable feat. (Dorothy Arzner was the other.) The sheer volume of directing work Lupino did over three decades makes her one of, if not *the,* most prolific female directors in American history. Yet now, several years after her death, recognition of her achievements as both actress and director has yet to truly emerge.

Born in London during World War I to a theatrical family that traced its acting roots back to the seventeenth century, Lupino entered the prestigious Royal Academy of Dramatic Arts at the age of thirteen. However, acting was not her first choice of career, and in later years she noted with some irony, "I know what it's like to do something you don't want to do. I was forced into being an actress, and I didn't want to be. If I had to do it all over again, I'd do it differently.

Films by Ida Lupino

Not Wanted

Never Fear

Outrage

Hard, Fast and Beautiful

The Hitchhiker

The Bigamist

The Trouble with Angels

I'd sit home and write lyrics and music."

In spite of her reluctant entrance into acting, Lupino rose fairly quickly to star status, though she maintained a defiant dislike of the limelight and an overwhelming interest in other aspects of film production—including writing, producing and directing. An accomplished screenwriter and producer, who most loved writing for films, Lupino directed seven films between 1949 and 1965 as well as over a hundred television shows. Though her acting career was stellar, the celebrity status of some of her diva contemporaries, among them Joan Crawford and Bette Davis, eluded her. Like the characters she often played and the roles she would later direct, Lupino was a hard worker, not a publicity seeker, maintaining a low—and, more importantly—*independent* profile in Hollywood. The understated personal style Lupino established would later serve as a model for other women attempting to break into Hollywood's all-boy directing network.

As a director Lupino set her own goals and standards and ultimately did what she wanted. Unable to choose her own roles as an actress under contract with Warner Brothers, where Bette Davis had first choice of lead roles, Lupino decided to direct at a time when only one other woman, Arzner, was behind the camera in Hollywood. For over a decade after Arzner left, Lupino would be the *only* woman directing. She would later say she began directing because she didn't like wasting time, waiting around on the set with nothing to do. A maverick and an iconoclast who integrated her various cinematic talents into her work, Lupino was as vital to changing the role of women in Hollywood as Lillian Gish had been a generation before and Barbra Streisand would be a generation later. (Lupino was the first woman in Hollywood to direct and star in her own film since Lois Weber at the turn of the century; Streisand would be the next.) Like some of the early women in Hollywood—Gish, Mary Pickford, Weber—Lupino used all her cinematic abilities, and like Pickford, formed her own company (Emerald Productions, later known as The Filmmakers and then Bridget Productions) to accommodate her work, allowing her to be writer, producer and director.

Despite her battles within the studio system, Lupino played the female lead in over fifty studio films and in countless television programs and television movies. As an actress, she epitomized the tough girl forced by circumstance to get what she wanted by whatever means necessary—even murder. Roles in critically acclaimed movies like *They Drive by Night* (1940), *High Sierra* (1941), *Ladies in Retirement* (1941), *The Hard Way* (1943) and *The Bigamist* (1953), which she directed and starred in, allowed Lupino to develop characterizations of women that were three-dimensional—women with ambition, desires (including sexual desires) and vulnerability. Later, as a director, she would refine those characterizations

Edmond O'Brien and Ida Lupino in *The Bigamist.* Lupino directed and starred in the film.

in her own films and add yet another dimension by broaching subjects vital to women that had previously been off-limits in Hollywood movies, taboo topics such as unwanted pregnancy and rape. She also focused attention on communities of women, like the convent school in *The Trouble with Angels* (1965).

To engage Lupino fully as a cinematic symbol, one must examine her skill as actor as well as director, because those skills impact each other so definingly in her work. Lupino would say late in her career that she learned a great deal as a director from other directors—what to do and what not to do with actors. Being a director herself, she noted, gave her added respect for both jobs, actor and director, and the difficulties inherent in each.

Lupino—actor and director—helped define the American film noir (she was the first woman to direct in the genre, predating current filmmakers like Lizzie Borden and Kathryn Bigelow). As an actress she, along with contemporaries like Barbara Stanwyck and Lana Turner, epitomized the "bad" girl. But Lupino's characters were just a little more three-dimensional—smart and vulnerable as well as intrinsically prone to bad choices. Thus the smoky-voiced Lupino, perennially unlucky in love, sears the screen in director Raoul Walsh's rarely seen tough little melodrama, *The Man I Love* (1947). Less well known than her other starring vehicle with Walsh, *High Sierra* (through which she rose to top billing along with co-star Humphrey Bogart), *The Man I Love* is the sort of film Lupino blazed through. With

Ida Lupino

the quintessential forties nightclub as backdrop, *The Man I Love* features Lupino as a tough-talking but vulnerable nightclub chanteuse. (Sadly, the torchy-voiced Lupino was not allowed to do her own songs, which were dubbed by Peg LaCentra. One must catch *Road House* (1948) to hear Lupino's sensual rendition of "One for My Baby." Singing was another of her many talents.) *The Man I Love* provides a perfect vehicle for Lupino, who really defined the female victim-turned-survivor role. Like all Walsh's films, *The Man I Love* has a tight, action-packed pacing with wonderful neo-camp dialogue delivered with subtle nuance by Lupino ("I know quite a few things—and I sing."). Like *High Sierra, The Man I Love* showcases Lupino's range as an actor, despite the limitations of the role itself.

Later in her acting career Lupino would be criticized for taking a plethora of mediocre roles in equally mediocre feature and TV movies. But Lupino suffered the same fate the majority of female actors have faced in Hollywood as they have aged; play "character" roles—which often involve portraying the mother of a male actor of the same age, like Angela Lansbury in *The Manchurian Candidate* (1965), who was a mere three years older than her screen "son" Laurence Harvey; Glenn Close, two years senior to "son" Mel Gibson in *Hamlet* (1991); or Kate Nelligan, six years *younger* than "son" Nick Nolte in *The Prince of Tides* (1991)—or stop acting.

Regrettably for Lupino, being relegated to such roles was not mitigated by a more expansive career in other areas of cinema; for while Lupino preferred screenwriting and directing, her access to those fields remained limited by the studio system in which she was enmeshed. Lupino attempted several independent directing projects (including, in 1974, a film version of the Frances Farmer autobiography, *Will There Ever Be a Morning?* in which she wanted to star Academy Award–winning actress Glenda Jackson), but was unable, for a variety of reasons, to succeed in bringing these projects to fruition.

A quarter-century ago women were directing few feature-length films in the United States. Lupino, in many respects, is the female director who links the past of studio-driven Hollywood to the present of female independent filmmakers. She certainly had the drive and ambition to be a major director and one to be reckoned with, but unlike the nineties, where it is not unusual for a well-known actor (Mel Gibson, Jodie Foster, Tom Hanks, Barbra Streisand) to turn to directing while also maintaining a solid acting career, in the forties, fifties and sixties, this was not done—especially in Hollywood, where even the roles stars were allowed to play were controlled by the iron fists of the studio moguls. It is evidence of Lupino's amazing drive and talent that she was able to circumvent that system enough to direct even a single film.

The films she *did* direct, however, are extraordinary. She portrays women and issues vital to women in a starkly social-realist style. In addition, she turns the tables on presentations of men, serving up portraits of vulnerability entirely at odds with the standard role of men in films then (and even now). *The Hitchhiker* (1953), Lupino's personal favorite among her feature films (and the first film noir directed by a woman), is a chilling tale based on the true story of a young California serial killer. Two men on a fishing trip to Mexico (Edmond O'Brien and Frank Lovejoy) pick up a hitchhiker, a simple response to another guy down on his luck. But this small act turns their vacation into the stuff of nightmare. O'Brien and Lovejoy were tough-guy actors of the era, yet in *The Hitchhiker* they become vulnerable, terrified by their innocent but deadly wrong choice. William Talman plays the creepy young killer in the tradition later set by Billy Zane in *Dead Calm* (1988). Lupino co-wrote the screenplay with her then-husband, Collier Young.

Hard, Fast and Beautiful (1951) is for lovers of *Mildred Pierce* (1945) and other tear-jerker dramas of the period. Lupino directed the marvelous Sally Forrest in this tale of a rising young tennis star and her oppressively controlling mother, played by veteran actor Claire Trevor with a steeliness that makes Joan Crawford's Pierce seem tame. Lupino appears briefly as a passerby, à la Hitchcock. As with her directorial work in *The Hitchhiker,* Lupino's focus is character-driven. Intent on the motivations of her characters, Lupino's vision isn't narrow, simply succinct. The interaction between mother and daughter, the impact of career and familial obligation on the young tennis star, the influence of romance—Lupino takes these conflicts and heightens them with the strength of the main performers. (In fact, this directing style had long been labeled "women's" directing in Hollywood and the resultant films, "women's pictures," even though it was men like Frank Capra directing films with that emotional style, not women.)

Hard, Fast and Beautiful is an uneven but interesting film, though indisputably a melodrama with an ending that will disappoint feminists (which Lupino claimed not to be). Darker and simpler than *Mildred Pierce,* the film explores the same kind of volatile mother-daughter dynamic.

Lupino's direction of Forrest, a powerful young actress who had a very brief career, is taut and excellent. A few years earlier Lupino's directorial debut film, *Not Wanted* (1949), had starred Forrest as well, as did her 1950 film *Never Fear.*

Lupino liked fresh faces, new stars and character actors over established studio stars. In a 1945 fan magazine interview, Lupino, then at the height of her acting career, made some prescient comments about her future in Hollywood, noting, "I see myself, in the years ahead, directing or producing or both. I see myself developing new talent, which would be furiously interesting for me. For I love talent. Love to watch it. Love to help it. Am more genuinely interested in the talent of others than I am in my own."

Which may explain why, despite her own strength and ability as an actress, Lupino was a superb and challenging director. She claimed to have learned her directorial skills while hanging out at the Warner Brothers studio, where she was on contract for eight years. "I paid attention," she noted. "I didn't like to stand around wasting time."

With *Never Fear* (1950; later re-released under the insipid title *The Young Lovers)* Lupino began a series of topical films that pegged her as an *auteur* of social realism. *Never Fear* stars Sally Forrest, once again giving an extraordinary performance under Lupino's direction of a screenplay co-written by Lupino and Collier Young. Forrest plays Carol Williams, half—with her fiancé—of a nightclub dance act. During a rehearsal she collapses onstage and is subsequently diagnosed with polio. The film explores what happens after diagnosis, interpreting the impact of the disease from the perspective of those who've contracted it as well as examining the physical and psychological hurdles involved in recovery. (Lupino herself had polio when she was a teenager.) The film has an almost documentary element to it in parts.

Forrest gives a wide-ranging performance, from dancer to bitter invalid to a woman recovering from a devastating illness that has totally altered her life. *Never Fear* broaches a subject very much on the minds of pre–Salk vaccine America, handling it deftly and seriously, but avoiding the melodrama of *Hard, Fast and Beautiful.*

Like *Never Fear*, *Not Wanted* (1949) and *Outrage* (1950) are part of Lupino's *oeuvre* of taboo subjects and two of her most important films, for which she also co-wrote the screenplays. Startling for both their content (unwed motherhood and rape, respectively) and their stark intensity, these films have a broader range than *Hard, Fast and Beautiful,* but incorporate the docudramatic element of *Never Fear.* It's difficult to explain to current film audiences, jaded from endless TV movies-of-the-week featuring every taboo subject from anorexia to incest, how groundbreaking these films were nearly fifty years ago. (In fact, even the word "rape" itself was taboo; it is never actually mentioned in *Outrage.*)

Like actor-director Penny Marshall, Lupino started out as a fill-in director (though uncredited at her insistence) after the original director of *Not Wanted,* Elmer Clifton, fell seriously ill during filming. *Not Wanted* was low-budget even by fifties standards, made for less than $100,000 but grossing well over $1 million. *Not Wanted* resembles the classic British film *Room at the Top* in its gritty exploration of class issues, but there is nothing similar to its examination of the choices unwed mothers had in a 1950s America defined alternately by the white, middle-class married perfection of Ozzie and Harriet and the fear, paranoia and suspicion of the McCarthy–House Un-American Activities Committee (HUAC) hearings.

The film debuts Lupino as director as well as debuting her interest in communities of women—here a home for unwed mothers, later convents and prisons.

Outrage (originally titled *Nobody's Safe)* shows Lupino's easy development as a director. Her third film, which she also co-wrote, *Outrage* is one of the best feature films about rape ever made, vying with the Australian-made *Shame* (Steve Jodrell, 1988). Starring a convincing and vivid Mala Powers as the young rape victim Ann Walton, *Outrage* actually delves into and explores the now-acknowledged double-victimization of the rape victim. When the film was released in 1950, none of the (male) critics could comprehend why Ann couldn't recognize the voice of her attacker (who works nearby), or how her friends and co-workers could reject her after the rape. Yet these issues explain why the film is groundbreaking: They are true to the reality of rape. Rape victims frequently exhibit what is referred to as victim amnesia. And the assignation of blame to the victim remains classic even now; it was commonplace in 1950.

What may bother modern audiences is the stagey atmosphere of the studio sets, yet these too seem to denote a real creepiness, evoking the sense of dread Ann Walton feels, defining the small-town environment as claustrophobic before, during and after the rape.

Criticisms of these Lupino vehicles abound. At the time, reviewers castigated Lupino for everything from indelicacy to melodrama to theatricality. Archivists have faulted the director for what they call the "dated quality" of films like *Outrage* and *Not Wanted*. Critics of the fifties and nineties, however, miss the point: Lupino was attacking taboo subjects, deliberately choosing both new and character actors as well as claustrophobic sets to heighten the intensity of her scrutiny of these issues. Hence a film like *Outrage* really does examine what happens to a young woman raped by an acquaintance; viewing the film, even through a nineties lens, one can seeehow *cinéma vérité* Lupino's vision was and how her development as a director was evolving. In 1950 sex was not a film theme; Lupino not only addresses sex, but addresses its unpleasant (*Not Wanted*) and brutal (*Outrage*) aspects.

That Lupino's focus on women disturbed and confused critics of her time is unmistakable; her early films—even the terrific *The Hitchhiker*—didn't receive much critical acclaim, and those focusing specifically on women and the complexities of their lives actually received a good deal of negative press. (Critics carped over the "indelicacy" and "crudeness" of a woman director's mentioning unwanted pregnancy or rape.) Nor were the films huge box-office successes.

Yet Lupino's major box-office success as a director, *The Trouble with Angels* (1965), also met with mixed reviews as typified by Robert Salmaggi's New York *Herald Tribune* review: "Director Ida Lupino has made an icky-poo precious movie from Blanche Hanalis's icky-poo precious screenplay of a Jane Trahey novel." Most critics (some of whom had panned her earlier films as too dark) found *The Trouble with Angels* far too sweet for their palates.

This last directorial effort (in film) is undoubtedly on the sweet side, far lighter than Lupino's earlier films, both in content and style. The film is, however, very much a movie of its era, when beach movies and airline-stewardess high jinks were all the rage—and meant big box office for the studios. The neorealism of postwar films had disappeared and the infiltration of European-born art films had yet to impact Hollywood. *The Trouble with Angels* has an almost Disneyesque quality to it, heightened by superstar child actress Hayley Mills in the lead role. The film was extremely popular, despite mixed reviews.

The Trouble with Angels stars Mills as a student ready to graduate from what she considers the stultifying atmosphere of a girls-only convent school. It was Mills's best performance, surpassing even her stunning portrayal of the troubled pubescent in *The Chalk Garden;* if critics lauded nothing else in the film, they applauded her performance as the rebel teen turned novitiate. Rosalind Russell is at her older/wise woman/crone best as Mother Superior (the original title of the film when it was made in 1965). A host of other strong female character actors round out the cast. Though *The Trouble with Angels* seems starkly different from Lupino's earlier films, it is actually part of the larger piece of her directorial *oeuvre.* A funny, smart and moving film about women's choices, spirituality and coming of age, it is in many respects Lupino's least flawed film, despite the fact that she didn't have a hand in the screenplay, reflecting how refined her directorial talent had become. Superb acting, a unique setting and a fast-paced story all compel the viewer, but like the director's other work, this film is intensely character-driven, with a strong story line about women's lives and intergenerational conflicts. Unquestionably, *The Trouble with Angels* functions as a comedy, but a comedy in which the strength of the story lies in its commentary on women's lives. Once again, Lupino breaks ground, exploring the concept of choices for women; what may appear to be a narrow or limiting choice, like entering the convent and choosing a cloistered life, is in fact a superb choice—solid and expansive. It is easy to imagine this film being directed today by Penny Marshall, Susan Seidelman or Joyce Chopra (*Smooth Talk,* 1985), because of the issues it raises and develops, and the manner in which the characterizations evolve.

In using two popular and well-established studio stars, Mills and Russell, Lupino diverges from her usual modus operandi, but elicits strong performances from each. Mills's shift from class hellion to novitiate seems believable, largely because of the influence of Russell and the manner in which the relationship between these two develops and deepens. And though there are many sentimental moments, an equal number of strong scenes between Mills and Russell as well as among the other women characters propel the action.

Though *The Trouble with Angels* was Lupino's last feature film, she directed television for over three decades. Herself a veteran actor of numerous television programs, Lupino became one of the first women directors on the small screen, directing episodes of everything from the sit-coms *Bewitched* and *Gilligan's Island* to westerns like *Have Gun, Will Travel* to classic television dramas such as *General Electric Theatre, The Twilight Zone,*

Alfred Hitchcock Presents, The Untouchables and *The Fugitive*. She continued to direct other television programs and TV movies throughout the fifties, sixties and seventies. Viewed throughout Hollywood as an extremely hard worker, Lupino was repeatedly called to direct TV because she kept to schedules and budgets and always garnered good performances from actors regardless of their status as classic film actors, serial television actors or neophytes. In addition, this kind of directing had its own challenges, like unreasonable schedules (Lupino was known to tell Method actors they had no time to do anything but "Just do it, Baby.")

How Lupino refined her technique and style as a director through this myriad of television programs often escapes mention in discussion of Lupino as director. But classic TV, now revived—like *Bewitched, Alfred Hitchcock Presents* and *The Fugitive*—gives students of Lupino's art an opportunity to see how innovative her work was. Techniques now associated with advances in film and television were used by Lupino back in the fifties, setting her work apart from other directors of the time. Lupino never liked static shots unless they heightened the reality of a scene; hence in a film like *Outrage* the camera stalks the rape victim, symbolizing her attacker. This film conceit has become a commonplace, as has the moving camera in television directing, particularly noted on shows like *NYPD Blue* or *Homicide: Life on the Street*. But in the brand-new and studio-limited sets of fifties TV where the camera tended to move only from A to B, Lupino's moving camera—in close-up, following the characters as they went about their comedic or deadly work—was starkly innovative.

Although she was in constant demand as a director, Lupino did complain that the pay wasn't equal to what Hollywood had to offer when she stood on the other side of the camera. She noted, "I have to direct five half-hour shows to equal the salary I get for one acting appearance." And then, as now, directing in television brought few rewards *except* money. In fact, Lupino's television directing has regularly been treated as a mere footnote, even though she directed well over a hundred shows in an amazing range of genres. (One doesn't today, for example, see the same directors handling *Frasier* or *Seinfeld* as well as *NYPD Blue* and *ER*. Lupino, however, did just that.)

Lupino's most compelling work as a director delineated the imperatives of women's lives, how events and choices define who women are or what they later become. In *Hard, Fast and Beautiful* a daughter tries to decide what *she* wants for her life, apart from her mother's ambition *for* her; this is more than a simple story of career choices. In *Never Fear* catastrophic illness disables a dancer, threatening first her life and then, as she begins to recover, her sense of self. *Unwanted* and *Outrage* explore what happens to women who transgress or are perceived to transgress the boundaries of social mores. *The Trouble with Angels* details a very different form of transgression, examining the lives of women, old and young, who choose a cloistered, spiritual and distinctly female existence over the more established social roles for women.

Lupino, who had worked since she was a child on the stage and whose film debut coincided with her thirteenth birthday, also addressed the issue of class in her films. The majority of her characters (just like those she most frequently played as an actor) work, and work because they have to, because they are driven to either by ambition or the need for a paycheck. In fact, it is at or through work that action most often occurs in Lupino's films. Ann Walton is raped outside her job on her way home from work in *Outrage;* Carol Williams collapses while working in *Never Fear;* the men in *The Hitchhiker* are getting away from work, taking a brief fishing trip, when calamity befalls them; *The Trouble with Angels* is about combining spirituality with work. In a period when work was decidedly unfashionable in the movies, or at the very least only a means to an end, Lupino acknowledges the reality that most people, like the director herself, work.

The small but powerful retinue of films by Lupino stands as a link between the work of women directors in the early days of filmmaking when it seemed women would be equals behind the camera and the work of independent directors in the present, still struggling to bring the lives of women to the screen in honest and compelling films. Lupino, largely ignored as a director, in fact almost singlehandedly kept women behind the camera in the male-only world of Hollywood. A powerful actor, a compelling director and a determined woman unwilling to sit on the sidelines when she could work, when she could "do something," Lupino was a maverick, a director of evolutionary import in the history of women and the cinema.

**Ida
Lupino**

Documentary Film

Allie Light

Learning About Metaphors

At sixty-two, Allie Light isn't resting on her laurels—even though her laurels would be envied by many filmmakers. Light's 1991 documentary *In the Shadow of the Stars* won the Academy Award for Best Documentary Feature, and her 1993 documentary *Dialogues with Madwomen* won the Emmy

Allie Light with footage from *Dialogues with Madwomen* (photo by Jim Block)

Award for Outstanding Interview Program, the Freedom of Expression Award at the 1994 Sundance Film Festival and the Grand Prize at the 1994 Atlanta Film Festival. Winning the Oscar, said Light, "had wonderful repercussions. One of the first things my youngest daughter said to me afterwards was,

Films by Allie Light

Mitsuye and Nellie: Asian American Poets

In the Shadow of the Stars

Dialogues with Madwomen

Rachel's Daughters

'Mom, your life has changed forever now, because no matter what happens to you in your life, even in your obituary it's going to say that you're an Academy Award winner.' It's very validating."

That said, Light is quick to note that the Academy Award "hasn't brought us any money at all. That's what happens with documentaries anyway." Light and her husband and co-producer, Irving Saraf, chose not to attend the Emmys: "It's very expensive to go to the Emmys; it's not like the Academy Awards, where they send you tickets. If we had had the money that it would have cost us to go to the Emmys, we could have put it into our new film instead. With the Emmys, the news and documentary awards aren't broadcast, so we just stayed home and sat by the phone, drank a bottle of wine and wondered if we were going to win. We were up against Diane Sawyer and Bill Moyers, and we thought just about budgets, we thought what *Dialogues* cost and what their segments probably cost, and it was overwhelming to us. We so much thought we weren't going to win."

Light, like many filmmakers, did not go to film school; her undergraduate work was in poetry writing, and her master's degree is in interdisciplinary arts. "What I wanted to do was get out of looking at words on paper, so when I got into graduate school I really wanted to do something that was visual, but I wanted to do it with poetry, somehow putting images of words on the wall. That's how I started, actually. That was my first project," said Light. "Eventually, I did make a small film in graduate school. It was a study of my youngest daughter. It was actually a nude study of her—it would probably be called pornography now."

The story of Light's involvement in film is also the story of her courtship and marriage to Saraf, who co-produced and co-directed *In the Shadow of the Stars* and co-produced *Dialogues with Madwomen*. "We met when he did his first show at KQED [a San Francisco public television station] on Bay Area poets, and I was one of the poets," Light recalled. "When we got together, I would write a poem, and he would make a movie out of it and give it to me, and I would make a poem from that movie and give it back to him, and that's the way we started working together."

Light's first major collaboration with Saraf was 1981's *Mitsuye and*

Nellie: Asian American Poets. "I was involved in raising money for the Women's Building in San Francisco, and a friend and I did an all-day screening of films by women writers about women writers. There were no films about Asian-American women writers," noted Light, "so we had a live reading in the middle of the day in order to make up for that, and both Nellie Wong and Mitsuye Yamada read. I made this rash promise to the audience that there would be a film, so we had to do it. We were lucky—we got full funding from the National Endowment for the Humanities for that film, and within a year we had made it."

Light and Saraf then produced *Visions of Paradise,* five half-hour films about folk artists. "All of our films have personal hooks. *Visions of Paradise* started when my daughter and I went on one of those trips where you take every side road you want," said Light. "In California, on the road to Las Vegas, we found this yard full of dolls that were moving in the wind. It was so strange and bizarre that we took pictures, and that's how I discovered folk art—I had never heard of it before. It's now called outsider art." Light's favorite film in the series is *Grandma's Bottle Village:* "She made these bizarre houses out of glass bottles, and I always felt that I was drawn to her because I grew up in a housing project where everything was the same. Every house had the same floor plan, everything looked identical, and here's this woman who is building these absolutely bizarre houses. I just thought they were wonderful. When you're inside [one of the houses] and the sun is shining through the bottles, it's like being inside a jewel."

Of working with her husband, Light said, "It's both the best and the worst. We have real battles, and they get carried over. We're both stubborn, and Irving always says we agree that we won't use anything that we both don't agree on, but then one of us has to convince the other that that viewpoint is the right one. It's a real process with every shot that gets cut together, especially so in the editing room. You fall in love with an image and you want to keep it, and you want to then fight for it. There were lots of times that I was wrong and finally had to admit that he was right, and he's had to do the same thing. It isn't easy, but I can't imagine making something so personal as a film with somebody that you're not personal with in every other way. We can talk about it around the clock. I can wake him up in the middle of the night and say, 'We should have done this,' and he does that too. We really do work well together. Irving knows how to cut at exactly the right place, as far as I'm concerned. He always says there's only one

Allie Light

39

place you can cut, only one frame that will work with the other frame."

Why did Light choose documentary as the form her films take? "Irving had a long history of filmmaking before we got together, but it was at KQED in San Francisco, so it was documentary film," noted Light. "It was *cinéma vérité* and it was exciting for him and other filmmakers because the camera became lighter and you could actually pack it around and capture things that were happening right then. There was a whole excitement around that and it was a sort of offshoot of news and what was happening at the moment, which I think is purely intoxicating. For me, I was always interested in autobiography—certainly a lot of my poems sprang from my life—and it was an easy move from writing poetry over to documenting lives—real things—but it was certainly a long shot for me. I think the evolution of our documentary filmmaking has more and more encompassed poetry in a way that I never thought would happen. Our films have really evolved, and they're now in some no-person's land—they're not documentaries per se, and they're not fiction, but they take the elements of both and try to tell the story in a real life."

Part of what Light and Saraf are attempting to do, Light explained, is "document the interior life, which was never done before in documentary film. I don't understand how the genre went so long without somebody trying to tell these stories, because it's not the whole story—*cinéma vérité* is wonderful and it's probably the backbone of documentary film, and the interview is the second one, but there's a third one, and that's trying to portray the past, dreams, the inner life. We can't substantiate [these things], but how can we leave them out?"

In the Shadow of the Stars, the film that won Light and Saraf the Oscar, studied the dreams and aspirations of the chorus members at the San Francisco Opera, the unsung but singing heroes who back up the opera's stars. But it was with *Dialogues with Madwomen* that the pair fully delved into portraying the inner life, the literal life of the mind.

Dialogues with Madwomen explores the world of women and madness: Through interviews with seven women, Light shows how women who do not follow societal norms are labeled mad by the medical profession, with diagnoses such as schizophrenia, multiple personality disorder, manic depression and euphoria. Lesbianism might be considered a diagnosis as well: As one woman, Deedee, says, "The counselor thought my problem was I wasn't sleeping with men." Women who do not fit into society's roles can be labeled outcasts, unfit or mad. At one time or another, for one reason or another, every woman has experienced some variation of this—Light shows what happens when women continue to rebel against society. One could say that *Dialogues* is the nineties version of Charlotte Perkins Gilman's novella *The Yellow Wallpaper*.

Hannah from *Dialogues with Madwomen*

Dialogues is not just a voyeuristic look at madness—Light herself is one of the seven women interviewed in the film. The women are a diverse cross section of society: Hannah, a manic-depressive obsessed with Bob Dylan; R. B., a Stanford Law School student who became a bag lady; Mairi, whose multiple personalities arose after sexual abuse at home; Deedee, diagnosed as schizophrenic, who was beaten by nuns at Catholic school; Susan, a truant and runaway who developed self-mutilating behavior; and Karen, an artist who was diagnosed as schizophrenic, and who was murdered before the completion of the film.

And then there's Light, who was institutionalized for depression as a young mother in the early 1960s, and who, despite her psychiatrist's advice, went to college and became a filmmaker.

Dialogues breaks with the traditional talking heads of the documentary form to include dark reenactments of the women's dreams, memories and fantasies. Light, in her reenactment segment, goes back to the experience of being sexually molested when she was four, in the basement of the building she lived in. In a piece she wrote for a book on surviving child abuse, Light said: "I had thought about this scene for several years—how it would look, what elements would be incorporated—but when the time came to direct it, I truly had to face my four-year-old self. I took with me into the basement all the fortifications I could gather. When my friend signed the property release for the use of her basement, she told me how she was molested by a priest when she was six years old, growing up in Chile. I took *her* story into the basement. I brought in (out of camera range) the mother of the child I was filming because my mother was not in the original basement of 1939. The molester is played by my adult son and the fact that this man whom I love, whom I gave birth to was a stand-in for a scary person from my childhood gave me command and power over a traumatic episode in my life. I was able to say to him, *'Move here,' 'Lift the chair from the wall,' 'Walk through again.'* I could control this dear actor. And, because film is magic, my son is also one of the men who walks by the window. He is the inside man *and* the outside man looking in."[1]

Dialogues is also a film about hope and healing: Light shows us how each woman's story (except Karen's) is resolved, how each woman comes to terms with her own madness. The film's message is both simple and complex: You're not crazy, and you're not alone. As Light herself says in the film: "Everything transcends what the reality of it is. You either go mad or you learn about metaphors."

When Light started work on *Dialogues,* she used what was at the time a unique fundraising approach: She sent a letter to every woman she knew, asking for a $25 donation to help fund the film. "That's how we got the first money—about $2000. Most everybody can afford to donate $25, and I did say [in the letter] that I didn't want people to give more because I wanted women who didn't have a lot of money to feel that they had the same input, and I think the people who wanted to give more sent me $25 at other times." But that $2000 was enough to pay for Betacam video equipment, a big step up in technology from the Hi8 camera used to shoot Karen's and Light's interviews for the film. Light and Saraf raised $20,000 for the film from grants and then funded the rest of the production—$43,000—with their own money. *Dialogues* actually turned a profit, and Light and Saraf were able to pay royalties to each of the women who appeared in the film.

Light and Saraf's latest project, like *Dialogues,* has a deeply personal hook: *Rachel's Daughters,* a feature-length documentary, is about breast cancer, the diagnosis their daughter received the summer that *Dialogues* was first touring the film festival circuit. "She's—so far—okay," said Light of her daughter. "We've learned so much about premenopausal breast cancer [while making *Rachel's Daughters*] that we're just going to be scared all the time, the rest of our lives, because it's almost a different disease than what older women get."

Rachel's Daughters is, said Light, "a detective story. Seven women with breast cancer try to find out what caused it. They interview researchers, scientists, doctors, other women with breast cancer all over the country. It has turned into an environmental film as well. I always liked Nancy Drew books when I was a kid, and it [the film] really is a detective story. It's a very plot-driven, narrative film."

Light also noted, "It's a sad film, because we've lost one of our detectives already. She was the youngest, and she died in April [1996]. And then a number of women who were interviewed [for the film] died, and sometimes I just want to bang my head against the wall afterwards, after talking to some of the other women in the film, finding out that now the cancer has metastasized. It's changed our lives—it's a dark, dark side of life."

As with *Dialogues with Madwomen,* Light and Saraf attempt to portray the inner life in *Rachel's Daughters,* "because," Light explained, "three of the scientists we interviewed also have breast cancer, so it's trying to blur that line between who is the doctor and who is the patient. Everybody is both. Mostly we're all trying to get someone to heal us or to heal ourselves. We just talked to a molecular biologist who has breast cancer. All of her research is in breast cancer. She's working fast, but I just heard this morning that she has metastases."

Stills from *Rachel's Daughters: Searching for the Causes of Breast Cancer* (top photo by Michelle Vignes; bottom photo by Rosalind Delligatti)

One of the scientists who has cancer, Sandra Steingraber, is asked in the film by one of Light's detectives if cancer is a feminist issue. Steingraber gives this insightful response: "It is a feminist issue because the parts of women's bodies that are affected—our ovaries, our uterus, our breasts—are the parts of the body that have been despised, objectified, fetishized, so we have strange cultural ideas about them. What it means to cut off a woman's breast in our society says a lot about our culture and the way we might value a breast over a woman's mind or a woman's life. The devaluation of women insinuates itself in reproductive cancer."

Light and Saraf raised $130,000 to fund the production of *Rachel's Daughters;* Light noted that they have another $100,000 to raise to complete the film. The Goldman Foundation gave them their first grant; the rest of the money came from "private money and individuals who have breast cancer in their lives," said Light. "We have as a co-producer one of the women who is in the film, and she was also the president of Breast Cancer Action, which means that she is very much an activist, and she's helped quite a bit with raising money."

Light noted that the biggest challenge in making *Rachel's Daughters* was to marry the scientific information gleaned from the many interviews with doctors and researchers with portrayals of the inner lives of women with cancer. Light added of the finished film, "We're going to make it very captivating. It's not going to be one of those voiceover documentaries people used to make."

In a letter Light wrote to us after our interview with her, she said: "I've been thinking of your question—why I make documentaries—and the answer is that I'm interested in my own life, so I'm also interested in the lives of others. The natural extension of this is to begin to *create* characters' lives and to eventually make dramatic films. This I've begun to do with my screenplays—one finished, two unfinished—and two unfinished novels. The unfinished are close to completion, but I've not had the time. Maybe when *Rachel's Daughters* is out. If my daughter remains well, anything can happen."

Notes

1. Allie Light, "Three Versions of *The Man in the Basement*," in *Writing Our Way Out of the Dark: An Anthology by Child Abuse Survivors*, ed. Elizabeth Claman (Eugene, Oregon: Queen of Swords Press, 1995), 148–149.

Pratibha Parmar

Warrior Marks

"I really cannot imagine a more terrible thing that could happen to you and you still go on living." Her rich voice rising with intensity, Pratibha Parmar's succinct description of her feelings about female genital mutilation (FGM) explains why she decided to take on the taboo subject with her most controversial film, *Warrior Marks* (1993).

Parmar is one of England's most prolific young filmmakers. Born in India and raised in Kenya, she emigrated to the United Kingdom with her family when she was eleven.

Pratibha Parmar (photo by Brigette Pougeoise)

Intensely political, Parmar is an ardent feminist, deeply engaged in addressing issues of race, class, gender and sexuality in her work, which is primarily documentary, though her films have a keenly dramatic and highly poetic flair. Tackling the political and cultural debate surrounding the practice of FGM, a major feminist issue in the United Kingdom, seemed

Films by Pratibha Parmar

Emergence

Sari Red

ReFraming AIDS

Memory Pictures

Bhangra Jig

Flesh and Paper

Khush

A Place of Rage

Double the Trouble, Twice the Fun

Warrior Marks

Memsahib Rita

The Colour of Britain

Jodie: An Icon

right to the filmmaker.

"There is so much of [FGM], really. People, *women*—especially in the West—just aren't aware of it," Parmar said. "Once you are aware of it, you can't forget it, can't get the images out of your head. I'm hoping people will get that from *Warrior Marks,* what it is to *live* with [FGM], to not be able to escape it."

Warrior Marks, like many of the films in Parmar's *oeuvre,* addresses a subject in which racism and sexism are inextricably connected. The filmmaking was done throughout Africa—in Senegal, Burkina Faso and Gambia—and was, Parmar said, long, arduous and intensely and personally painful. The film explores the variant aspects of FGM, explaining that in the world today, including the United States and Europe, over one hundred million women and girls are victims of FGM. FGM, often wrongly called female circumcision, is the practice of removing the clitoris, labia and parts of the vulva in a ritual "cleansing" to ensure the sexual "purity" and marriageability of women in some African, Asian, Muslim and other cultures. The ritual is nearly always performed without anesthetic, most often by a group of women or a ritual excisioner using a sharpened rock, bone or knife. (In Europe and the United States, the procedure is sometimes done in a doctor's office or hospital.) FGM is performed on girls as young as one month old and women as old as thirty, but most FGM is done just before puberty. The results are always significant and last throughout the life of the girl or woman: infection, disease, pain, sexual crippling, difficulty with childbirth and occasionally death.

It was those facts, plus the distinctly human side to this suffering, that Parmar wanted to elucidate for her audience. Part of that explication is of the taboo itself (the filmmaker does not show the actual act of FGM being performed, but does interview girls and women who have just experienced it) and how silence over the issue works to perpetuate the practice.

Warrior Marks, notes Parmar, explains why FGM remains a hidden crime against women, with very few people fully aware of the extent of the mutilation and how widespread the ritual is, how hideous the manner in which it is performed is, and how shattered the lives of the women and girls who are its victims are—even though the United Nations task force on women has cited FGM as a crime against women and a consistent cause of physical, emotional and psychological trauma, disfigurement, infection, disease and death among women worldwide. The International Tribunal on Crimes Against Women lists FGM as one of the five most prevalent crimes against women and girls in the world.

Unlike with her other films, Parmar did not work alone on *Warrior Marks.* Pulitzer Prize–winning African-American novelist Alice Walker, who writes about FGM in her novels *The Color Purple* and *Possessing the Secret of Joy,* approached Parmar about doing a film on FGM in December 1991. Parmar's film *A Place of Rage* (1991), about African-American women and their achievements, had featured Walker as well as African-American poet June Jordan and political activist Angela Davis. After her experience with Parmar's filming of *A Place of Rage,* Walker was convinced that the filmmaker was ideal for the project Walker had conceptualized, which would involve an exploration of FGM through a documentary trip to Africa. She put a significant amount of money toward the project, using the royalties from *Possessing the Secret of Joy,* and participated in many aspects of the filming, traveling throughout Africa with Parmar.

The film intercuts the documentary elements with Walker's commentary and rumination on the issue of FGM. Walker is credited as executive producer of *Warrior Marks,* and she and Parmar also compiled a book about their experience making the film called *Warrior Marks: Female Genital Mutilation and the Sexual Blinding of Women,* printed by Walker's publisher, Harcourt Brace. The book chronicles the filmmaking process—including diaries the two women kept, poems by Walker written during the filmmaking and interviews with survivors—and reproduces stills from their travels and the making of the film. It also provides resources related to abolishing FGM worldwide.

Walker had a significant impact on the film and its focus, said Parmar. The filmmaker has always addressed the political elements of racism and sexism in her work, and *Warrior Marks* does not deviate from that thematic structure, despite the more poetic elements engendered by Walker's participation. Parmar explicates how FGM is practiced in many countries, while few have made it illegal. (England, for example, did not make the procedure illegal until 1985.) *Warrior Marks* emphasizes how in Africa, Asia,

Still from *Warrior Marks* (courtesy of Women Make Movies)

India and the United Kingdom, women have been organizing to make the practice illegal and prosecutable so that women and girls are protected. But in many of the nations in which FGM is most prevalent, women are not marriageable if their genitals have not been excised, and some are driven from their homes as "fallen women." The situation keeps women economically and socially enslaved.

Parmar said all her films are "very personal" in individual ways, but that *Warrior Marks* had particular resonance. Parmar is very aware of her cross-cultural status as a woman of color in a predominantly white country. She has been deeply involved in political and community issues involving women of color and lesbians for years, and her films and videos reflect those interests. *Warrior Marks* incorporates Parmar's feminist and activist sensibilities, and as in her other documentaries, the viewer sees with Parmar's vision, through her personal lens.

Warrior Marks rivets the viewer. Exquisite, painful and with a haunting lyric quality, the film is rich with telling scenes between women in Africa. Fascinating and terrifying interviews with survivors of FGM, the perpetrators of the practice and health care providers working to eradicate FGM provide the nexus of the film, with Walker's commentary filtered throughout.

Walker said of the film—in her characteristically elliptical way—"When I saw the completed *Warrior Marks* I recognized it as a symbol of our [Parmar's and Walker's] mutual daring and trust. It is a powerful and magnificent film, thanks to Pratibha's brilliance as a director, constructed from our grief and anger and pain. But also from our belief in each other, our love of life, our gratitude that we are women of color able to offer our sisters a worthy gift after so many centuries of tawdriness, and our awareness of those other 'companion spirits' we know are out there."

Parmar, who has made several films since, is more direct about the impact *Warrior Marks* had on her. "This is the kind of project that simply stays with you," she explained. After the film premiered, she spent months with Walker promoting it, in the United States, United Kingdom, Europe and Mexico. She spent a grueling year working on the film, editing it, getting distribution and finally previewing the film in a ten-city tour. Parmar works as an independent filmmaker for London's Channel 4 television. She noted that in many respects working on *Warrior Marks* was no different from her other films, but that working with Walker altered the filmmaking process significantly. The work exhausted her, physically and emotionally.

Still from *Sari Red* (courtesy of Women Make Movies)

"I was very emotionally involved in this film; it was very visceral for me," she said. "It was difficult to separate myself from the project, although that has happened with other films I have done. I made a film called *Sari Red,* which was about the racist killing of a young Indian woman on the streets of London. That brought up a similar range of feeling for me. Very deep, very visceral, almost physically painful."

Warrior Marks, however, said Parmar, "is not the kind of film one makes to further one's career. You have to be very committed to women and to changing women's lives to do this kind of film, this kind of work. It's controversial, sensitive. I wouldn't have taken it on without that commitment."

But despite these disclaimers, Parmar admits that as soon as Walker suggested the collaboration, she was intrigued, even though she had never done a collaborative project before.

"I've never done this, worked with someone else on a film," she said. "It was different from my usual way of working in that sense. But Alice let me be the director; she didn't intrude in any way, so I was able to work as I normally do."

Working with Walker was a "very valuable experience," added Parmar. "I felt supported by Alice at all times during the project. I felt supported by her clear thinking about what we were doing. She had such clear faith in me. It was really quite wonderful."

It was in part Walker's own personal experience that brought about

Pratibha Parmar

some of that "clear thinking" about FGM and her desire to make a film on the issue. When Walker was only seven, she was shot in the eye by her brother with an air rifle. The injury blinded her instantly—and permanently—in one eye.

"After caring for me the week it happened, my parents ignored the injury," Walker explains in the book *Warrior Marks.* "They referred to what had happened as 'an accident.' *Alice's* accident. When I failed to adjust to a new school environment because of the resulting handicap and hostile curiosity of my classmates, I was sent away to live with my grandparents. For a long time I felt completely devalued. Unseen. Worthless. Because I had been blamed for my own injury, yet could not accept that it was my fault, the thought of suicide dominated my life." Added Walker, "What I had, I realized only as a consciously feminist adult, was a patriarchal wound." Walker explores the larger aspects of what she terms the "patriarchal wounding" of women in the film, from rape and assault to eating disorders to hair straightening.

For Parmar, the exploration was equally broad and equally unsettling. "I think Alice's perspective, the way she links all these different aspects of oppression together is good, really important, because it helps people to see that genital mutilation isn't the only thing here—there are lots of ways in which we are mutilated and oppressed by the society, by different cultures."

She explained that this linkage is important because it disallows "any distancing from the issue. It might be easy for some people, even some women, to say that genital mutilation doesn't affect them, because it isn't happening where they live—or so they think. But what Alice does forces them to make the connections."

Those connections were, however, clear to Parmar at the outset. As a woman of color, a woman born in Africa, where the majority of genital mutilations are performed, and as a lesbian, Parmar felt deeply galvanized by Walker's concerns about stopping the practice globally.

"As a lesbian, I think I felt very, very strongly about this issue," she said with a tinge of anger. "I kept asking myself if I was feeling as intensely as I was because as a lesbian, I know how much sexual pleasure I get from my own clitoris."

Parmar added that many of the women she interviewed had experienced the "milder form" of mutilation in which just the clitoris is excised, but there is no infibulation, which is the excising of the labia and sewing shut of the vulva, leaving only a small hole for menstrual excretion. An infibulated woman is reopened by her husband on their wedding night, usually with a ritual knife or razor, so that he can then have sex with her.

"*These* women told me that they enjoyed sex with their husbands, that they could be penetrated without extreme pain," she explained. "But in lesbian sexuality, our clitorises are so important. Many of us discover our lesbian sexuality through masturbation, and I think we focus on our sexual pleasure there more than straight women do."

Coming out as a teenager and while in her early twenties, Parmar said she experienced her first sexual pleasures as a lesbian "through my clitoris. Personally, when I first came out I was very much involved in the pleasure of my own body as a lesbian and so for me much of this discussion and filming had a lot of implications. As a lesbian, the implications of having your clitoris *cut off,* your genitals *cut off,* were dramatic."

It was not merely the actual physical trauma, said Parmar, but the psychological damage that unnerved her, during the filming and since.

"There is so much shame about this," Parmar explained. "As lesbians we talk a great deal about pride, including pride in our sexuality. But if your genitals are *cut off,* then the implication is clear. That is something to be really ashamed of, something to fear or hate about one's self. I think that there are a lot of cultural manifestations of this shame. In the West, for example, masturbating is frowned on, made shameful."

But genital mutilation, noted Parmar, is the most extreme form of this shaming of women over their sexuality. "It is an attack on the whole body of a girl child," said Parmar vehemently. "It is so terrible, and it stays with her forever—the pain, the shame, the trauma. When we talked to these women, years later—years after they went through this—they still feel the pain in so many ways. How can it be seen as anything but a terrible, terrible assault?"

Parmar and Walker both had such visceral reactions to seeing and talking with women and girls who had undergone the excisions that each had actual physical responses to the pain involved in their African journey. Parmar had nightmares from which she awoke sweating and screaming; Walker had terrible insomnia and couldn't sleep for days at a time. Parmar found herself making transcontinental phone calls to her lover during which she would sometimes simply sob hysterically. "I just desperately needed comforting after dealing with this experience," Parmar acknowledged. Walker remembers becoming so angry with one of the woman excisors that she later said she was ready to go "off my head." The struggle to maintain an emotional equilibrium was difficult for both women, particularly given the extended period of filming, the harsh conditions and the arduous travel.

"There is no question that this was a painful and difficult journey to do," said Parmar. "That's why you'd have to be very personally committed to do this kind of film. But there are so many people who don't even know about this [FGM], that it happens, today, now, in our very own countries. This isn't something distant and far away. That is what is so truly extraordinary—it *is* happening here [in London, where Parmar lives, in the United States, where Walker lives]."

Parmar is no stranger to long and difficult journeys. At twenty she decided to "go on my 'Roots' trip to India. I did volunteer work there. I worked with Mother Teresa for a while." At the time, it was still possible to travel via land to return to England—which Parmar did. "It wasn't so dangerous as it is now," said Parmar, "and none of the countries were closed, so I was able to travel overland back to London. At one point I was very low on money, so I sold a pint of blood for cash. I guess I have been through very difficult journeys before."

As important as her trip to India was to her personally, Parmar believes the work with Walker will have lasting impact.

"When we took the film out on previews," she said, "we found that many people hadn't even *heard* of female genital mutilation. I was rather surprised, because there has been organizing about it here in England for some years now. But in the United States, for example, many people just hadn't heard about it."

Others had taken some wrong turns in their identification with the issue. "We had a screening in San Francisco that was rather disappointing," Parmar explained. "There was a group of white gay men, men who had been circumsized, and they all had to talk about their own experience and how they could understand the pain of women who had been circumsized because *they* had been circumsized. I mean, it's hardly the same, is it? It's just a little piece of skin [lost in male circumcision], it isn't having your genitals cut off. But these guys couldn't even give space to the women who were there. The women booed the men down, but the men just really took over. Alice and I were very disappointed. We asked these guys to step out of themselves and listen to the women, but it didn't happen."

Other experiences were more rewarding, said Parmar. "On the whole, the discussions were good, and about a thousand people attended each screening. We also did a lot of interviews. Alice did CNN and Charlie Rose [on PBS], and I did CNN International. I think that the more we talked about the issue, the more it gives strength to African women."

"If just one girl child is saved from genital mutilation" by the work she and Walker have done, Parmar said, then it will all be worthwhile.

"We are trying to put this issue into a global framework," she said. "It isn't *just this* crime against women—it's what is going on in our own backyards. Rape, battering, all our warrior wounds are just as unacceptable as female genital mutilation. The film and the screenings and the book all open up a way for women to connect," Parmar explained. "It is crucial that women make these connections. It's not useful for women to see this as something far away and removed from themselves."

The filmmaker believes women in the United States and Europe can most easily make links to the violence of FGM, although she hopes the film will continue to be shown worldwide and affect audiences still suffering from the oppression of the practice. She thinks her film will have the most impact, however, on audiences already cognizant of crimes against women.

"The level of violence that the media perpetrate against women in the United States and Europe is so extreme," Parmar said. "We watch in a cinema women being raped and mutilated—the majority of women accept that as a reality. *Warrior Marks* is about changing *all* this violence against women."

Parmar said that the importance of crimes against women continues to be minimized, however, which is one of the reasons she makes the films she does. When she was touring with *Warrior Marks* an interviewer asked about the Lorena and John Wayne Bobbitt incident. "I was being interviewed before the [Washington] D.C. premiere of the film," she explained. "It was on Fox [television network] and it was live, and they asked me about Bobbitt and I said, 'Well, what about his abuse of her? He's only getting all this attention because a penis was cut off and because he is a white, heterosexual man. One hundred million women are having their genitals cut off, and they are seen as disposable—because they are women and because they are primarily women of color. He comes at the top; they are negligible.' I don't think they liked my response," she laughed, "but it was live, so they couldn't edit it out, for which I was very glad. People need to hear this."

One of the criticisms leveled at Walker and Parmar for instituting their fight against FGM comes from cultural purists who think excision is part of the cultural heritage of people of color and Muslims. It is an accusation that the filmmaker is more than ready to answer. She makes the point that there is nothing culturally sacrosanct about FGM. She cites the medical evidence of raging infections and deaths from the procedure and the ensuing pain and later deaths in childbirth that women experience. She also notes that the spread of HIV among women in Africa and Asia, where women are contracting HIV in greater numbers than men, may be directly related to the use of the same excision knife on twenty to thirty girls and women at a time. Finally, Parmar quotes Walker from *Warrior Marks,* "Alice says there is a difference between torture and culture."

Said Parmar, "Making this film has made me realize how much more confident I am as a filmmaker; it's pushed me to a different level as a filmmaker. The subject is haunting, it's controversial, it's emotional, it stays with you. That is what I wanted all along. I wanted these women, their pain and their survival to stay with the audience. I wanted to push the boundaries as a filmmaker and an artist. Filmmaking is so often the preserve of white heterosexual men. I believe my filmmaking is about representation and self-representation, about political engagement with the issues. I don't come from a film school background; I come from a community-organizing background. So my films are very much about making marginalized issues heard. In *Warrior Marks* I wanted to make these women heard. I don't believe millions of women should be marginal, disposable. We need to care what happens to these women, to these young girl children. What I hoped to do was make people see what is happening."

Despite the controversies, *Warrior Marks* won prizes at film festivals in Paris and Madrid. Although Parmar discusses *Warrior Marks* as her most challenging and controversial film, in fact her work has always elicited controversy, particularly because the themes of race, gender and sexual choices form the nexus of her *oeuvre*. And Parmar is prolific, making at least one film a year for over a decade. Focusing attention on difference, alienation and "otherness" in society, whether that society is Western, as in *Sari Red* (1988); Indian, in *Khush* (1991); African, in *Warrior Marks;* American, in *A Place of Rage;* or lesbian, in *Flesh and Paper* (1990), Parmar consistently juxtaposes the position of the "other" with the so-called normative within a given society. This contrapuntal approach is what imbues Parmar's films with such depth and power.

One of her most powerful pieces has particular resonance for her as an Asian woman. Just as she explains how *Warrior Marks* raised numerous emotions in her as she went through the process of documenting FGM, Parmar noted that *Sari Red* "could have been about me or any other Asian woman here [in Britain]. That is the horror, right there."

Detailing a grisly racial murder in England, *Sari Red* was made in memory of Kalbinder Kaur Hayre, a young Indian woman murdered during a racist attack in 1985. Parmar said, "The violence against Asian women is always there; it's all around you. It isn't *just* racism—that is only a part." And *Sari Red,* like *Warrior Marks,* delineates the range of violence Asian women experience, explicating that violence in both private and public spheres.

In *Sari Red* Parmar also broaches the subject of women's sexuality, a taboo she returns to in other films, like *Khush.* The word *khush,* Parmar explained, means "ecstatic pleasure" in Urdu, a major language of India, and the film delves into the complicated history of homosexuality, race, gender and personal pleasure for Indian lesbians and gay men. In *Khush* Parmar uses interviews with Indian lesbians and gay men in Canada, the United States, the United Kingdom and India to explore the panoply of Indian queer experience within those various cultures and within the larger tradition of Indian sensuality. The confluence of race, gender and sexual expression receives vivid treatment through Parmar's use of images of Indian culture and sensual identity.

Homosexuality is illegal in India, making it more difficult for lesbians and gay men to express their *khush.* Parmar said, "I wanted to explain what it was to be Indian and lesbian, Indian and gay. The experience is different in different places—you get that from the ways each person talks about those emotions."

Parmar addresses the exoticization of Indian queers in other countries as well as their alienation and their sense of "otherness," but juxtaposes the problematic aspects of sexual expression with the solidarity of sharing a cultural bond that has an historical as well as a personal locus.

Parmar examines other "marginal" issues, such as disability in the lesbian and gay community in *Double the Trouble, Twice the Fun* (1992) and the political and social backlash AIDS has created within the lesbian and gay community in *ReFraming AIDS* (1988). In *ReFraming AIDS*, Parmar challenges societal constructs over sexuality and oppression; in *Double the Trouble, Twice the Fun*, she tackles the invisible nature of disability within a community that often overvalues the perfect body.

Parmar also maintains a keen interest in the arts, and a significant number of her films focus specifically on artists and writers and the role they play in political consciousness-raising through re-creating and reinventing culture in a different image from the mainstream. *Emergence* (1986) presents four black and Third World women artists, including African-American poet Audre Lorde and Palestinian performance artist Mona Hatoum, discussing their work and their lives as artists, women of color and lesbians. This video explicates the artist in her role as political voice, repeating that Parmar theme of "otherness" by expressing the isolation often felt by the artist and woman, particularly as she struggles to find her place in her own community and to find her own identity as artist and woman/lesbian/person of color.

Memory Pictures (1989) covers similar ground as it examines the life of Sunil Gupta, a gay photographer, while also showing footage of a show of the filmmaker's own photographs, titled "Wall of Images." *Flesh and Paper*, about lesbian-feminist Indian poet Suniti Namjoshi, examines the intricacies of cultural and personal identity. Other work—notably *A Place of Rage, Bhangra Jig* (1990), a fantasy with music and dance about ethnic identity in the nineties, *The Colour of Britian* (1994), about the ghettoization of ethnic writers in the nineties—addresses that confluence of race, gender and politics.

Jodie: An Icon (1996) is a kitschy tribute to Jodie Foster, actress, director and producer and a lesbian icon who may or may not be a lesbian herself. Parmar's treatment is wholly nineties and very ironic, presenting Foster as the Marlene Dietrich–style butch/femme icon phenomenon of the millennium for lesbians, replete with World Wide Web pages for fans and look-alike contests in San Francisco's Castro district. In some respects, *Jodie: An Icon* represents a bit of a departure for Parmar, if only in tone: The film is light, funny and full of ironic nuances; however, it still deals with the marginalizing issues that form the foundation for all of Parmar's work.

Parmar's work as a documentarian is distinctive, particularly for its lyricism. As the director has noted, art and politics are inextricably connected in her life as well as in her films, and Parmar often imparts a rich tapestry of lyric imagery, music and dance as counterpoint to the seriousness of her subject.

Parmar has developed a weighty body of work in the past decade that makes her one of the most important young women documentary film-makers. *Warrior Marks* solidified her place as a documentarian willing to take serious risks in her work and art, but the repertoire of her films over-all illuminates a filmmaker for whom the personal is indeed political, a filmmaker whose goals are activist as well as artistic, a filmmaker whose vision compromises neither her own ideology nor her subjects.

Pratibha Parmar

Michelle Parkerson

I Just Do My Work

Michelle Parkerson (photo by Leigh H. Mosely)

Michelle Parkerson is one of a handful of African-American women making films in the United States. She is one of even fewer black lesbians making films. Those facts alone make it surprising that Parkerson is amassing a prestigious complement of films.

Parkerson—who has done some outstanding work in what she calls "docutainment" with African-American legends such as jazz singer Betty Carter, male impersonator (from the Jewel Box Revue) Storme DeLarverie and the a cappella group Sweet Honey in the Rock—has reached an even higher level of achievement in her work on the late poet Audre Lorde, *A Litany for Survival* (1995), co-directed with Ada

Gay Griffin [a profile of whom appears in this book].

A Litany for Survival—the title taken from a poem by Lorde—shows the poet in all her complexity and diversity: reading the title poem to a university audience, working with a writing group of young women of color, talking to the directors about her life as a "black lesbian warrior woman," attending a poetry reading/ book signing, surviving being black and lesbian in America and struggling with breast and liver cancer.

A Litany for Survival is a compelling document in which Lorde shows her strengths and her vulnerabilities, her humor and her anger, and how she managed to use all these to become an unofficial poet laureate of lesbians in America. Lorde talks about how her first poem was published in 1947 in *Seventeen Magazine,* even though her writing teacher told her it was not a good poem. "I made more money from that poem than I made for the next ten years," Lorde says ironically in the film. She also explains how between 1947 and 1960 her poems went unpublished, effectively "leaving me with no voice."

This point is also a metaphor in Lorde's work. As the camera rolls, Lorde explains, "We [women, African Americans, lesbians] were not meant to survive. We are not seen, we are not heard." Giving voice is what Lorde's life work was about, and *A Litany for Survival* shows that with a delicacy and subtlety that are truly marvelous.

There are other nice touches in the film that anchor this point—such as a scene from the book signing in which African-American lesbian writer Jewelle Gomez is talking to a white woman and says, "Did I tell you, I have a book coming out." The woman asks who is publishing it, and Gomez laughs and says she is publishing it herself.

Parkerson's first film was ... *But Then, She's Betty Carter* (1980), which the filmmaker said "has all the flaws of a first film." But the film, which stars Carter, Lionel Hampton and some fabulous music, is so delightful and engaging one has to concentrate on the flaws to notice them. Parkerson gives Carter free rein—both musically and personally—to tell the story of her rise from a teenaged be-bop queen to one of the most respected jazz singers in the United States.

"I choose my subjects from my growing up," Parkerson said. "Betty

Films by Michelle Parkerson

. . . But Then, She's Betty Carter

Gotta Make This Journey: Sweet Honey in the Rock

Storme: The Lady of the Jewel Box

Odds and Ends (A New Age Amazon Fable)

A Litany for Survival: The Life and Work of Audre Lorde

Michelle Parkerson

Carter was a voice I heard then, along with the Modern Jazz Quartet and Miles Davis. Motown came later. In my house, jazz was the predominant thing. In my twenties, I really liked the group LaBelle [Patti LaBelle, Sarah Dash and Nona Hendryx], and when I got out of Temple [University] I wanted to do a major piece of my own that didn't belong in part to the school. LaBelle liked the treatment but couldn't do it, because Don Kirshner had them tied up for media stuff. So my mind naturally went to Betty Carter, because she embodied the same ideals of black women surviving in a predominantly white male business. Betty Carter had been doing it for thirty years. She's the mother of two kids, has a record company. Now she's got the Grammy award and the world is discovering her, and that's wonderful.

"That's probably the start of *all* these films: I just want people to discover these artists because they're so fantastic. Moreover, artists always do have such an overt political direction in how and why they do their art. I call these films 'docutainment.' They're like propaganda films. These women *do* have a definite political perspective that many status quo women consider radical. But the politics slip in very softly as you're being entertained by their singing. Suddenly you may pick up why they're singing 'Biko' instead of whatever. It's a subtle way of producing propaganda films. It broadens the audience's idea of entertainment and their political outlook. They hear another's perspective as a black woman or lesbian."

Parkerson frequently speaks about her work as a filmmaker and also about the work of other African-American filmmakers (including Spike Lee, whose work she doesn't like but whose business acumen she admires). One film that Parkerson admires is Euzhan Palcy's *A Dry White Season* (1989). "There's the racist presumption that she [Palcy] must do a film about blacks," said Parkerson. "That's as racist as anything else. Or, because she's a woman, the protagonist must be a woman. Those are stereotypes, limitations and *isms*. I can't respond to the media—the racist, homophobic, sexist institutions that comprise America. I strive to be in her [Palcy's] same creative stream. There is some camaraderie by dint of being in the same field—and especially when another black woman makes it big, I'm for it. She did the work so beautifully. Her idea of violence: the use of violent *sounds*, as opposed to seeing it; the lighting—the use of amber gels to bring out the luminosity of the African land. A great rendering."

Parkerson originally planned to go into theater, not film. "My mother was a very avid theatergoer who also loved old films, so I had a sense of theater and film from her. My dad built hi-fis, so I had a grounding in the arts and gravitated that way," Parkerson noted. "What surprised me is that they nutured me in this, because most black parents just try to set their children up to live in this society, granted its racism. Perhaps African-American parents had to steer their kids toward more status-quo jobs, and artistic leanings were fostered to be avocations. Even though they fostered mine, no little black girl in the fifties or sixties was thinking about being a film director.

"I went to Temple University in 1970 for a degree in theater arts. I wanted to know more about the technical side. As a teenager, I was really active in regional theater in Washington, D.C., community theaters, and my parents were also very active in the civil rights movement, so the political side was included too. When I got to Temple, there were not only technical but also performance requirements to be filled. So, thinking I was a really good actress and wanting to move up in that sphere as well as learning the technical aspects—like sets and lighting and directing and even extending the writing, which was, for me, mostly poetry at that time—I learned at Temple there were few opportunities for black students to have any starring roles in the college theater repertory. So I was immediately confronted with the apartheid of that community.

"At that time the Afro and feminist movements were influencing my life and how I intended to spend it. I didn't think politics should be separated from my work and career. It didn't make sense to join IBM with my radical thinking. I talked to a black woman who was a senior at the time, who told me I would get nowhere in my current program and that I should try going across the hall to the radio, television and film department. It was like all the doors opened, and the writing and directing were things I could use in film and radio and in being in control of a product. Temple was a good training ground in that area. I actually went back there to teach for a semester in 1986.

"So I got into film because I was an artist, but also because it was going to serve my politics," Parkerson said. "I'm learning to make a living at making films. More and more I'm getting the chance to direct, and that's a great joy just to be able to do one thing at a time. Independents are usually doing most of the jobs: producer, director, editor, et cetera. Not to have to worry about the producing is a great joy at this point. It shows me there's progress."

Michelle Parkerson

61

After graduating from Temple, Parkerson landed a job in television. "I worked for NBC in 1975 as a TV engineer for commercials, and then I worked for Metromedia—now Fox—which allowed me to get into the union, get my first-class licenses and get a technical reference for the industry, which has helped me enormously as a producer-director. I left the TV media around 1981. At that time, there were very few women, though now the numbers have increased. Affirmative action also *eased* the doors—didn't *open* them—but eased them. I had been through the throes of technology. Once you can push buttons and read oscilloscopes, it's a tremendous empowerment. I try to make my female students pay attention to this because I think a lot of young women feel that working with machinery defeminizes you. I think it empowers you and lets you get a lot more jobs. If you can edit, you don't always have to be waiting for the directing jobs. You can make a great living as a technician—especially if you've got a union to oversee the company you're working for. When I worked at NBC, there were five black women there who had already been there for two to three years. My generation was at the end of that affirmative action wave."

Parkerson is acutely aware—without being angry—of white privilege in the field of filmmaking. "We know we sort of have to try the doors one at a time," said Parkerson of black women filmmakers. "The feminist movement has given more visibility to us, too, as it's turned its eyes toward restoring white women to film history texts—Dorothy Arzner and Alice Guy-Blaché. Also, the black press and foreign press have acknowledged us. African cinema gets the spotlight once in an orange moon."

She also points out that the media play a large part in how films by African-American women are received. "If you're not Steven Spielberg, we're not going to read about you in *Ladies Home Journal*," she noted. "You've got to be a mega-entity for the masses to know of you nationally. People don't feel it's legitimate if you haven't done a Hollywood film. Documentaries make you a second-class citizen in the film industry. No matter how many you've done, if you haven't done a feature, you're not a 'real' director. That built-in bias keeps people like Debbie Allen and Neima Barnett from being more prominent. People look at documentaries and sit-coms as something less than a 'real' movie.

"I think people are looking for a change from what Hollywood and television are offering. But we don't have a consistent venue for it: The distribution and exhibition ends have got to be marketed well. People are making political films, but people aren't seeing them at their local theaters. We've got to get them out in the world. How are these films being marketed and reaching audiences—being advertised in papers? How many reviews are they getting, critical analyses outside of academia? If it's in 16mm, most theater chains don't have that anymore. That's part of the exclusionary element."

Money is another exclusionary element: "There is a limited amount of funding for alternative cinema," Parkerson said. "Women and blacks have been most affected by the cutbacks in this area. This is good in a way, because all of us want to move beyond subsidized filmmaking, and now we're forced to, since Reagan. So we're broadening our world. This *is* a business. You've got to find MBAs out there to find other funding sources: limited partnerships, co-production deals with foreign companies and cable companies, holding fundraising benefits to get money.

If women or blacks owned a theater chain, what changes would that effect? Oprah Winfrey's owning a studio is a major bit of history here. *If* we owned chains, could we raise the money to begin making films and our own particular exhibition circuit? It's not only content and analysis, but money. Introspection is interesting and important, but ultimately it's the *making* of the film that gives you something to talk about."

Parkerson has a measured and gracious delivery that is reminiscent of some of the women she filmed in her as yet uncompleted documentary on black women clergy, *Upon This Woman Rock*. Parkerson frequently thanks God in the credits of her films. When asked to explain her ability to combine a lesbian-feminist perspective with her attention to God, Parkerson skirted the issue of lesbianism and religion, answering that she was a spiritual person and was not involved in the "organized side of [religion]," but saw that organized religion helped others and therefore she wasn't judgmental about it. She did not address the complex problem of the role of lesbians in the African-American church community.

Latina filmmaker Frances Negrón-Muntaner asked Parkerson at a screening about Parkerson's focus on "elite artists." Negrón-Muntaner's point was that it was relatively easy to deal with homophobia, sexism and racism in the queer community, but that class issues were almost never raised.

"I found myself wanting to have people say things better," Negrón-

Still from *Storme: The Lady of the Jewel Box* (courtesy of Women Make Movies)

Muntaner said of her own classism. Parkerson agreed that classism was an important issue to deal with, but noted that for many women documentaries were not the best style of filmmaking, that "narrative fiction [filmmaking] offers you the opportunity to put words in people's mouths. It gives you more power to direct what you are saying."

Parkerson also said that she had found the same problem in making some of her films, particularly *Storme* (1987). "It's not politically correct to be butch and femme, it's not politically correct to use dildoes. I found myself coming from my post-Stonewall consciousness to [Storme's] and wanting to take words out of her mouth or make her say them differently." But Parkerson also made the point that this is how "our herstory" gets edited out—that editing was the primary power in filmmaking because "you control the images that get seen. People are always telling you to tone things down, like tone down that S/M thing, or tone down that African thing. The editing process alters the images—it decides which images will be seen."

Parkerson noted that she herself is moving away from documentaries, a change heralded by her 1993 video *Odds and Ends (A New Age Amazon Fable),* which takes place in the year 2096 and features black women warriors. "I've done industrials, commercials," said Parkerson. "I've edited for others. So I've earned my living in ways people don't recognize as 'a film by Michelle Parkerson.' I've also done black history promos for TV, but with no name recognition. I don't see myself as only a documentary filmmaker. I'm trying to move into feature filmmaking. For the last ten years, I've been content to reflect *my* politics through the politics of other women, because I subscribe to the politics they have. *Then* it was important for me to have the artists speak for themselves—'ahs' and 'ums' included—so that the audience gets a sense of the person, their cadences of speech and thought processes and any politics involved. *Now* I want to put words into other people's mouths—that's why I'm moving more into feature narrative or feature dramatic films. I think documentaries prepare you for dramatic films, because the best documentaries have an element of drama—the human drama of things—and constructing

Documentary Film

images and sound in a way that does unravel the story.

"I just do my work offering a black, lesbian experience," said Parkerson. What sorts of films does she, as a black lesbian filmmaker, want to see? "All kinds. Experimental, animation, documentary, commercials. But first you have to assume a society that could tolerate diversity. *If* we had such a society, one with a holistic approach, seeing everyone as part of a whole and not as segments or chunks. But that's idealistic and very far away; I can only work to have my voice heard, and my voice will be joined by others because I'm not out here alone."

Michelle Parkerson

Catherine Saalfield

Art and Activism

Catherine Saalfield (photo by John Hall)

At thirty-one, filmmaker Catherine Saalfield has started her own nonprofit corporation, Aubin Pictures, to produce and distribute her work. Her most recent video, the activist documentary *When Democracy Works* (1996), a look at the tactics of the radical right wing on civil rights issues, is just one of the many places where her art and activism meet.

"I can't separate my work into either art or activism," said Saalfield unequivocally. "For me, filmmaking is the most efficient, creative and satisfying form of activism."

In 1995, she co-produced *Positive: Life with HIV*, a four-part series about HIV-related issues that aired on public television in 1996. *Positive* was the largest project Saalfield had undertaken and the first series about HIV-related issues that included people in all stages of the disease. "It is very much a grassroots series," noted Saalfield. "We gathered over forty people in the HIV community—people with HIV, their lovers, family, children, social workers, doctors, nurses—for a meeting and asked them what they wanted to see, what HIV-related issues they felt should be addressed." Part of what makes *Positive* so unique is that "it assumes the viewer is HIV-positive, has relationships with people who are positive, or is working in the positive community," said Saalfield.

Each of *Positive*'s four episodes is made up of five- to ten-minute segments that include dance, music video, animation and short documentaries. The segments explore many of the issues faced by those who are HIV positive, including homophobia, racism, homelessness, activism, access to health care, treatment, care provider burnout and planning for death.

Art and activism also intersected in Saalfield's role as director of the Television Production Workshop at New York City's Hetrick–Martin Institute, a position she held from 1994 to 1996. Hetrick–Martin houses the Harvey Milk School, the only high school in the nation specifically for lesbian and gay teens, as well as other social services for lesbian and gay youth. Saalfield worked directly with lesbian and gay teens, overseeing the production of eight half-hour shows that are written, shot and edited by youths at the institute. The series, appropriately titled *BENT TV* (*bent* is the British slang word for queer), was underwritten by a grant from New York City cable access station Manhattan Neighborhood Network, which aired the finished pieces.

The student work explored the range of lesbian and gay teen experience—from the humorous to the horrendous. *BENT TV* segments included a public service announcement on diversity, a spoof commercial for "Fruity Loops" breakfast cereal, a parody about coming out in which a student goes through emotional turmoil when he thinks he might be straight and a documentary about a male-to-female transsexual who lives and works on the street. Most were short pieces, and many used humor—sometimes ironic—to help get their messages across.

"I teach the kids how media works and how powerful it can be, how they can use it for their own ends," Saalfield explained. "At the same time, I teach them about what a big responsibility working in media is and how every

Videos by Catherine Saalfield

Bleach, Teach, and Outreach

Ends and Means

Keep Your Laws Off My Body

Among Good Christian Peoples

Bird in the Hand

I'm You, You're Me: Women Surviving Prison Living with AIDS

Sacred Lies, Civil Truths

B.U.C.K.L.E.

Cuz It's Boy

Outta the Blue

Positive: Life with HIV (co-producer)

When Democracy Works

Catherine Saalfield

step in the production process requires important decisions. What's important," said Saalfield, "is that everything that gets broadcast has been made by the kids themselves."

Saalfield is not merely a producer; her own videos are perennial favorites at queer and women's film festivals across the country. In *Keep Your Laws Off My Body* (1990), a video indictment of legislation against privacy, Saalfield and co-producer Zoe Leonard juxtaposed footage of lesbians in bed with footage of police breaking down the door. *Bird in the Hand* (1992), which she co-produced with Melanie Hope, follows two lesbian lovers as they try to get out of town for the weekend. *Among Good Christian Peoples* (1991), co-produced with African-American children's author Jacqueline Woodson, is based on Woodson's humorous essay about growing up as a black lesbian who is also a Jehovah's Witness. In *Cuz It's Boy* (1994), Saalfield uses the murder of Brandon Teena [the transgendered person who was murdered in Nebraska because of her/his relationship with a young woman in the area] as the jumping-off point for her pixelvision exploration of gender and the differences between "being a boy" and being a lesbian or a woman who passes as a man.

Saalfield often combines documentary work with an activist agenda: Saalfield's video *Sacred Lies, Civil Truths* is a documentary study of the religious right and its tactics that she co-produced in 1993. The documentary, which has been shown across the country, analyzes the religious right's campaigns for anti-gay initiatives in Oregon and Colorado in 1992. It also examines the role religion plays in lesbian and gay communities. "I hope it can be used as a learning tool," she said, "particularly in communities and schools."

Saalfield followed the success of *Sacred Lies* with the 1996 video *When Democracy Works,* which she both produced and directed. The film is an activist look at the strategies of the radical right in an election year: David Duke's failed political campaigns in Louisiana, the battle over anti-gay Amendment 2 in Colorado and the fight over legal and illegal Mexican immigrants in California. "The right doesn't discriminate in its targets," said Saalfield, "and the targets need to stop being so single-issue focused. It [the video] really concentrates on kinds of scapegoating, how scapegoating works." The video was funded by the Interfaith Alliance Foundation, the National Campaign for Freedom of Expression, the National Lesbian and Gay Task Force and Political Research Associates.

When Democracy Works cost $63,000 to produce and another $60,000 to distribute. Over eighteen hundred copies were distributed at low cost to schools, churches and organizations between the Republican National Convention in August 1996 and the presidential election in November. Saalfield noted that the video was used as a premium giveaway for the pledge drive at Pacifica Radio Stations in California, was aired more than three times on Free Speech TV and was distributed to the leaders of fifty-seven different organizations represented at the Southern Human Rights Organizing Conference held in September 1996.

Still from *When Democracy Works*

Saalfield's résumé has all the earmarks of a rising star. The Ohio native studied semiotics and women's studies at Brown University, graduating magna cum laude and Phi Beta Kappa in 1988. In spite of her semiotics background, she doesn't sound like a film theory textbook whenever she speaks: "I had to actively get away from that," Saalfield mused. "Semiotics is a great place to come from, but you have to be able to communicate with other people, and all the semiotics jargon really gets in the way of that." Saalfield worked as a production assistant on legendary filmmaker Yvonne Rainer's film *Privilege* (1990). Later, she was an assistant director on African-American director Julie Dash's *Praise House* segment (1991) of the PBS series of *Alive from Off Center*. In 1990, she founded New York's annual LOOKOUT Lesbian and Gay Video Festival.

"She's a dynamic figure in the lesbian and gay media arts world," noted Jenni Olson, a film curator and the former co-director of the San Francisco International Lesbian and Gay Film Festival, adding that Saalfield's work has appeared at the festival every year since 1989. "She has been important in drawing attention to women and AIDS, particularly with the video *I'm You, You're Me: Women Surviving Prison Living with AIDS* [1993]. The work

Catherine Saalfield

she did as an Astraea National Lesbian Action Foundation board member was invaluable in providing funding for projects that otherwise wouldn't get funded. She's also very generous in helping other people get access to media equipment and in networking with people," Olson said.

Saalfield is just as much of an overachiever in her personal life—her ice hockey team won a silver medal at the Gay Games IV. And Saalfield and her lover, African-American poet and playwright Melanie Hope, recently celebrated the birth of their daughter. Saalfield is clearly intoxicated by their relationship: "It's really good for us, because we both love everything about each other, and it gives us lots of space to be welcoming and nonjudgmental about all the ways in which we are different from each other."

One is bound to wonder where Saalfield gets all her energy. "Having a really hot lover," she laughed in response. "Seriously, just being in the world gives me all the impetus I need. My work *and* my activism are comments on what I see around me."

Funding is a big issue for Saalfield. As part of the Astraea board, she reviewed applications for film and video production grants. "It hurts to see a production that would be great on film be shot on video because the funding isn't available," she said. "One of the great things about having ITVS [Independent Television Service] fund *Positive* was that we could actually pay people for their work. Often, you have to work for nothing, especially if you're doing something about AIDS or about being lesbian." Her latest concern is Newt Gingrich and his attacks on funding for the National Endowment for the Arts (NEA) and public television. Said Saalfield, "*Positive* was funded by ITVS, which is funded by Congress as part of the Public Broadcasting System [PBS]. Funding cuts to PBS and the NEA directly hurt filmmakers and indirectly hurt the lesbian and gay community because ITVS and the NEA have regularly funded lesbian and gay projects."

Saalfield's brand of activism underscores the importance of the old feminist slogan "the personal is political." As Saalfield says simply, "You can't separate your activism from your art any more than you can separate your sexuality from your identity."

Experimental Film

Barbara Hammer

Filling the Blank Screens

Quixotic, quirky and quintessentially questioning—all apt descriptives for the queen of queer cinema, the doyenne of dyke video, Barbara Hammer, who has been the preeminent lesbian experimental filmmaker for three decades. In the era of lesbian B-movies about bar girls and trips to the lesbian moon, in the age of postmodernist art and post–

Barbara Hammer (photo by Geoffrey Nelson)

postmodernist politics, Hammer's cinematic and political vision set her apart from the new wave of lesbian film and video makers with work that is sharp, daring, controversial and—nearly thirty years and over seventy films and videos since her filmmaking debut—still iconoclastic.

Nearly sixty, Hammer is lesbian filmmaking's *grande dame,*

Films by Barbara Hammer

Schizy

A Gay Day

I Was/I Am

Menses

Sisters!

Dyketactics

Jane Brakhage

Women's Rites or
    Truth Is the
    Daughter of Time

"X"

Superdyke

Psychosynthesis

Multiple Orgasm

Moon Goddess

Available Space

The Great Goddess

Sappho

Double Strength

Eggs

Haircut

Home

Dream Age

Women I Love

Our Trip

but her work is as maverick today as it was when she virtually created the genre of lesbian experimental film; her film *Dyketactics* (1974) was the first film depicting lesbian sex to actually have been made by a lesbian filmmaker. Her films have been shown everywhere from church basements to the most prestigious film festivals in the world. She has won numerous awards for her work, had premieres several times at the Whitney Museum of Art Biennial, been given retrospectives at the Berlin Festival and Museum of Modern Art in Paris, taught filmmaking on both coasts and given master classes from Marin County, California, to Soweto, South Africa.

Hammer said she was "born to make movies. I am—literally—a child of Hollywood." Her grandmother was a cook for Lillian Gish, and her mother was determined to make Hammer into a child star. Hammer was born in Hollywood in 1939, the year director Victor Fleming barraged the box office with back-to-back blockbuster epics, *The Wizard of Oz* and *Gone with the Wind;* the highest paid actress in Hollywood was Shirley Temple. Hammer said she "expected to be an actress, because I didn't realize that *I* could be making the pictures, that I could *make* the movies, not just act in them."

Thirty years old before she made her first film (after being given an 8mm Bolex camera), Hammer previously had tried her hand at art. Painting interested her; she studied with William Morehouse. "I wanted to create," Hammer said. One day Morehouse brought "a leather-clad woman model with her motorcycle into the class, and I was so inspired," she recalled, "that I stretched the largest canvas yet and, in an attempt to show the movement I felt her figure implied, gave her extra arms, hands, legs and feet."

Other experimentation with the idea of movement followed, Hammer explained. "Later I painted with materials that would change under varying lights and constructed color wheels or black-light paintings that moved while viewed." But it was the experience of making her first film that made Hammer the creative artist she had always known herself to be. Her first film, *Schizy* (1968), dealt with the duality of masculinity and femininity. That film began Hammer's long expression through film and video of the complicated terrain of lesbian life.

"Two things happened with that first film that helped me to continue in filmmaking," explained Hammer. "It won an Honorable Mention at the Sonoma County 8mm Film Festival, and the experience of watching it projected with an audience was incredible. The film was larger than any canvas I'd painted, and the audience was captured by the darkness and direction of light to watch my work in a way no one had looked at my paintings. That was it. I was a filmmaker."

Arequipa	Optic Nerve
Machu Piccu	Place Mattes
Sync Touch	No No Nooky TV
Pools	Endangered
Picture for Barbara	Two Bad Daughters
Pond and Waterfall	Still Point
Audience	Sanctus
Stone Circles	Vital Signs
Bent Time	Nitrate Kisses
Doll House	Eight in Eight
Parisian Blinds	Out in South Africa
Tourist	Tender Fictions

The next step for Hammer was to begin to develop her own gaze, which evolved surprisingly quickly into a distinctly lesbian cinematic perspective—and a totally new genre of filmmaking. Hammer credits Maya Deren as her most defining influence, with *Meshes of the Afternoon* (1943) as her most pivotal early experience of cinema.

"I knew there was room for a woman's vision on the screen," Hammer said. Her first 16mm film, *I Was/I Am* (1973) "pays direct homage to Deren." The theoretical writing Deren did on film also impressed Hammer, as did the later work of French feminist theorists like Luce Irigaray and film theorist Teresa de Lauretis. Deren, Irigaray and de Lauretis, Hammer said, "confirmed my intuitive creative processes and have helped give me words to name my endeavors."

Hammer said as a filmmaker she was looking to express a new experience—that of lesbianism—which hadn't been given cinematic expression previously. "Although I didn't have the theory or the words to form it," she explained, "I worked through the seventies to make films of my lesbian experience. These stand outside the heterosexual discourse on gender and its representation. I was propelled in numerous films to represent one lesbian identity/experience by making images that were unique to my renaming myself as a lesbian. I believed that in making films that represented at least one lesbian's experience—my own, as I knew no other—I could contribute to abolishing lesbian invisibility."

Those themes—the abolition of lesbian invisibility and the breaking of silences—repeat in Hammer's work. She approached the complexities of her own life and personal lesbian history in *Tender Fictions* (1996), a feature-length autobiographical film and a view of the lesbian and gay community over the past thirty years. Like much of Hammer's work, there is an interconnectedness between the filmmaker and the film's subjects; Hammer said she cannot separate her lesbianism from her filmmaking, her life from her art: "*Tender Fictions* is really just another part of my entire life work."

The piece is rich with personal and political meaning for Hammer; even the title reflects her immersion in lesbian history—it's a take-off on Gertrude Stein's autobiographical collection, *Tender Buttons*. Hammer describes the film as a sequel to her award-winning documentary and favorite film, *Nitrate Kisses* (1992), which was lauded at such prestigious venues as the Sundance and Berlin film festivals, where it was called a documentary masterpiece of gay and lesbian cinema.

A feature-length documentary about the loss of vital pieces of collective lesbian and gay history, *Nitrate Kisses* incorporates found footage of lesbian and gay life from the 1930s to the 1990s. Hammer said, "It is a definitive statement about the importance of chronicling our collective queer history. In that film I told people to save their scraps of paper, diaries, letters, photos—anything—to make a community biography. We need every available thread of our history for the future."

Tender Fictions continues the historical theme begun with *Nitrate Kisses*. "I am a documentarian in many ways," Hammer explained. "I am recording lesbian life in the late twentieth century. I want to create a record. I don't want there to be missing pieces, empty pages, blank screens like there were for me" [when she came out as a lesbian]. Hammer said the idea was to make a "post–postmodern autobiography. The imagery is full of performances." Always looking for new ways to accommodate her lesbian-feminist politics in her art, she also altered her voice in the narrative parts,

Experimental Film

using a "male authority figure voice and a female authority figure voice" to illustrate how women's work and ideas are often received in the world of art and politics.

After two years of work and five months of editing together film and video clips from her own life since 1967 and tying them together with narrative vignettes, Hammer showed the finished hour-long, 16mm film at the top festivals: New York, Sundance, Berlin and Toronto to enthusiastic response.

"It's a major film," she noted with characteristic forthrightness. "I was scared and nervous, but I made it for myself and the community and I want everyone to see it—not just the gay and lesbian community, but all the other people who need to know who we are, what we've accomplished."

What Hammer has accomplished since her days as a film school student in the years of avant-garde filmmaking icons like Stan Brakhage and Maya Deren is to become an icon in her own right—the first out lesbian of the avant-garde and experimental cinema who has shaped filmmaking since the post–World War II era.

Hammer didn't realize that what she wanted to do with film, and later, video, would be groundbreaking. "Of course I didn't realize then, when I was looking at Maya Deren's work, that she was the *only* one, that there *was* no women's cinema—and that when I started doing this work, *I* would be the only one, that I would be a pioneer," she explained. Now, however, like Deren before her, Hammer's work is classic, studied by film students around the globe. But it was the closed society of middle-class 1950s America that led Hammer in the direction her work has taken.

"It was the impetus for my work, I think," she said. "In the fifties, middle-class homogeneous homes were silent. When I came out I didn't want to be silent. And I didn't want to take silence into the lesbian community." As a result, she said, her films are very explanatory, very much about language and speech and what we say to each other—and what other people say about us.

"My films talk about all the things we [women, lesbians] were told never to talk about: orgasms, personal desire, the body, sex. I wanted desperately to break that taboo of not talking, to smash through all that silence I had been raised to believe was the way women had to be—the way we *all* had to be."

As a consequence, many of Hammer's films are discourses on the

Still from *No No Nooky T.V.*

body—often through language. She explores many of the pivotal areas of women's lives in films like *Dyketactics, Menses* (1973), *Women I Love* (1979), *Sync Touch* (1981), *No No Nooky TV* (1987), *Sanctus* (1990), *Vital Signs* (1991) and, of course, *Nitrate Kisses.* Her video and mixed-media installation piece, *Eight in Eight* (1995), tackles another formidable aspect of women's lives: breast cancer. Like much of her earlier work dealing with taboo issues, *Eight in Eight* has fielded more than its share of controversy.

The title refers to the public health statistics that one in every eight women will get breast cancer in her lifetime. "But the figures are much higher for some women," noted Hammer. "For lesbians, African-American women, poor women, women with other illnesses, breast cancer is an even bigger threat. And no woman is untouched by the impact of the disease."

Featuring video interviews with eight women of different classes, races, sexual orientations and ages who have survived the disease, *Eight in Eight* tells the story of breast cancer in America. The eight interviews play on one video monitor while another plays news clips from the three major television networks from 1967 through the 1990s. All these news items give various reports on breast cancer—including the often conflicting advice and information women receive through the media. In a pool below the video monitors, Hammer placed bones that had been treated with photographic emulsion and then exposed to other headlines about breast cancer and deaths from the disease. In front of the monitor with the interviews is a plastic breast form that hides small nodules representing incipient cancers. When the viewer finds one of these, the monitor turns on and one of the interviews plays.

Experimental Film

The installation had its premiere at the San Francisco Arts Center and traveled to several museums and galleries across the country. But while *Eight in Eight* met with critical acclaim, it also met significant controversy. "People don't want women to see it," Hammer noted with some surprise. "I have heard so many rumors about what was in this exhibit—like a mastectomy and other very graphic images of mutilated bodies that were simply not in the piece. What I wanted the piece to show was how breast cancer affects women physically and emotionally, and how the media presents the disease in a misinformed and hyperbolic way that only serves to confuse and frighten women further."

Hammer added that the breast has also been negatively sexualized in a way that makes women afraid of touching—and examining—their own breasts, which is part of why she used the breast form in the installation.

Hammer's earlier films and videos are unequivocally experimental, and she has explained repeatedly over the years that she could not adopt a conventional cinematic style. That style, Hammer said, like the Hollywood that surrounded and dominated her childhood, replicated the heterosexual/heterosexist dynamic that she was trying to break away from and get beyond. Hammer's films may be experimental, but they are also their own distinct genre because she truly is an iconoclast, actually creating a new form within cinematic culture: lesbian experimental cinema. The impact of her work and its influence are difficult to measure; it can be suggested that the increasing number of young lesbian filmmakers have benefited from her work, both directly and indirectly. Certainly, a retinue of lesbian experimental filmmakers using Hammer as their model has developed in the last decade.

Hammer said, "It is difficult for me to say how I have helped to pave the way for women and feminists in experimental film. History provided the conjunction of theory with my artistic production. I found an experimental film-going audience devoid of feminist theory and practice and, similarly, a feminist audience that knew little about experimental cinema. I have tried in personal presentations to address those issues by talking about the importance and contributions of feminism to an audience of avant-garde film lovers, and [talking] about the viability and expansion of possibilities that experimental cinema provides a feminist audience."

The confluence of the lesbian-feminist with the avant-garde has not coalesced as smoothly as it seems to today. Hammer's work has always been

Barbara Hammer

controversial because of her desire to portray lesbians and lesbian sexuality on screen and because her work is intensely political. She funded all her own films for nearly twenty years; only in the last decade has she begun to receive grants after, as she noted with some irony, "applying every year for twenty years." It was 1984, for example, when, after sixteen years of filmmaking, Hammer received the Jerome Foundation Grant for Emerging Filmmakers. Hammer made *Tender Fictions* on a budget of $27,000, most of which came from the National Endowment for the Arts in a program that no longer exists, the Western Media Regional Film/Video Program. She noted that money for filmmaking has become scarcer than ever as funds and grant monies continue to dry up.

As a consequence of her determination to depict lesbians, lesbian imagery and a lesbian vantage point in her work, for many years that work was rejected by the very film festivals that now recognize her as an established and important avant-garde filmmaker and seek out her work.

"My lesbian films were often rejected by avant-garde showcases across the country and in museums everywhere during the period I was actively and expressly engaged in making lesbian representation," Hammer recalled. "It wasn't until I 'depopulated' my cinema, that is, took the women out, that I began to get the invitations I had so long sought. Believe me, there were calluses on my knuckles from knocking at locked doors, for I am not one to accept a 'no' and go away quietly."

Hammer also found, as have other women directors such as Lizzie Borden and Mira Nair who have dealt openly with women's sexuality, that female sexuality presented by a woman director was more taboo than blatant, even pornographic, extremes of sexual violence against women portrayed by male directors. At one point a lesbian-feminist friend of Hammer's was selected as curator for one of these film festivals. Hammer recalled, "I was so excited. Now, I thought, I would be able to show my films somewhere besides the women's coffeehouses. I will never forget the profound disappointment that shook me to tears when I received a letter back from my 'friend' informing me that not only was she in the closet, but that she thought she'd lose her job if she included my films. Russ Meyer [*Faster, Pussycat! Kill! Kill!*, 1966] was in the program, but not me."

Censorship has dogged Hammer; her films have been previewed by vice squads searching for child pornography and banned from church basement screenings by pastors who discovered her films celebrated lesbian life. She is candid about the experiences: "It was mortifying. No person should have to undergo the humiliation of censorship."

Though they continue to incorporate experimental elements, Hammer's later films have taken on a decidedly documentary tone, including the mixed-media piece *Eight in Eight*. *Vital Signs* (1991), which won the grand prize at the Black Mariah Film Festival, examines Western perceptions about death. *Nitrate Kisses, Out in South Africa* (1995) and *Tender Fictions* all explore various elements of lesbian and gay history. Hammer said the difference in her later films "has something to do with maturity, I think. I am suddenly very aware of history, of leaving records, of documenting everything. Until recently lesbians were unnamed in film, on radio, in the popular press. At most we were named historically by patriarchal medicalizations," she explained. "I was thirty years old when I first heard the word 'lesbian.' That word wasn't heard or written until the second wave of feminism in

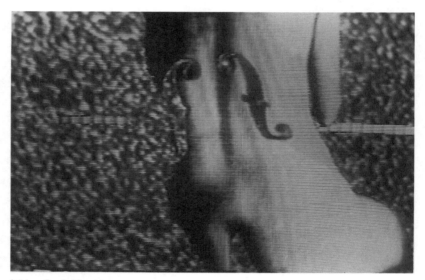

Still from *Two Bad Daughters*

the 1970s. With the word came a change of lifestyles for many of us who immediately or slowly recognized emotional, sexual and physical attractions to women. Some women, I'm sure, are more precocious than I was, but it took the name, the 'L' word, for me to rename myself and act on hitherto unnamed desire. Amazing."

That power of naming and self-recognition continues to intrigue Hammer, who has found that documenting history in her films is part of the process of breaking silences that she began when she first started making films. *Out in South Africa,* her sometimes lyrical and often disturbing narrative of lesbian and gay life in postapartheid South Africa, represents Hammer's first foray into an almost wholly documentary narrative that is

Barbara Hammer

Analie and Nomkitha in *Out in South Africa*

also definingly historical in many of the same ways as *Nitrate Kisses* and *Tender Fictions*.

In 1994 South Africa became the first country in the world to include lesbians and gays in its constitution, a move by Nelson Mandela and the new Pretoria government that thrilled lesbians and gays globally. *Out in South Africa* explores how lesbians and gay men have yet to feel the impact of the new constitution. In fact, the legacy of apartheid—sexual as well as racial— remains stark and painful, particularly in the black townships like Soweto.

Invited to South Africa for a retrospective of her films in June 1994, Hammer documented weeks of traveling through the countryside giving film workshops to lesbians and gay men. Neither linear narrative nor straight documentary, *Out in South Africa* begins and ends with short, explanatory commentaries by Hammer, with similar bits scattered throughout the film as she travels from place to place. But primarily the film is a pastiche of Hammer's interviews with lesbians and gay men in the townships, at her workshops, at a *shebeen* (a township gay bar that is like a speakeasy in someone's house), at the film festival, over meals and on the road.

An intensely moving look at the personal and political struggles of an emerging lesbian and gay culture, Hammer's explication takes the viewer deep into the savagely poor black townships where the legacy of apartheid is far from over for lesbian and gay South Africans.

"There were so many stories to tell," said Hammer. "It was difficult to choose just the few I did, because these lives, these women and men, they have so much to tell us."

As realized in Hammer's film, the tales are of bravery and struggle against a culture and a political heredity that disallow queerness. Other women and men Hammer interviewed talk about their sexuality and how it has made it hard for them to stay in their villages. And hovering over the underground nature of gay life in the townships is the specter of AIDS, which is epidemic among South Africans.

"Many of the men I talked to have male lovers but are married to women," explained Hammer. "But they don't use condoms to protect all of their partners—especially their wives." As a consequence, along with giving her money to young lesbians in trouble, Hammer found herself imploring men to use condoms—and handing them out at the film workshops she gave.

Hammer had agreed to go to the film festival only if she was able to "give something back" to South African lesbians and gay men; that "something" was film workshops for lesbians and gays in the black South African townships.

"I decided that what I wanted to do," Hammer recalled, "was chart gay life and desire after the new constitution was in place. But what I found were shocking and heart-filling stories of apartheid. Things really haven't changed much yet. Especially in the townships. This is emergency filmmaking," she added. "The situation for many of the lesbians and gay men I met is a real emergency. Things are happening now, and I wanted people to know about them right away."

Hammer, who has spent much of the last decade living in San Francisco and New York, admitted, "I'm not used to living like I did there. It wasn't just the place," she explained, although she traveled hundreds of miles by car and van from the cities into the countryside and the black townships, filming with only a small, hand-held camera. "It was what I was doing and how I was doing it. Living on the edge, everything pretty unplanned, pretty much minute by minute. It was very electric. It was very exciting. I want to do more of it."

The electricity of her documentation came from her experiences in the townships. Remnants of the legacy of apartheid, the townships are desolate, often incredibly grim areas, divided from the cities by long barren stretches, often bordered by hazardous waste sites. "I'd never been to South Africa before," Hammer said, "and I had no idea what to expect. There are so many powerful stories."

One that touched her most was that of sixteen-year-old Zandile, a black lesbian from Soweto. "She told me how the boys and men in her area and at her school threaten to rape her every day," Hammer said. Because Zandile sleeps with another woman, the men say she is a virgin, she isn't a lesbian, and so she is fair game for sexual predation. "She wanted me to adopt her; she wanted me to give her money to leave and move elsewhere," Hammer added. "I gave her as much money as I could and tried to get other women to give her money to leave. She was so desperate; she thinks about suicide because her situation is so terrible."

In the film, Zandile looks incredibly young and fragile with her very short hair and her thin body dressed entirely in men's clothes. But her strength comes through much more powerfully than her fear as she explains about the daily threats of rape.

Patric, a nineteen-year-old black gay man, echoes the same fragility as Zandile and explains that young gay men are subject to some of the same threats as the women are. Patric has been threatened with rape in his township, where being gay is not accepted.

"There are a lot of other problems," said Hammer. One is AIDS and misperceptions about transmission. Hammer spent part of her time in the townships doing safe sex education. "The perception about AIDS in the rural areas and in the townships is that the disease is transmitted by vaginas," she explained. "Nobody thinks that gay men get it. So the use of condoms becomes really controversial, really misunderstood. One gay man talked about how he uses condoms with his male lovers but not with his wife—many of the gay men are married. And this man is a health care provider and so is his wife." He is also, as the film shows us, lover of the nineteen-year-old Patric. Hammer said she "got down on my knees with some of these guys to beg them to use condoms with their boyfriends *and* wives."

Hammer said she wanted to show the range of stories of lesbians and gay men and tried very hard to balance the tales between the positive and the negative. She also had concerns that the majority of the women and men in her film are black and she is white. "This was one of the reasons I wanted to do the workshops," she explained. "I think it is important that these women and men tell their own stories on film. But for now, just getting the information out, so people will know what is happening, what the struggles are for these people, is really important."

The struggles differ depending on the influences surrounding the individuals, Hammer said. "One young man, Bebe, told me about how he had had a woman teacher who was very supportive of his sexual preference and that made things much different for him than it was for others I talked to."

Bebe's experience was the antithesis of Vera's, a young black lesbian from a rural area, Utata, between Durban and Capetown. Hammer said Vera was ostracized by her family and her village for her lesbianism. As a teenager

Vera became involved with another young woman. When the elders in her village found out, Vera was taken to the village chief, where she was forced to undress so he could determine whether or not she had both male and female genitals.

"In many areas," explained Hammer, "it is believed that gays and lesbians are hermaphrodites, that they have male and female gentalia." When Vera was found to be wholly female, she was lashed and caned and then sent to live with her grandparents outside her village.

"Many of the women are butch," Hammer explained, "or what we might call cross-dressers—they dress in men's clothes. It is difficult for them to meet other lesbians and gay men, often because there is so much actual physical isolation in the townships—transportation is a terrible problem." In the film these women discuss how they met their first lovers, how some of them spent time having sex in the toilets of bars in the cities or were initiated into sex by older women.

Labels are often ignored in South Africa. The married men, for example, don't consider themselves bisexual, which often has the connotation of hermaphrodite, but gay. And many of the women, Hammer said, although they have been in long-term relationships with other women, don't call themselves lesbians. An Afrikaner lesbian who has a black lover talks in the film about how coming out was deeply connected to the English language—her own language, Afrikaans, has no word for homosexuality. For a filmmaker who has chronicled the language of lesbianism for so many years, and been so focused on issues related to naming and claiming identity, the experience was challenging.

It has taken time for Hammer to distance herself from the South African experience. "I guess it was that electricity," she said, "that energy of living on the edge, nothing planned, things just really happening all around you. I want to go back for several months. I'd like to set up some video collectives, do some work with groups. That would be more revealing than just people telling their stories."

"I want to see if things have changed," she said succinctly. "Apartheid history is being whitewashed in South Africa. There's a real denial, like in Germany after World War II. I want to see if equality is really being achieved. And I want to see those women and men again, because their lives are so powerful, their lives are so incredible, their struggles are so real. That's something we all can learn from—and should."

Out in South Africa was considered for but didn't make the final cut at the 1996 Sundance Festival, where Hammer has been a juror and where *Nitrate Kisses* received such warm response. She was disappointed.

"I realize it's not the smoothest film," she explained, "and that I did it on a really small budget, and it's competing with films with really large budgets. But this is guerilla-style filmmaking; it's shot from the hip. And it's a real departure for me [from her experimental style]. I completed this film in only five months. I funded it out of my own pocket. I had an honorarium from the film festival [in South Africa], but I gave it away to the women and men I met."

The film hasn't shown in South Africa, and Hammer isn't certain how it will be received when it does get shown. But the experience has been defining for her and added to her concerns about documenting lesbian and gay history.

In her quest to continue breaking silences and new ground, Hammer has extended the attention she gave to lesbian and gay history in *Out in South Africa, Nitrate Kisses* and *Tender Fictions* to cyberspace. Hammer began an online "lesbian community biography" on the World Wide Web as part of her commitment to recording community history, setting up a computer archive where lesbians can "tell their stories. They can scan art, photographs, tattoos, they can put in their diaries, letters, dreams, life stories—anything they want to be part of history."

Community has been the foundation for much of Hammer's work. Hammer urges young lesbian filmmakers to look to their communities for ideas as well as support. Hammer's main objection to the spate of lesbian films in the 1990s is that, unlike her own work, they don't reflect real lesbian lives. There is an assimilationist aspect to some of this narrative filmmaking, which Hammer has never sought to replicate in her own work. "I had this idealistic view that a lesbian should take chances, challenge tradition, challenge form, which is also what I think an artist does," she explained. "I never wanted to make films that are simply representative. I wonder if the desire some lesbians express for films that tell stories with lesbian characters in the Hollywood tradition comes out of this need to fit in."

Hammer noted that despite the handful of lesbian-themed narrative films currently garnering mainstream attention, the concept of the closet and the struggle for visibility are certainly not over. "Until there is a naming and a construction, there can't be a deconstruction," she asserted. "I think that during the seventies we were naming ourselves—it was a community affair. In the nineties we can deconstruct the social identity we gave ourselves. With that ability to reexamine, we can then reconstruct with greater consciousness and permission the self-representations we desire."

A point that Hammer continually makes, however, is that there *is* a broad range of work from lesbian filmmakers and that diversity is essential. Diversity has certainly been a hallmark of Hammer's own work, from the early celebratory identity shorts to the complex features of the last few years. Hammer is unequivocal when she says, "We need different voices, different work. There is no feminism but *feminisms,* there is no lesbian cinema but lesbian *cinemas.* People ask me, Do I want to see the work of other lesbians? Of course I do. We've only begun to speak the language of lesbianism on screen; how can anyone think we've exhausted the imagery and ideas?"

Filmmaking is Hammer's life work. One project is barely in postproduction before she begins another. Some might say she's obsessed, others that she is compelled. What has held Hammer's interest in her art for nearly three decades, she said, is the daily challenge art presents for the artist and the challenges within the world itself that art must address. "I'm most excited by art that changes things," she said, "that hasn't been seen before, that isn't realistic in that it merely repeats the world, but art that creates a new world, a new way of seeing."

Barbara Hammer

Su Friedrich

Damned If You Do

Su Friedrich may not have the name recognition value that her colleagues who direct feature films have, but her black-and-white visions end up being films that are hard to forget. Friedrich has been making films since 1978, and her work has been shown in retrospectives at New York City's Whitney Museum of American Art, the Rotterdam International Film Festival in the Netherlands, the Wellington Film Festival in New Zealand, New York City's Anthology Film Archives and the Cork International Film Festival in Ireland. Her films are in the permanent collections of New York's Museum of Modern Art, the Art Institute of Chicago and the National Library of Australia.

Still, only in 1996 did Friedrich get what many experimental filmmakers consider the big break: Independent Television Service (ITVS) funding for the hour-long film *Hide and Seek,* which, like all of Friedrich's films, has racked up an impressive résumé of festival screenings. And because *Hide and Seek* was funded by ITVS, it will be available for broadcast by public television stations across the United States.

Friedrich didn't attend film school, but worked as a black-and-white photographer before taking the plunge into filmmaking via Super 8mm film, the format made popular by home movies in the 1960s. Friedrich would shoot her work on Super 8mm film and then have it blown up to 16mm for projection—a practice she still continues, editing the blown-up segments in with original 16mm footage.

Hide and Seek also represents a departure for Friedrich: It is the first of her films for which she did not shoot the majority of the footage herself, but instead hired a cinematographer so that she was free to focus on directing the film.

Friedrich's first film was the 1979 release *Cool Hands, Warm Heart,* a sixteen-minute silent film that shows four women performing what Friedrich described as "women's beautification rituals"—shaving, putting on makeup—on a stage on New York City's Orchard Street. Because Friedrich shot the film in Super 8mm, she was able to capture the reactions of the crowd of people who stopped to watch. *Cool Hands, Warm Heart* put Friedrich on the map as a feminist filmmaker who wanted to push the boundaries of our concepts of spectacle and spectator.

The 1981 short film *Gently Down the Stream* allowed Friedrich to explore new territory: She culled phrases and recurring visual images from dream journals and etched the phrases directly into the edges of the film negative. To emphasize the dreamlike quality of the film, Friedrich instructs projectionists to run the projector at the slower speed of eighteen frames per second, rather than the standard twenty-four frames per second. The result is a languid montage of repeating visual motifs.

As with *Cool Hands, Gently Down the Stream* is a silent film. Friedrich noted that she is hesitant about using music as a background to her films: "I feel that it distracts from the visual rhythm of the film," she said.

In 1984, Friedrich began to delve into the rich material her parents' lives offered her. The hour-long *The Ties That Bind* is a look at the life of Friedrich's mother, who lived through Nazi Germany. As with *Gently Down the Stream,* Friedrich scratched her film negative, this time with questions for her mother. *The Ties That Bind* was Friedrich's first foray into blend-

Films by Su Friedrich

Cool Hands, Warm Heart

Gently Down the Stream

The Ties That Bind

Damned If You Don't

Sink or Swim

First Comes Love

Rules of the Road

Lesbian Avengers Eat Fire Too

Hide and Seek

Top: Su Friedrich and her mother in *The Ties That Bind* (courtesy of Women Make Movies), bottom: Peggy Healey and Ela Troyano in *Damned if You Don't*

ing documentary and experimental genres through the use of archival footage, footage of contemporary Germany and dialogue between Friedrich and her mother.

Friedrich toured extensively with *The Ties That Bind* and received two offers to teach filmmaking during the tour. Although she turned down permanent teaching posts, Friedrich has run filmmaking workshops in New York City and taught for a month at the University of Wisconsin.

For her next film, Friedrich chose to fuse narrative story with experimental footage. The result, 1987's *Damned If You Don't*, tells the story of a novice nun who falls in love with a lesbian. In addition to being a compelling tale of sexual desire, *Damned If You Don't* is also cutting-edge low-budget filmmaking; shot with a 16mm spring-wound camera that didn't require batteries and using a nonsynchronized soundtrack, the film offers a startling deconstruction of Michael Powell's 1946 classic, *Black Narcissus*. Rather than pay the exorbitant costs of leasing footage from the Powell film, Friedrich chose to use distorted footage of the film playing on a television screen.

Damned If You Don't continues to be one of Friedrich's most frequently shown films and is emblematic of her approach to filmmaking in general. Although Friedrich has said that she uses black-and-white film because it costs less, anyone who has seen her films will note a strong aesthetic from her days as a black-and-white photographer, a love of the interplay between light and dark. Friedrich tends to perform all the filmmaking roles herself—writer, director, producer, cinematographer, sound recordist, editor—which she noted is another way of saving on production costs, but which has also been a way of maintaining creative control.

In 1990, Friedrich examined her relationship with her father in *Sink or Swim*. The film's title is a reference to her father's method of teaching his daughter to swim. The film takes as its reference point the study of language and alphabets—her father's field of academic expertise—and, starting with the letter *z* and progressing to the letter *a,* tells twenty-six brief tales about her relationship with her father, both as a child and as an adult. In one of the stories, the grown-up Friedrich watches,

Still from *Sink or Swim* (courtesy of Women Make Movies)

chilled, as her father treats her young half-sister in the same dismissive manner he once treated her. "*Sink or Swim,*" said Friedrich, "is about the damage either parent can do when trying to shape their child in their own image. One of the most painful things I realized in making the film was that we all inherit so much sorrow and hurt from our parents. We aren't the product of perfectly balanced adults—we are each created by people who have a legacy of their own, which goes back through each family line. On my good days I try to believe that each generation rids itself of a bit of the violence of the prior generations."

Whereas *Damned If You Don't* put Friedrich on the map as a lesbian experimental filmmaker to watch, *Sink or Swim* brought her critical acclaim from mainstream reviewers, including an article in *Premiere,* the glossy magazine for movie enthusiasts.

In 1991, Friedrich returned to her lesbian activist roots with the film *First Comes Love,* which contrasts traditional marriage ceremonies with a listing of all of the countries in which homosexual marriages are forbidden. *First Comes Love* was one of the first salvos in the campaign for civil rights for lesbians and gays, but was largely critically ignored.

Friedrich once again blended the narrative with the experimental in the 1993 film *Rules of the Road,* about a fractured lesbian relationship. She uses the traditional American station wagon—the wood-paneled vehicle of countless family vacations and road trips—as an emblem of the nostalgic past. The two lesbians in *Rules of the Road* have shared such a station wagon, but now that the relationship has ended, one retains the car, while the other sees it and others like it all over town—Friedrich deftly using the American love of automobiles to mirror our personal relationships. *Rules of the Road* marked Friedrich's first use of color film.

In 1996, Friedrich completed *Hide and Seek,* which again fused narrative with documentary. It is the story of a young girl's coming of age and learning about sexual desire; this principal story is intercut with women

Alicia Manta, Ariel Mara and Chels Holland in *Hide and Seek* (photo by Joyce George)

talking about their early lesbian experiences and archival footage from scientific and instructional films. Friedrich set *Hide and Seek* in the 1960s, and added a soundtrack to match, with songs by the Monkees, the Supremes, Bobby Darin and Del Shannon. "It's about being at an age when sexual feelings are still vague and about how a girl might know even then that her Prince Charming is a Princess," said Friedrich of *Hide and Seek.* "The film ranges over the last forty years of American social life and looks at the issue both as witnessed by the child and as hypothesized by adults/experts. It shows that the childhood experiences of a lesbian are often quite innocent but can be seen in retrospect to have a significant bearing on her adult life."

Friedrich has been involved in only one video project, which she co-directed with Janet Baus: the 1993 documentary *The Lesbian Avengers Eat Fire Too,* a look at the activist group that served as a catalyst for lesbian and gay political action in New York City.

"Whenever I set out to make a film," noted Friedrich, "my primary motive is to create an emotionally charged or resonant experience—to work with stories from my own life that I feel the need to examine closely and that I think are shared by many people." Friedrich added that her work is, of necessity, both personal and sexual, and although she doesn't start out with a specific political agenda, politics is a part of the feminist, lesbian and female filmmaker's work.

"I really believe in film, I believe in its power. It is the most comprehensive way I know to explore all those various aspects of my life and the lives of other women and men. Film is compelling in a very definitive way. It can touch so many people in visceral ways they cannot ignore. I like that impact—feeling it and reproducing it. Filmmaking makes me feel more a part of the world—it makes me feel I have a voice and the power that comes with that."

Su
Friedrich

Trinh T. Minh-ha

Surname Viet Given Name Nam

Trinh T. Minh-ha

The name Trinh T. Minh-ha will be completely unfamiliar to those who have not seen her films or studied with her in the film department of San Francisco State University. Part of the problem is that Trinh makes difficult films: films that require active thought rather than the passive experience that most viewers undergo when they watch most—if not all—mainstream releases. Trinh, who originally hails from Vietnam, is more interested in making films about what goes on in our minds.

"I was trained as a composer," said Trinh, "and I actually have my degree in comparative literature, more specifically, in Francophone literatures. My involvement in film started out more in film analysis. Later on, many of my friends were filmmakers, and I got involved in their work and ended up making films myself. I learned almost everything I know about making films from those friends."

Trinh funds her films with a combination of grants and

self-funding. She will start making a film regardless of how limited her funds are—if she has only $5,000, she does everything herself, but if she has $100,000, she hires others to work on the project. *Reassemblage,* her first 16mm film, was entirely self-funded, but opened the door to grants for future films.

Trinh's first films were shot on Super 8mm film in early 1980; her first professional film, *Reassemblage,* was shot on 16mm film in 1981 and released in 1982. *Reassemblage* is a study of women in rural Senegal; it is also a film about the documentary genre and how we represent other cultures when we make films about them. Trinh further studied West African rural cultures in her second film, 1985's *Naked Spaces: Living Is Round,* which she shot in Senegal in 1983 for three months and in Mauritania, Mali, Burkina Faso, Benin and Togo in 1984.

Naked Spaces incorporated Trinh's musical background in that the film presents the rhythms and rituals of rural life as a symphony or fugue, rather than as a *National Geographic* documentary. *Naked Spaces* brought Trinh awards and critical acclaim despite its nonlinear structure. "For me, to move from literature and music to film seems to be a very natural step," noted Trinh, "precisely because film can be considered as a composite art. I do not mean that you can just put together a number of arts to make film, but rather that it pulls together my interests in poetry, in the visual arts, as well as in music."

Music still plays an important part in Trinh's work. "The soundtracks of all my films are just as important an element as the visuals," she noted, "even when the soundtrack is composed of many moments of silence."

Still from *Surname Viet Given Name Nam* (courtesy of Women Make Movies)

Films by Trinh T. Minh-ha

Reassemblage

Naked Spaces: Living Is Round

Surname Viet Given Name Nam

Shoot for the Contents

A Tale of Love

For her third film, Trinh returned to her Vietnamese roots with 1989's *Surname Viet Given Name Nam,* a look at the role women play in Vietnamese society. In it, Trinh gives voice to women from both North and South

Trinh T. Minh-ha

Vietnam, as well as to Vietnamese women who have immigrated to the United States. Trinh looks not only at the role that women play in contemporary Vietnam, but also at the historical role of the Vietnamese woman.

Trinh followed *Surname Viet Given Name Nam* in 1991 with *Shoot for the Contents,* a look at allegorical naming and storytelling in China and how the student protest in Tiananmen Square served as a catalyst for change. *Shoot for the Contents* shares nonlinear structure with Trinh's earlier *Naked Spaces,* but also incorporates formal interviews, as did *Surname Viet Given Name Nam.* Trinh's compelling use of imagery in *Shoot for the Contents* led to the best cinematography award at the Sundance Film Festival.

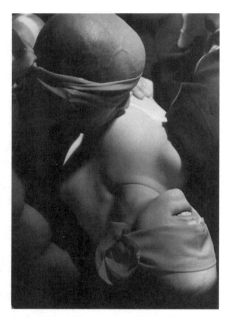

Still from *A Tale of Love* (courtesy of Women Make Movies)

In 1995, Trinh made the narrative film *A Tale of Love,* which is loosely based on the Vietnamese poem "The Tale of Kieu," a love poem viewed as a mythical biography of the Vietnamese nation. In the film, Kieu, a writer by profession, also works as a model for a photographer who is intent on capturing the headless female body. *A Tale of Love* explores the confluence of voyeurism, sensuality, love and, ultimately, identity in a narrative where reality, dream and memory mix. Trinh also uses this particular tale of love to deconstruct traditional love stories, using voyeurism as the master key that fits all of the stories.

Trinh's emphasis on women is a problem many male viewers cannot overcome. At a screening of *Surname Viet Given Name Nam* in New York City, a man in the audience asked the filmmaker, "There are so many important things to make a film about; why did you make a film about women?" Trinh calmly asked the man to apply the same criteria to films about men: Why make them?

"One thing I thought was very interesting," said Trinh of that evening, "was that while he [the man who asked the question] was talking, I heard some agreement coming from one or two women in the audience. That is the part that is in a way more baffling, in a way expected, because that kind of question coming from a man is somehow obvious, but coming from women—and I have seen it in many other forms coming from women— is somehow baffling, in that we live in such a context that even when a tool is being offered to a woman for 'empowerment' or for looking at herself no longer in negative terms, but in affirmative *and* negative terms, she wouldn't recognize it or she wouldn't take it. I've heard that question in other public debates as well: Why would you focus on women? So when I heard that agreement in the audience, I thought maybe there is so much more work to be done, in the sense that every time we talk about the female perspective, we always have to indicate how it opens up rather than duplicates the spirit that these kinds of questions come from, the vision of a compartmentalized world in which the individual cannot see society in the individual and vice versa. It is such a compartmentalized vision of the world that allows a person to say that to focus on women [in *Surname Viet Given Name Nam*] is not to focus on the [Vietnam] war.

"Cinema is dominated by men," Trinh points out. "Film theorist Laura Mulvey, who wrote about visual pleasure, made this analysis of how the look is always owned by men and that whenever women are presented in film, they are either the object of the look, or, if they look, it is only to signify man's desire. I think this is an important point. In my case, for example, I would transfer it to the kind of things that I would want to bring out in films and that I would never find or recognize in any other films, especially in documentaries. The only affinity that I have with a number of women's work is that I recognize certain desires to break with a notion, for example, of cinema that equates movement with action. In the case of women, there is the notion of time that is quite specific, that does not just depend on the overall editing of the film, nor on the movement of the camera, but a notion of time that comes through in the image itself. By that, I do not mean simply a cultural difference, because one can very easily say, 'Well, the film is slow because it is an African film or because it's from a culture different from ours.' So it's very easy to classify difference by saying that it's a cultural difference. I think the question of gender is involved and the question of looking at things differently; for example, breaking with accepted, established notions of cinema."

Trinh added that the question of gender and the question of race are related, "but it would be too easy to say that they are the same. Many people have done that—it is the trap in which a certain number of women writing in theory equate the problems of gender with the problems of race. Hence, the reaction of many women of color against that kind of stance.

Still from *Surname Viet Given Name Nam* (courtesy of Women Make Movies)

Trinh T. Minh-ha

97

In equating the two, I have the feeling that what happens is, on a certain level, either the problem of gender is rendered invisible, or the problem of race is rendered invisible. There is no easy solution, and there is no solid ground that we can stand on. We constantly have to be careful of how oppression works and how it circulates, whether in the context of race, or in the context of gender.

"Women of color and people of color in general are always asked to stay in their territory," Trinh added, "that Asians make films about Asians, that Africans make films about Africans—that they write on their own culture. So you have a recognition of difference, but only when these differences are carried out within the territory that has been demarcated, authorized. On the other hand, you realize that, being a Vietnamese woman making a film on Vietnamese women, you cannot really bloom without a certain form of recognition from the dominant culture, whether it comes from white women or from the male establishment."

Trinh has no plans to make a mainstream film. "It is the doom of many independent filmmakers to make films that look mainstream," she said.

**Experimental
Film**

Frances Negrón-Muntaner

The Politics of Identity, Part One

Frances Negrón-Muntaner describes herself as a "Puerto Rican who is island-born, light-skinned, middle-class and a lesbian." This self-description informs her film *Brincando El Charco: Portrait of a Puerto Rican* (1994) and *Puerto Rican ID* (1994), her segment of the public television series *Signal to Noise: TV Inside Out*. At thirty-one, Negrón-Muntaner is one of America's premier Latina filmmakers. Her work is known for its dramatic explorations of race, class, sexual and national identity.

Puerto Rican ID studies the "hybridity of culture," noted Negrón-Muntaner. Starting with home movies that she shot as a child in Puerto Rico, Negrón-Muntaner "follows the responses of one particular TV viewer over time."

Brincando El Charco, which Negrón-Muntaner produced, directed and wrote, continues to be screened at film festivals across the country. She noted, "*Brincando El Charco* started out as a documentary, with the premises of realism and truthfulness. But in making a film about identity, I felt the insufficiency of the documentary form and instead chose to use forms that represent ambiguity. The material demanded it." Negrón-Muntaner also chose to use mixed media to represent "the multiple realities of Puerto Ricans."

Brincando El Charco is the story of Claudia Marin, a Puerto Rican lesbian photographer, and her return to Puerto Rico for her father's funeral. Negrón-Muntaner's hour-long experimental narrative uses interviews, poetry, dance and soap opera to chronicle the three days Claudia spends

Frances Negrón-Muntaner in *Brincando El Charco*. Negrón-Muntaner directed and appeared in the film. (courtesy of Women Make Movies)

on her native island. During those three days, Claudia reflects on mass migration, racism and homophobia. Claudia's third day addresses "issues of desire and how gay politics are articulated," explained the filmmaker, including a sex fantasy sequence and footage from a gay and lesbian pride march.

"*Brincando El Charco* follows the conventions of autobiographical filmmaking," said Negrón-Muntaner, explaining that the film is not autobiographical, even though she does portray one of the film's characters. "My appearing in the film caused a lot of confusion," she commented, "and I don't intend to appear in any of my future films."

It was Negrón-Muntaner's maternal grandfather who introduced her to film. "He studied film at the University of Miami in the 1940s. After he returned to Puerto Rico, he did commercial work, documentaries and medical photography for the Puerto Rican Veterans Administration. He always wanted to make feature films. Ever since I was very young, he's been putting cameras in my hands, encouraging me to be a filmmaker."

Her grandfather has not seen any of her films. "He knows what they're about," noted Negrón-Muntaner. "I know he wouldn't approve of their content." Still, when she visits her grandfather, "He quizzes me on filmmaking—if you have this scene and this camera angle, how would you light it, things like that. It's his way of acknowledging that we're both filmmakers." Negrón-Muntaner eventually wants to make a fictional film about her grandfather and their relationship—"a tribute to him as a filmmaker," said Negrón-Muntaner, who plans to use some of his film footage in the project. "He is very ill—he has sickle cell anemia—and because of how my family feels about my work, I probably won't be able to do any real work on the project until after his death."

Negrón-Muntaner was born and raised in Puerto Rico, where her family still lives. When she was nine, her family moved to Long Island, New York, for two years while her father worked on his doctoral degree.

She went not knowing any English. Her mother put her in a regular public school class. "It was the sink-or-swim method of learning English," said Negrón-Muntaner. "I was speaking English within two months." Both her parents are professors at the University of Puerto Rico, where her mother teaches English and her father teaches history. Frances was groomed for an academic career as well—she followed her parents' wishes by studying sociology at the University of Puerto Rico, even though she originally wanted to major in English literature.

Negrón-Muntaner eventually moved to Philadelphia in 1986, where, after studying visual anthropology at Temple University, she switched to Temple's graduate film program, from which she received her master of fine arts degree. Now she is a doctoral candidate in comparative literature at Rutgers University in New Brunswick, New Jersey. She is studying literature of the Caribbean and African diasporas and is, in a sense, following in her father's footsteps—his specialty is nineteenth century Caribbean history.

Negrón-Muntaner's success hasn't pleased her family. "My parents cherish their privacy," said Negrón-Muntaner. "The fact that I have such a public career causes them a great deal of stress, not only because my success invades their privacy, but also because my lesbianism forces them to either defend me or to stay silent. In many ways, my family serves as a self-censoring mechanism for my work."

Until *Brincando El Charco*'s release, Negrón-Muntaner was best known as the co-director of the 1989 documentary film *AIDS in the Barrio*, which studied AIDS in Philadelphia's Puerto Rican community. *AIDS in the Barrio* has also been broadcast on PBS.

Negrón-Muntaner is currently working on *What a Beautiful Flag/Que Bonita Bandera*, which started as a documentary about the Puerto Rican responses—from outrage to support—to superstar Madonna's rubbing the

Frances Negrón-Muntaner

Puerto Rican flag between her legs at a concert in Puerto Rico. "It is," said Negrón-Muntaner, "a look at the profound dissension that surrounds the basic elements of everyday life in Puerto Rico." Negrón-Muntaner has expanded *What A Beautiful Flag* into a feature-length narrative film that "parodies nationalism while using the thriller genre"; she is working on the screenplay and planning to shoot the film in New York City.

Although most of Negrón-Muntaner's work is about identity, she said that she is "leaving identity politics behind. When I was working on *Puerto Rican ID*, the people at ITVS [the Independent Television Service, the program's funder] kept coming back to me and saying, 'Tell them who you are.' Consequently, much of the piece is specifically about me—who I am, where I am, what I am. It was an instructive experience, but I'm tired of legitimizing my voice."

Negrón-Muntaner believes that "the dominant images and representations of Puerto Ricans both in the often racist mainstream culture and in the narrow elitism of dominant Puerto Rican cultures must be challenged and radically diversified. In order for Puerto Rican voices and experiences to be more broadly consumed, we must stress the similarities, rather than the differences, between Puerto Rican and American cultures.

"*Brincando El Charco* is a personal meditation with the hope of provoking others, particularly Puerto Ricans, toward self-reflection," said Negrón-Muntaner, who hopes that viewers will "take a serious look at not only the racism practiced against us, but also the productive alliances many Puerto Ricans have created with other communities, such as African-American communities and multiracial gay and lesbian communities." Negrón-Muntaner explained that "the film hopes to break with narrow notions of the Puerto Rican experience for audiences that have little knowledge of the complex racial, class and migratory histories of Puerto Ricans in the United States. *Brincando El Charco* is not a film designed to explain or make Puerto Ricans sympathetic to the mainstream," she said. "It is a film that attempts to capture the complexity of the Puerto Rican experience through the eyes of one specific Puerto Rican."

Negrón-Muntaner is quick to point out that she isn't just a filmmaker— "I engage in other things that creatively feed each other," noted Negrón-Muntaner, who also writes creative fiction and scholarly articles. She is the editor of the anthology *Shouting in a Whisper: Latino Poetry in Philadelphia* (Asterion, 1994). "I had it drummed into me by my parents to get a doctorate degree—they are concerned that I will end up being marginalized without the right credentials to teach at a university. And in spite of everything, here I am working on my doctorate."

Frances Negrón-Muntaner

Michelle Mohabeer

The Politics of Identity, Part Two

Michelle Mohabeer

In 1974, Michelle Mohabeer's family moved from her native Guyana to Toronto, Canada. She was thirteen. Although Mohabeer has lived in Toronto ever since, she has not forgotten her Guyanese roots: Her experimental films explore the diversity of cultural identity and the politics of gender, sexuality and colonialism.

Mohabeer studied film theory and criticism at Carlton University in Ottawa, where she earned her bachelor's degree; she went on to get a master of fine arts degree in film production from Toronto's York University. "My work tends to have theoretical elements to it," said Mohabeer of her bachelor's degree. "If you look, it's there." Thirteen years ago, "I was the only person of color in film school, woman or man," noted Mohabeer. "When I did my MFA, there was one other woman of color. There still aren't that many people of color in film schools in Canada."

Her first professional film, the eight-minute short *Exposure*, was commissioned by the National Film Board of Canada's *Five Feminist Minutes* series in 1990. Working with a budget of $10,000 (Canadian), Mohabeer used a dialogue between Japanese-Canadian writer Mona Oikawa and African-Caribbean poet Leleti Tamu to study the issues of sexual and ethnic identity, racism and homophobia. "It explores their interconnections and their differences within various kinds of contexts about Afro-Caribbean culture in terms of how Africans arrived in the Caribbean and the whole colonial background experience," Mohabeer explained. "It also looks at Japanese-Canadian internment in the camps here in British Columbia [during World War II]."

Films by Michelle Mohabeer

Exposure

Coconut/Cane & Cutlass

Two/Doh

Child-play

In 1994 Mohabeer followed the success of *Exposure* with the thirty-minute film *Coconut/Cane & Cutlass*, an exploration of Indo-Caribbean womanhood in Guyana from colonial days to the present. The haunting experimental film, which layers location footage, dance and poetry over Mohabeer's narrative structure, follows the filmmaker's search for personal

identity as a woman, a lesbian, an Indo-Caribbean and an outsider. The film's $85,000 (Canadian) budget allowed Mohabeer to shoot in Guyana as well as in Toronto. Breathtaking cinematography and optical double-printing allowed Mohabeer to segue between the film's documentary and erotic footage. In *Coconut/Cane & Cutlass*, Mohabeer juxtaposes the colonization of the Indo-Caribbean people with the colonization of women's sexuality, raising many questions about the confluence of culture and sexuality.

Sonia Dhillon and Sharon Lewis in *Coconut/Cane & Cutlass*

"When one does filmmaking that could be perceived as political, it's hard to marry that with anything that also explores a poetics, a sensualness in terms of the imagery and the way the imagery is constructed," said Mohabeer. "I don't believe in producing work that is really seventies and politically correct, very didactic, very instructive, boring and not beautiful

Michelle Mohabeer

and poetic in any way. That's why I love Patricia Rozema's *When Night Is Falling*, which has been criticized a lot, but I think it's one of the most beautiful Canadian films ever made. Canadian cinema tends to be a certain kind of cinema; it's almost like a working-class cinema in a way, but it lacks that poetics which I find much more prevalent in international cinema, whether it's from India, Iran, Europe, wherever."

Mohabeer also cited the work of writer and filmmaker Marguerite Duras as an influence. "She's amazing—I love her work, being a writer and the kinds of films she made. They may be challenging to some people, but

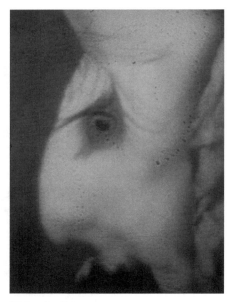

Still from *Two/Doh*

work like that, when it's poetic, it has a soul, it speaks to you on so many other levels. Very little work here [in North America] is like that. It's a kind of cultural dogma, a way of only seeing realities and life and art in a very narrow and sometimes simplistic way. And it means art has to unfold around plot and various devices furthering the plot."

In 1996, Mohabeer shot two more films: the five-minute *Two/Doh* and the thirty-minute *Child-play*. The experimental *Two/Doh* was shot on Super 8mm film that was then blown up to 16mm, allowing the film to be made at the low cost of $7000 (Canadian). Mohabeer described the film as "an evocative pastiche tying in intercultural and interracial connections between two dykes—one is Persian-Armenian, and the other is South Asian–Sri Lankan—just their different connections culturally and erotically." Mohabeer intercut the film's footage with various erotic haikus and called the finished project "in a vein like *Coconut*, kind of rich, evocative and colorful. Various emblems from both the cultures are in it."

Child-play (1997) is Mohabeer's first drama, although it does contain experimental elements. "It's a surreal allegory about, for want of a better word, the colonial rape," said Mohabeer. "The film is from the perspective of a woman in her late sixties who recalls this incident that happened to her when she was a young girl of ten. The woman is visited by the spirit of a Dutch man she had encountered previously. The style of it is surreal, impressionist—it's very complex in terms of what it interweaves between dream, memory and reality. Ultimately, the film is a dream, so the woman doesn't ever really confront the spirit, who it turns out is a child molester. There is this whole Caribbean mythology surrounding it—[the molester's] name was Georgie de Roos, and he was killed and buried near the house where his mother lived; a tree was planted over his grave, and since then the tree has only borne rotten cocoa buds.

"It very much has to do with children, power, a kind of spirit element—for want of a better word, magic realism, like one would find in Latin American authors," Mohabeer said. "It's a bit of an unusual film—something like the work of the Aboriginal filmmaker from Australia, Tracey Moffatt [*Nice Colored Girls, Bedevil*]. Actually, Debbie Zimmerman from Women Make Movies [American distributor of both Mohabeer and Moffatt] said that our work is similar, that when she saw *Coconut*, she thought of [Moffatt's film] *Night Cries*. The other work people might compare *Child-play* to is that of a filmmaker from Curaçao who lives in Holland now, Felix de Roos. He's gay, and his work ties in a lot of mythology and folkloric myths and sexuality and just the milieu of the Caribbean and various contradictions about race and culture and identity."

When Mohabeer finished postproduction on *Child-play*, she went back to work on a feature-length screenplay, *Chameleon*, which is "about the idea of passing, both in terms of gender and in terms of race, about a relationship between two people who are passing for different reasons and enter into a triangular relationship," Mohabeer explained.

Most of Mohabeer's funding comes from the various Canadian arts councils, although she has also used some corporate fundraising, such as donated plane tickets so that she could shoot portions of *Coconut/Cane & Cutlass* in Guyana. "More and more independent filmmakers are having to use other strategies and ways of raising money, because it's very difficult right now in Canada; funding is drying up and it's ultracompetitive," said Mohabeer. She noted that there are more foundations in the United States that will provide funding to filmmakers than there are in Canada.

Surprisingly, Mohabeer's work is not screened often in Toronto. "Because of the themes that I deal with in my work, it's not often embraced in Canada, but it's embraced outside of Canada," Mohabeer said. "That is a difficult thing for me, because my work doesn't often get programmed in the Toronto International Film Festival—for various reasons, usually it's political—whereas it gets programmed elsewhere in the world, wins awards elsewhere. It happens to other people here as well, and not just women of color. It's a struggle to be a filmmaker, period, no matter who you are. When you add a cultural difference or racial difference or sexuality on top of it, and you make work with that [difference] there, that can marginalize your work even more. When you make work that's not traditionally a drama or traditionally a documentary, again, that can take the work out of the mainstream.

"Sometimes it's just damn hard—it's really hard not to lose faith in yourself and in your work, especially when you don't get support in your own backyard. I find that really tough, and the older I get, the tougher it is to say, 'My god, I have no money, I'm always broke, and this is what it means to be an artist, to be a filmmaker.' I've had jobs and I've worked, but I find that I get really down or depressed because I think it's too damn difficult. You do it because you're really passionate about it. It sounds clichéd, but it's very true. That's why I do it. I can't imagine doing anything else but being a filmmaker."

Margaret Tait

Blue Black Permanent

When her first feature film, *Blue Black Permanent*, was released in 1993, the British press made much of the fact that Margaret Tait, its director, was seventy-four years old. In fact, Tait has been making films—short films—since she was thirty-four, but it took *Blue Black Permanent* to make people outside her native Scotland take notice.

Tait started her career not as a filmmaker, but as a doctor. In 1944, she was drafted into the British war effort and sent to India. Tait had always loved movies, and during the war she considered writing a screenplay for the Crown Film Unit about the Chindits, the British soldiers who went behind enemy lines in Burma.

But it wasn't until after the war that Tait really got her feet wet in the art of film. When the war was over, she returned to Scotland and bought an amateur movie camera. Her plan was to work as a doctor for six months and then spend six months making films. She worked as a doctor in a variety of surgeries in Scottish villages, driving from one to the next,

Films by Margaret Tait

Portrait of Ga

Orquil Burn

The Drift Back

Where I Am Is Here

Hugh MacDiarmid—A Portrait

The Big Sheep

A Pleasant Place

On the Mountain

Aerial

Colour Poems

Place of Work/tailpiece

Some Changes

The Look of the Place

Land Makar

Blue Black Permanent

Experimental Film

saving money by sleeping in her car.

In 1950, she had saved enough money to enroll at the Centro Sperimentale di Cinematografia in Rome, Italy—Italy's premier film school, frequented by the top Italian film directors of the time and housed at the Cinecittà studios.

Back in Scotland a year later, Tait started making films, including *Portrait of Ga* (1952), a study of Tait's mother; *Orquil Burn* (1955), "from sea to source, the whole course of the burn" (*burn* is Scottish for stream); *The Drift Back* (1956), a study of two families who return to farm on the Orkney islands on the coast of Scotland; and the thirty-five-minute *Where I Am Is Here* (1964), a poetic tribute to Edinburgh.

Where I Am Is Here put Tait on the map of experimental filmmakers to watch. In the program notes to a 1993 retrospective of her work at London's National Film Theatre, Tait said of *Where I Am Is Here:* "Starting with a six-line script which just noted down a *kind* of event to occur, and recur, my aim was to construct a film with its own logic, its own correspondences within itself, its own echoes and rhymes and comparisons, all through close exploration of the everyday, the commonplace, in the city, Edinburgh, where I stayed at the time."

In 1981, she made her last short film, the thirty-two-minute *Land Makar*, which Tait has described as "a landscape study of an Orkney croft [farm], with the figure of the crofter, Mary Graham Sinclair, very much in the picture, and enriched throughout by her vivid comments. Filmed over several seasons between 1977 and 1980, it takes in many of the human activities which alter the look of the land. The croft is on the edge of a small loch [lake] where swans and other birds nest in the grass. It is worked in the old style and, although mechanized aids are brought into use when appropriate, much is done by one woman's labor." Tait also noted that *makar* is a Scottish word, meaning poet, and that "the film is worked out so that the sequences are like a number of canvases."

In 1981, after the release of *Land Makar*, Tait decided to devote her time to developing feature-length screenplays. In 1992, she began shooting *Blue Black Permanent*, which was financed by England's Channel 4 TV and the

British Film Institute. *Blue Black Permanent*, set in the 1950s, is about Greta, a poet who drowns herself in the sea, and her daughter Barbara, who is haunted by memories of her mother.

Blue Black Permanent isn't Tait's first fictional work. Some of her short films, such as 1969's *A Pleasant Place*, which portrays a marriage from which passion has long ago fled, provide a meeting place for the experimental and the narrative. As Tait told Jan Moir of *The Guardian* when *Blue Black Permanent* was released, "Like all of my films, every single moment is based on my own life and all the characters are me. But it is not the story of my life."

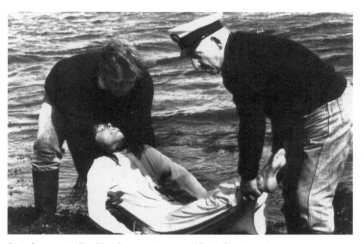

Gerda Stevenson in *Blue Black Permanent* (courtesy of British Film Institute)

The majority of Tait's work is self-funded with revenues from rentals of her films. Tait also credits her ability to "live cheaply" as playing a major role in funding her films. Until 1983, when she was able to afford an office, Tait edited her films in her kitchen.

Tait's husband, writer Alex Pirie, summed up her work when he said that she "searches for what Gaels call *an seann stugh* [the real stuff]—got by doing what Rilke mentioned, 'looking at the object until it speaks from its nature'; using, too, Gongora's method, as defined by Lorca, of 'stalking the image.' From this dedication has come the mastery of a form that contains, indeed becomes, a poetry of presence, offering 'the privilege of the instant,' perspectives of duration, of time moving, of time being moved in."

Yvonne Welbon

Memory

Yvonne Welbon (photo by Catherine Crouch)

"There have always been black lesbian filmmakers—they just haven't been out," said Yvonne Welbon, who, not content with an undergraduate degree from Vassar in history and a master's degree in fine arts from the School of the Art Institute of Chicago, is working on a doctorate in radio/TV/film from Northwestern University. Her dissertation topic: black lesbian filmmakers. "We are definitely seeing more films by black lesbians—before 1990 we had one publicly known black lesbian filmmaker, Michelle Parkerson. In the 1980s, there were five films and videos by out black lesbians in distribution—four of them by Michelle Parkerson. While other black lesbians created work during the 1980s, these women were, for the most part, closeted.

"Between 1985 and 1990, the number of videos, films and interactive computer media created by out black lesbians increased to approximately seventy pieces. In five years we've seen an incredible amount of growth—this group of artists [in the period 1985–1990] grew from two to twenty-one."

Welbon herself has helped continue that growth. In 1991, she produced the three-minute black-and-white film *Monique*, which used a childhood experience of racial biogtry as the foundation for a meditation on racism in American society. In 1992, she made *The Cinematic Jazz of Julie Dash*, a video documentary in which Dash talks about the making of the feature film *Daughters of the Dust* (1991).

In 1993, Welbon fused narrative and documentary genres in the film *Sisters in the Life: First Love*, which explored both first young love and its mature adult counterpart. In documentary footage, African-American lesbian Donna Rose talks about her first experiences with teenage love and about falling in love with her current girlfriend. In evocative and idyllic flashbacks of Donna's life at age fourteen, Welbon captures the spirit of first, innocent love—sleeping over, painting fingernails, talking about boys.

Welbon followed *Sisters in the Life* with *Missing Relations* (1994), which once again fused narrative with documentary. Welbon has two half-sisters who are twins. When they were six months old, the twins were kidnapped by their father, and Welbon did not see them again for twenty-four years. *Missing Relations* explores Welbon's "childhood feelings in association with this loss. My intention was to create a cinematic space for grieving and healing. Through re-creations of time and place, I explore my childhood memories and the constructed memories of my siblings, my mother and the twins' father," Welbon stated. "It's about family secrets, and about how a lie can, after time, be considered a truth—I didn't really have any sisters, because they weren't there."

Welbon's latest film, *Remembering Wei Yi-fang, Remembering Myself: An Autobiography* (1995), which aired on public television's *P.O.V.* series, is an autobiographical piece in which memory once again plays a key role. In it, Welbon looks back both at her years as an African-American lesbian living in Taiwan and at her grandmother's migration from Honduras to the United States.

Films by Yvonne Welbon

Monique

The Cinematic Jazz of Julie Dash

Sisters in the Life: First Love

Missing Relations

Remembering Wei Yi-fang, Remembering Myself: An Autobiography

Yvonne Welbon

"Re-creations of time and place are presented through memories, historical documents, photographs and video and film footage," said Welbon. "These re-creations move from my family's ancestral home in Honduras to South Dakota to Chicago to Taipei, Taiwan—creating intersections between Latin-American, African-American and Chinese cultures. The narrative is created through dialogue in English and Chinese between myself and my Chinese persona, Wei Yi-fang, and through my grandmother's stories of 'home.' The film gives voice to my grandmother, a woman who immigrated to America in 1948 as a domestic worker. By linking our stories, I offer two seldom seen portraits of African-American women."

Welbon's grandmother in *Remembering Wei Yi-fang, Remembering Myself* (courtesy of Women Make Movies)

Welbon said of living in Taiwan, "One of the things that was really important there was that people really knew where they were from, they knew a lot about their history and their ancestors; so part of the message of this piece is that in knowing where you come from, you know a lot more about yourself and you're less likely to feel low self-esteem because of some name somebody else decides to call you. As long as you know what your own name is or who you are, it doesn't affect you as much."

Welbon, who started taking film classes in 1990 and earned her MFA in 1994, said, "*Remembering Wei Yi-fang* is my first accomplished piece. It's my fifth piece, and the first one I'm really happy with. I feel I had enough time [in which to produce it], and this was the first film where I had funding to have it professionally cut by an editing house. I felt mature enough as an artist."

Welbon noted, "I've never really had production financing problems, partly because I was in school and I had access to equipment, but that meant I might have to edit a piece myself or one of my classmates would. With *Remembering Wei Yi-fang*, I could afford to have a professional editor do it. I felt I had more skilled technicians involved in this production, partly because I did pay them money, instead of doing the in-kind route and just using what I had at hand." *Remembering Wei Yi-fang* was funded by an impressive list of grants, including the *P.O.V.* Minority Investment Fund, the Center for New Television's Great Lakes Regional Fellowship Program, the Sidney Poitier Emerging Black Filmmaker Fellowship and the Robert Lathrop Memorial Fellowship.

"The first film I made [*Monique*] only cost $100, and it immediately won an award for $200," noted Welbon. "I developed the film [stock] myself—I was at the Art Institute [of Chicago], where they teach you how to do everything yourself—you shoot it yourself, you process the film yourself, you cut it yourself. That's why the cost [of *Monique*] was so low. There were a lot of facilities right at the school that you would have to pay an arm and a leg for in the real world." *The Cinematic Jazz of Julie Dash* was also a low-cost project, with Dash supplying film clips and Welbon using the school's 3/4-inch video equipment. *Sisters in the Life* cost about $1500 of Welbon's own money in addition to the equipment she used at school. With *Remembering Wei Yi-fang*, Welbon said, "I got about $30,000 from *P.O.V.*, which meant I could even pay myself a salary while I worked, and I was able to pay an associate producer to help me, someone who had volunteered on some of my previous projects."

Part of what has helped Welbon in managing production financing is her background as a businesswoman. Welbon started and ran a tourist magazine in Taiwan for five years. But, after a motor-scooter accident, she closed the magazine and returned home to Chicago, where she started taking video and film classes.

"When I was at Vassar, you were told that it was really important for you to do something to make this world a better place. You were told, 'You are a Vassar woman, and there's nothing you cannot do.' I'm glad I went there for my undergraduate work, because I think if I had gone somewhere else I would be a different person. When you're eighteen, you're so malleable. I didn't realize that going to live in Taiwan was so unusual, and I explore that in my film."

Welbon is now busy finishing her dissertation, which deals with four African-American "firsts": "I'm working with Julie Dash, the first black woman to have a feature film with a major theatrical release in the United States; Leslie Harris [*Just Another Girl on the I.R.T.* (1992)], the first black woman to have a film released by a major distributor; Darnell Martin [*I Like It Like That* (1994)], the first black woman to do a studio feature; and Cheryl Dunye [*The Watermelon Woman* (1996)], who did the first black lesbian feature." Welbon sees her dissertation as becoming a book that may help other filmmakers: "I fully advocate that all filmmakers write a business plan for whatever they are doing and be very clear about what they are getting into. I hate these stories of people who are in debt for the rest of their lives around a film they didn't realize there was no market for."

And, as if that weren't enough, Welbon recently formed a production company with a friend from film school and is developing a feature-length project about the civil rights movement. "The feedback we've received has been good," she said, "so now we're looking at fundraising."

Ayoka Chenzira

I Really Wanted It to Move

"I'm the child who got everything that my mother didn't get," noted Ayoka Chenzira, dancer turned filmmaker, "dance lessons, trips to the opera and the theater. When I was about sixteen years old, I started to get interested in still photography. I did that for quite some time, along with the dancing, and it consumed a great part of my life. It was a very exciting time to be black and be involved with the arts. One day I looked at one of my stills and thought, 'It's just not enough.' I really wanted it to move, to say other things. Then I moved into film.

"The other attractive thing about film," added Chenzira, "is that we live in a society where you're supposed to pick one thing to do, or else you're considered a 'jack of all trades and a master of none'; at least that's part of the working-class ethic. With film I could call upon everything I had been taught to do, painting and dance and theater and music, and put all of that in film, and people would just leave me alone. So film gave me an opportunity to incorporate my other interests and skills. Wanting to incorporate my other interests and skills has

117

Films by Ayoka Chenzira

Syvilla: They Dance to Her Drum

Hair Piece: A Film for Nappy-
Headed People

Secret Sounds Screaming: The
Sexual Abuse of Children

Five Out of Five

The Lure and the Lore

Zajota and the Boogie Spirit

made me a very hands-on person as it relates to my work. Every year I'm clearer about things that I don't want to do in terms of ways of working."

Chenzira made her first film as a student in 1971. "I was very influenced by the music of John Coltrane and he has a song called 'After the Rain,' which is one of my favorite songs and always sends me off into deep fantasy/meditation, and I did a short, black-and-white piece about a woman dreaming, and the song was the jumping-off point for the dream."

While at New York University, Chenzira shot a documentary about African-American dancer Syvilla Fort, but wasn't happy with the finished film. So she raised the money to re-edit the film, which became *Syvilla: They Dance to her Drum* (1979). "Syvilla was the dance training link between the Katherine Dunham period of dance and the Alvin Ailey period of dance," explained Chenzira. "She was one of those unsung women who existed primarily through the oral tradition. She was a friend and teacher, and I also performed for her company."

With *Syvilla* completed, Chenzira moved into the distribution business. "It started because I couldn't find a distributor," said Chenzira. "When you get out of school you think you're going to conquer the world, and suddenly things you don't learn at school hit you in the face. So I bussed and trucked my film [*Syvilla*] all over the place and, because it was a dance film and because I was a dancer, and because I also wrote dance history and was very much involved in the black dance community, I put together this—what seems to me now ridiculous—incredible package, because I didn't think people would rent just a little 25-minute black-and-white film, which of course is what the distributors were telling me. With the package, a school could get the film, a slide lecture presentation on black women in dance and I would teach a master dance class and do a Q-and-A session. I stayed on the road for almost three years doing that. Part of it was my own naiveté, thinking that people wouldn't rent the film separate from these other things. Also, it helped me to bring to a close the performance aspect of my life."

Chenzira would continue to self-distribute her own films for ten years, eventually becoming program director for the distribution company the Black Filmmaker Foundation. She no longer self-distributes her films, because, as she said, "I cannot speed up production the way that I am doing and continue to distribute."

After the success of *Syvilla*, Chenzira moved in a different direction with the 1985 animated film *Hair Piece: A Film for Nappy-Headed People*, possibly her best-known film. In *Hair Piece*, Chenzira takes a satirical look at how the self-image of African-American women is bound up in how they feel about their hair, complete with a historical look at how to straighten one's hair. The message is serious, even if the tone of the film is lighthearted.

After completing *Hair Piece*, Chenzira produced what she terms an "experimental documentary" called

Still from *Hair Piece: A Film for Nappy-Headed People* (courtesy of Women Make Movies)

Secret Sounds Screaming: The Sexual Abuse of Children in 1986. Unlike *Hair Piece*, there is nothing lighthearted about *Secret Sounds Screaming*, which uses interviews with survivors of childhood sexual abuse, parents, abusers and social workers to highlight social attitudes toward sexual abuse and why and how abusers are able to get away with their crimes.

The following year, Chenzira made the rap music video *Five Out of Five*, about child and teen sexual abuse. The video featured New York Women Against Rape's Acting Out Teen Theatre, and brought the issue to the MTV generation of television viewers.

In 1988, Chenzira turned her camera on performance artist Thomas Pinnock in *The Lure and the Lore*, in which Pinnock discusses his immigration to the United States from Jamaica and the wild differences between what he expected ("the lure") and the reality with which he was faced ("the lore"). In the film, Pinnock explains how these two different views of the United States influenced his choreography. After two pieces about child sexual abuse, Chenzira was moving back to her first muse: dance.

Chenzira returned to animation in 1988 with *Zajota and the Boogie Spirit*, which she described as "the history of African Americans told through dance, through animation." In the folktalelike *Zajota*, the Zajota people use dance as a way of confronting challenges. "Dance is life," Chenzira noted. "It is the way the body responds to its environment, as well as what is taking place internally. When most people think of dance, they think only of its entertainment aspect; however, dance has been used to announce birth, prepare for war, ask for forgiveness, assist in healing, satirize events, and in the case of *Zajota and the Boogie Spirit*, dance is used both as a survival tool and a way to predict the future."

To finance her films, Chenzira does "the patchwork quilt of funding through traditional sources that have been set up to support the independent film and video community, and I also raise private money. Money is a real stumbling block, and it takes up a lot of time and a lot of energy. Using other people's money is not always easy. I don't know that I know how to do it—my films take a long time to do, and people who invest have to realize that. *Zajota and the Boogie Spirit* is eighteen minutes of animation that took almost three years to make. It's a hand art. Usually, when people work in animation, they have teams of people who are inkers or painters. People who put money into [my work] know that it's going to take a while. I do know that if you're just looking for grants, you're probably not going to survive for very long and your frustration level will be really high."

At City College of New York Chenzira teaches screenwriting and directing and oversees senior thesis film and video projects. Because her teaching schedule is limited—she teaches no more than three days a week—Chenzira also has time to work on her own projects. "What I do in the winter is write," she said, "so that I can prepare to go into production in spring and summer. I've also found that I can teach and edit [a film] at the same time."

Chenzira noted that many perils are attached to the making of a feature-length film. "I took a piece to the Sundance Institute in 1984 and shopped it around a bit; and [I found] people have trouble when you have all black characters. Suddenly it's not universal, and they don't know how to market it. Finally, a friend of mine called and said, 'Why don't you take it over to Columbia Pictures?' And I said, 'Because I have no intention of dealing with a studio.' The friend said, 'Well, [producer] David Puttnam [*Chariots of Fire*] is over there.' That really made a big difference, because I have a lot of respect for David's work. I didn't know much about him as a businessperson, but really admired him as a filmmaker. I got a yes from

Columbia, went off to Brazil to work on another project with a friend, and when I came back David was on his way to being fired, and everything went into turnaround.

"People are being pressured into feeling as though they have to make features," said Chenzira, "and people don't even talk about 'my story' or 'my film'; they say 'my feature.' I like working in all different kinds of formats, everything from video 8 to 35mm film, and I still like still photography, even though I don't do it very much anymore. I like producing short pieces—*Hair Piece* is very short, and every time I show it the response is just tremendous. So I don't feel pressured to make a feature. The problem that I run into now in listening to audiences is that everybody is set up for the long film; so, since I'm exploring a lot of things with home video right now, I'm looking for ways that people can be satisfied with a series of short pieces that add up to what their expectations are."

Chenzira also pointed out that a filmmaker cannot please everybody. "Whatever you do, there's going to be someone telling you it's not right, you shouldn't be, you shouldn't be. And when you drop dead, and you're either cremated or buried in this box, people will weep and talk about how much they miss you, but no one, no one, *no one* will say, 'Please cremate me too, move over, let me in the box.' So that should not dictate what a filmmaker does or doesn't do.

"I know so many people who have dropped out of the business," Chenzira said, "who were frustrated by the fact there was no consistency, that there were more scripts than there were screens. That's what I want to do right now—work, get it from head to screen."

Chenzira noted that the economics of the box office still drive what films the studios put their money behind. "Certainly, in terms of commercial cinema, people go to the theater to relax. The idea of going to the cinema still is done in the context of an outing. I remember when my mother took me to see my *My Fair Lady, Camelot* and *The Ten Commandments:* You dressed up to go to the movie theater because it was considered an outing. Now there's a lot of other stuff that comes with going to the theater. If you live in a place like New York, you've got parking, or you've got a terrible transportation system; if you've got a family, then there's the cost of popcorn and the ticket price; to take yourself and another person and kids to the theater is expensive. So people feel they're somehow getting more if they go to something that has certain stamps of approval and also is going to fit into enough space to be considered leisure time."

In spite of the emphasis on African-American characters and African-American culture in her films, Chenzira sees them as holding universal messages. "I don't really know if I think that there are things that are considered black issues," she explained. "Because of certain political structures, in any society there seems always to be a group of people who are having to go through specific fires at specific time periods, but I'm not sure that I would put that in the context of black issues. I have an interest in black people who are going through certain experiences."

Chenzira explained her working methods as being different from those of Hollywood. "I work from the inside out," she said. "I only do things that interest me, only do things I care about and only do things that are bothering me. It's the 'bothering me' aspect—what I'm doing in film is trying to get comfortable with spaces where I'm not always so comfortable. Out of that evolves a certain language or a certain physical presentation.

"I think the problem with a lot of films made not necessarily by men, but within the Hollywood structure or a really tight business structure, where money is the focus and not the character or the story—although they seem to pretend that it is—is that you're already at odds; the marketing people are involved with trying to figure out the ancillary products—that's a very exterior way of working. Sometimes it will hit an interior by accident, but most times it seems to miss the mark. There's a real concern with the illusion of a perfect reality, so you get scenes where people are either waking up or just going to sleep, and they look just gorgeous. It's as if the American public couldn't take it any other way. Women being lit for what is considered their best features. I would like to present women in a way that they've never been presented before, or I would like to show women doing X, Y and Z. Most of the women I remember and know—their lives, their stories, their history, what they looked like—have never been presented. I don't think about presenting them—I think about the story I want to tell, and they then emerge."

Sadie Benning

Teen with a Toy Camera

In the late 1980s, toy company Fisher-Price decided to cash in on the home video boom by marketing a video camera—the PXL2000—specifically for

Sadie Benning (photo by Fotografia Studios; courtesy of Women Make Movies)

kids, with the low price of $100. Instead of using videocassettes, the PXL2000 used standard *audio* cassettes, recording both sound and a black-and-white image. The end product, termed pixelvision (a pixel is a line of resolution on a TV set—pixelvision has considerably fewer lines of resolution than standard video), was a muddy, grainy picture within a black

Videos by Sadie Benning

A New Year

Living Inside

Me and Rubyfruit

Jollies

Welcome to Normal

If Every Girl Had a Diary

A Place Called Lovely

It Wasn't Love

"frame," not much compared with the smooth, color images adult video cameras produced. The PXL2000 also required lots of light and a steady hand. Needless to say, kids—those most discriminating of consumers—weren't impressed. By 1989, Fisher-Price had pulled the cameras from the market.

But on Christmas, 1988, fifteen-year-old Sadie Benning was given a PXL2000 by her father, experimental filmmaker James Benning. Benning immediately made the video *A New Year* (1989), essentially an artistic camera test that catalogued her possessions. Benning then turned her new camera on her working-class Milwaukee neighborhood and her own burgeoning lesbianism, and the videos *Me and Rubyfruit* (1989), *Jollies* (1990), *If Every Girl Had a Diary* (1990) and *A Place Called Lovely* (1991) quickly became favorites at lesbian and gay film and video festivals across the country.

They also catapulted the teenaged Benning to celebrity status in the experimental film and video community. Benning's crisp images spoke to a generation of frustrated women filmmakers, who then picked up cameras—even PXL2000 cameras—and started making experimental works. Before Sadie Benning, the PXL2000 had simply been a children's toy. After Benning's success, the remaining PXL2000s still available through mail-order catalogues and toy stores were quickly snapped up by independent filmmakers; now the cameras are sold and traded in the classified ads sections of independent film magazines.

Benning's work influenced other lesbian filmmakers as well: Wendy Jo Carlton used pixelvision to make her video *Bumps* (1993), a personal chronicle about venereal disease, and Catherine Saalfield turned a PXL2000 on her friends to explore lesbian gender identification in *Cuz It's Boy* (1994), which takes the murder of Brandon Teena as its starting point.

Only one feature-length project has been shot with pixelvision: Michael Almereyda struck big in 1992 with *Another Girl Another Planet*, a science-fiction love story that garnered lots of press because of its unusual format. *Another Girl*'s $12,000 price tag included 16mm film prints—Benning's works cost considerably less.

One of the hallmarks of Benning's video pieces is the use of phrases of text followed by caustic video images. In *A New Year*, for example, one line of text reads, "A friend got raped by a black man," which is followed by footage of a sink being scrubbed with cleanser, and which in turn is followed by the text, "now she's a Racist Nazi Skinhead." Benning made her second video, *Living Inside* (1989), after she turned sixteen and dropped out of high school. But it wasn't until she made *Me and Rubyfruit*, where she comes out as a lesbian, holding a dialogue with herself, that the video world began to take notice. Lesbianism is the theme of her next three pieces, *Welcome to Normal* (1990), *If Every Girl Had a Diary* and *Jollies*. In *Jollies*, Benning talks about the beginnings of her sexual desires: "It started in 1978 when I was in kindergarten / They were twins / and I was a tomboy / I always thought of real clever things to say / Like I love you."

What is perhaps most extraordinary about Benning's work, other than her youth, is that the majority of her footage was shot in her bedroom. Benning's taped introspections made her an Everywoman for teenage lesbians struggling with their sexuality and stunned adults with their precociousness.

As Benning told fellow director Ellen Spiro for an article in *The Advocate* in 1990, "My dad said to me, 'You know, I'm really worried that all your work is just going to be on one subject.' And I was like, 'Yeah, my life.' He makes [experimental] films. What are his films about? They're about his life. It just so happens that his sexuality isn't something that people are going to label or talk about or say, 'He's the heterosexual artist.' The art world is not white, heterosexual and male-dominated anymore. There's definitely homophobia in the art world, but I don't care. That's not my audience. My work right now is for gay and lesbian people. We are *starving* for work."

Benning's strongest pixelvision piece was also her last, *A Place Called Lovely*, which isn't about lesbianism so much as it is about childhood and gender. *A Place Called Lovely* may well be considered her last journeyman piece, one that shows she has mastered camera movement, lighting and editing.

In 1992, at the age of nineteen, Benning received a $35,000 Rockefeller fellowship; in 1993, she began working on a feature-length film about two sixteen-year-old lesbians. Her pieces have been shown at the Museum of Modern Art and the Whitney Biennial, both in New York. Despite her early success, Benning keeps a low profile and has moved from Milwaukee to Chicago. Her videos continue to be shown at film and video festivals worldwide.

Sadie Benning

Narrative Film

Lizzie Borden

Let's Talk About Sex

"We are living in a very anti-sexual time; lack of sexual desire is epidemic," said Lizzie Borden. "It's more than the fear of AIDS, it's more than the influence of the Republican culture of Reagan–Bush and Newt Gingrich. What I want to know is, why have we become so afraid of sex?"

For Borden the question is more than rhetorical. Hollywood has fallen victim to the de-sexing of the nineties—and as a consequence, so have her films. There is high irony attached to this turn of events, how-

Lizzie Borden

ever, because it was Borden's iconoclastic depiction of sex that brought her to Hollywood in the first place, lured by producers intrigued by her ideas and impressed by her success as an

Films by Lizzie Borden

Regrouping

Born in Flames

Working Girls

Love Crimes

Let's Talk About Sex

independent director unafraid to tackle taboo topics on screen.

Borden's 1986 film *Working Girls,* detailing a day in the life of a New York City prostitute, was an international award-winner. Her first Hollywood feature, *Love Crimes* (1992), starred Sean Young and Patrick Bergin and dealt with sexual obsession, repression and sadomasochism. Her work since *Love Crimes* includes a documentary for the Playboy channel on phone sex. Her current projects continue to delve deeply into the recesses of women's sexual identity and expression, while also addressing the outlaw nature of female desire. "It seems to be very taboo, what I'm doing," Borden explained.

What she's doing is making films that investigate sex, race, class and power from a female vantage point. All Borden's films, from her early short pieces to her most recent features and cable television work, break more than lesbian and heterosexual sexual taboos—each also addresses class, capitalism and the power money bestows. Each depicts interracial relationships. This is another theme Borden explores in her films and another taboo subject; after sex, race may be the most complicated issue in American society. Unlike the majority of white directors, who tend to position people of color in the background of their films as cinematic filler, or into what black director Julie Dash calls the "impeding roles" where a black character stands in the way of the white hero or heroine, people of color are never just "dropped in" a film by Borden. For the director, the feminist admonition that "the personal is political" has always been a *dictat* to live by. Borden's deepest emotional relationships have been with black women and men; her films reflect, in part, the issues raised by such interracial couplings. She is as interested in how whites and people of color work (and love) together as she is in the interworkings of male/female and female/female sexuality. But she also recognizes that just as forthright portrayals of female sexuality are still considered a pushing of the proverbial cinematic envelope, so too are realistic depictions of interracial relationships, whether in the workplace or at home. However, Borden is quite succinct about what she wants to do as a filmmaker, asserting, "I make films to answer questions. It has to do with asking questions that there are no absolute answers to, and creating a film in which there's enough ambiguity that people from different sides can jump into the fray with opinions on both sides."

The question of what prostitution is really about gets addressed with almost documentarian detail in *Working Girls*. (A source of annoyance to Borden is the fact that the film is often written about and discussed *as* a documentary, rather than as a narrative fiction film. "How can people mistake the two?" she asked, mystified. "It's like if you do a realistic portrayal of how women live, it must be a documentary." Other women directors have experienced the same problem, however, such as Indian director Mira Nair with *Salaam Bombay!*, her narrative film about Bombay's street children.)

Gritty, humorous, poignant, complex and uncompromisingly unsentimental, *Working Girls* depicts the specifics of life in a downtown brothel run by a superficial madam with bourgeois interests and prosaic desires. The film, which won the premier independent filmmaking award—Best Dramatic Feature at the 1986 Sundance Film Festival—was lauded as the first dramatic feature film to depict prostitution realistically from the vantage point of the prostitute and from a distinctly female perspective.

Louise Smith in *Working Girls*

The film is vintage Borden: about the complications, complexities and confluence of sex and sexuality in a culture both deeply desirous of and abundantly shamed by both. The narrative of *Working Girls* revolves around the mesmerizing performance of Louise Smith, who plays Molly, a lesbian artist who lives with her black lover, Diane, and their young daughter. Molly bicycles to work at the brothel, where the other women players are equally intriguing and, unlike previous films about prostitution, highly individuated in Borden's script. They include a college student working her way through school, a Latina woman in a rocky relationship with a man who doesn't know what she does for a living, an elegant but aging former model who needs to know she is still desirable and the strident and unctuous madam driven by conspicuous consumption. A new girl, badly dressed, a bit too timid and clearly out of her depth, gets interviewed in the course of this day in the life, but ends up leaving before the night is over; the work is too hard—not what she saw in the movies, not the easy money she'd hoped for. The madam, Lucy, continually berates the women for not acting enough like ladies, arguing that they musn't chew gum or smoke cigarettes, telling Molly to get her bicycle out of the hallway, or ordering Dawn (the student) to get her feet off the sofa as if the women are wayward teenagers rather than the prostitutes she pimps and makes a good living from. Lucy continually reminds her "girls" that putting the phones on hold is very bad for business.

The roles are difficult in *Working Girls*, the women tough, vulnerable and realistic (including their looks—they are all attractive but in a very ordinary way). The film is very much, despite the focus on Smith's strong central portrayal, about the ensemble nature of a brothel; the women support each other in many different ways: lying to the madam to protect each other, telling each other secrets to make the tricking easier, helping each other get through the work day much as they would in a factory or a restaurant. Each woman is individuated, rather than the generic prostitute model seen in other films; each depicts variant aspects of the *business* of prostitution and the life lived outside that job.

Borden scripts the men who buy these women's services with equal care: businessmen, entrepreneurs, college professors; older, middle-aged, deceptively young; married and single; regulars and first-timers; attractive and creepy; confident and unsure; charming and downright brutal; they are just like men in the world outside the brothel—diverse and occasionally perverse. Some want things they can't get at home, others want dramatic scenarios involving sex toys and fantasies, others are simply avoiding the complications of intimacy. Part of the real complexity of the film is Borden's insistence that human sexuality exists in shades of gray, not the black and white of the anti-sex culture the director rails against. Just as the prostitutes themselves are real women with totally separate lives outside the brothel, the men also defy stereotyping—they are, for the most part, just regular guys; some deserve the audience's sympathy, others its censure. But both the female and male characters in *Working Girls* are part of the cultural tableaux of sexuality that fascinates Borden—and worries the censors.

Borden believes it is her avid interest in depicting the complicated nature of female sexuality and desire that makes producers uneasy. Borden is manifestly disinterested in the established stereotypes of female desire and sexuality; her women characters are never timid or withdrawn—if they appear to be on the surface, something else is roiling just below that seeming passivity or aloofness, as in her film *Love Crimes. Working Girls* ignores the stereotypes of prostitution established by Hollywood. There are no exaggerated, overdressed black pimps terrorizing their young, white, drug-addicted whores as featured in (the so-called) realistic films about prostitution, nor are there the happy-go-lucky whores-with-hearts-of-gold who regularly populate the other prostitution films from Hollywood. If there is a villain in *Working Girls,* it is the madam, clearly representative of the capitalistic drive that makes sex equivalent to power and just one more commodity in our consumption-driven and deeply acquisitive society.

A prostitutes yells at Lucy, the madam, in *Working Girls*

Although *Working Girls* was the feature film that established Borden's status as a director to be reckoned with, her first foray into film in Hollywood after that unmitigated success, *Love Crimes,* was a bleak disappointment for both the director and her fans. Despite having been drawn to Hollywood from New York by people "terribly excited" by her work, Borden found that once she began presenting her ideas—all focused on the outlaw nature of female sexuality—the enthusiasm was a little less pronounced.

"The problems really came down to sex," she lamented. "My vision of what I wanted, of how I wanted to explore the character [played by Sean Young in *Love Crimes*] and her sexual needs and desires just wasn't acceptable or accepted. The sadomasochistic element of the film as *I* envisioned it was too scary for the people writing the checks. And then I didn't get final cut."

Borden is far more open about the various problems facing women directors in Hollywood than most women in Tinseltown. Some directors have had to adopt public personas that are very different from their real personalities just to continue to get their work made. Penny Marshall, an extremely bright woman and an excellent director who is also one of the biggest moneymaking female directors, is notorious for what insiders refer to as her "Laverne act" (a reference to the not-so-bright character she played for years on the hit television sit-com, *Laverne and Shirley,* before she became a director); pretending to be a bit flaky has made her less threatening to male producers and directors and allowed her to forge ahead with her own projects. Several other women directors who started out with small, intriguing independent features have become victims of Hollywood's directorial typecasting now that they are enmeshed in the studio system, making generic Hollywood films—slapstick comedies geared toward teen audiences or sure-fire box-office hits like action films.

Borden has had a tougher time, largely due to how uncompromising she really is and her continued unwillingness to make films she doesn't feel passionately about. She has a clearly delineated concept of what kind of filmmaking she wants to do and is willing to wait to make those films rather than accept any vehicle she's offered. After *Love Crimes,* she said, "All I was offered were erotic thrillers. And while I wouldn't mind doing an erotic thriller that *I* wanted to do, I didn't want to get pigeonholed as a director who only does erotic thrillers. The fact that this was how *Love Crimes* was perceived was a real disappointment to me, because that wasn't what I was aiming for."

What Borden was attempting ended up on the cutting room floor—literally. ("A lot of people don't realize how important final cut is to a film," she explained.) In fact, as released with the Hollywood final cut, *Love Crimes* was universally panned by critics as "murky" and "unfocused," while the release of the director's cut was uniformly well-reviewed. (For example, Leonard Maltin in his *1997 Movie and Video Guide* rated the studio cut of *Love Crimes* a "bomb" but gave the director's cut three out of four stars.) The experience with *Love Crimes* jarred Borden, who acknowledged, "You can't complain, especially as a woman, or you end up being categorized as 'difficult'—someone, a *woman,* who won't compromise, who can't be worked with. And frankly, you can end up never making another film in this town, whether it's done independently or with a studio. What I hate most about having other people decide how my films get altered, though, is that people will think I'm a sloppy filmmaker."

Negotiating that fine line between trying to do what you want cinematically and trying to do *something* is the tightrope Borden has been walking since she moved to Hollywood, hovering in a kind of movie limbo between being an independent director and a Hollywood director. Basically uncompromising, proud of her own vision and dedicated to realistic and feminist portrayals of female characters in what she calls *"real* dramatic roles—really big, exciting stories about the important things in women's lives" has kept her walking that fine line in a town that doesn't allow for safety nets.

In the film world Borden has a reputation for being an independent director who can make a really good film on a shoestring budget, and as such she has become somewhat of an icon for young women filmmakers. *Working Girls* was made for a mere $100,000. Borden built the sets in her loft in New York's Chinatown district and shot the entire film there, except for a few shots that were filmed on the streets of New York. Her groundbreaking early feature, *Born in Flames* (1983), took her four years to make in 16mm on the amazingly low budget of $40,000. Borden worked as a film editor while she worked on *Born in Flames*. "When I taught myself how to make films," she explained, "I immediately gravitated toward editing, because it's so much like writing—it's about logical ideas fitting together. (Borden had previously worked as a critic for *Art Forum* magazine.) So I could support myself doing that, and had an editing machine in my house so I could edit *Born in Flames* at night."

The work was grueling but has paid off for Borden—literally. "Both *Working Girls* and *Born in Flames* really made money for me, and allowed me to be selective about what I've done since," the director acknowledged. "I get money from the distribution of these films every year. *Born in Flames,* which has just gone to videotape (in 1997), has had this amazing cult following for years—it gets shown in classrooms and at festivals and in women's groups. It's really amazing how many people are still so interested in that film. But that's exactly what I wanted to have happen—I wanted people to be discussing that movie in a group, together, and that's what's happened."

The first lesbian feature film made by a woman (and to depict positive images of lesbians), *Born in Flames* is a futuristic allegory set in New York in a postrevolutionary society. Ahead of its time, the film explores the role of the media in culture and society within the context of a lesbian and feminist guerilla war. Borden's juxtaposition of pseudo news clips and media commentary lends a gritty authenticity to the film. Scripted as the film was being shot over the course of several years and filmed with nonprofessional actors who helped in the evolution of the script, *Born in Flames* is a tight and cohesive narrative. Borden's editing incorporates the use of a lot of innovative montage editing techniques later used by the director whose work

Lizzie Borden

Still from *Born in Flames*

inspired her to make movies, Jean-Luc Godard. (Jenni Olson, film archivist and former co-director of the annual San Francisco Gay and Lesbian Film Festival, called *Born in Flames* "one of the most dynamic feminist films ever made. We've shown it repeatedly [at the festival]. It's over ten years old, but it is still as timely today as it was when it was released. It's a feminist classic.")

Exploring the factionalism that occurs postrevolution among a series of women's groups—white, black, lesbian, intellectual—it is the first of Borden's films to develop her most prevalent theme: the marginalization of women by society, either through sexuality, race or class. As in *Working Girls, Born in Flames* features a searing focal performance by Honey as the DJ of Phoenix Radio, a black women's underground radio station. And also, as in *Working Girls,* money, class and power form the foundation for the questions the film asks—and attempts to answer. But while *Working Girls* veers away from the truly dark side of prostitution by examining the brothel, which is a somewhat more controlled working environment for prostitutes than the street, *Born in Flames* has echoes of the same dark underside of life that Borden later tried to explicate in *Love Crimes;* there is a death/murder of a lesbian revolutionary while under police interrogation. The startling nature of life's twists and turns, the dangers that lurk everywhere for women, particularly where the power is not their own, is an element of what Borden explores in the film. We see the characters pulling together and out of their own factions, bonding in an effort to rise against the anti-woman, anti-lesbian, anti-black forces while also crossing barriers of race, class and sexual identification. The film also presumes a female (and feminist) audience, which is fascinating, especially in retrospect, as films by women directors so often attempt now to neutralize singularly female identification, promising a "film for everyone." *Born in Flames* is fundamentally and unapologetically a film for women, as was her early feature, *Regrouping* (1976).

"*Regrouping* was a way to deal with the idea of women's groups and what could be gained from the solidarity of those groups," Borden explained, "only to find that the solidarity was, in some ways, fleeting, and not really as substantial as I thought, but still valuable. *Born in Flames* is about energy and action, and it's about marginalization. I shot it a particular way and worked on it in this kind of evolutionary way because I wanted this intensity, this guerilla quality, this immediacy of something happening to be sustained in the film, and I think it works, though I don't think I would ever do a film that way again."

The concept of *Born in Flames* was as evolutionary as the process by which the film itself was made, explained Borden. "*Born in Flames* actually came out of *Regrouping*. I saw that a lot of the motives of feminism and a lot of the women's groups themselves were really controlled by white, middle-class women. I didn't see many black women involved—or women of any other color or nationality. So the premise of *Born in Flames*," said Borden, "was to have black and white women working together after an evolution toward a more socialist government. I wanted a multiplicity of voices, as opposed to one unified voice, which seems to be the inherent demand of a white, middle-class movement—which is that everyone has to speak this common language. But what I found," Borden explained, "was that one didn't have to speak that kind of language to have the same goals. There can be a way of joining without assimilation, without becoming homogeneous. Because I think that destroys individuality and destroys cultures." Borden readily admitted that making the film was itself a kind of guerilla action—shooting quickly at airports or on Wall Street, filming only the first take because she was working with nonactors she had literally gotten off the streets of New York and found that because there was no actual acting technique, the first take was usually the most intense and direct.

In recent years Borden hasn't had to deal with the constraints that come with shoestring budgets and guerilla tactics. But she still feels very much like she's fighting a kind of cultural war as she tries to make her films. *Let's Talk About Sex* premiered in 1994 at the annual San Francisco International Lesbian and Gay Film Festival, the world's largest lesbian and gay film festival. The film played to a sold-out audience at the Castro Theater on a Saturday night, but not without some controversy regarding the content: The film is about a Latina phone sex worker and, even in the traditionally more accepting gay community, Borden's films still push limits. (The film predated Spike Lee's box-office bomb, *Girl Six* [1996], about a black sex worker, by three years and has Borden's distinctly female gaze.) There continues to be resistance to Borden's portrayal of women sex workers as positive characters with deep emotional lives whose "work" in the sex trade is both valid *and* real work.

Perhaps one of the aspects of Borden's *ouevre* that leaves audiences confused is her consistently feminist vantage point; as *Born in Flames* presumed a female and feminist audience, her more recent work presumes an audience that accepts female sexuality and desire as a given. And these films, while not being lesbian per se, are strongly reflective of her love of women.

That love of women and their individuality has also led Borden to demystify both sexuality and the body itself. Despite her own admitted addiction to working out, she actively chooses to cast actresses in her films who don't have the stereotypically perfect female body. "This image of the perfect female body that men created has damaged a lot of women," she argued. "I get a lot of criticism for how I depict women, because I don't portray idealized women's bodies or a male view of female sexuality. I like to see real women on screen."

The director has had some problems with this conceptualizing of female body image as she's dealt with the Hollywood image of women, however. Combined with the censorship questions and the problems devising projects that everyone can commit to, things have gotten dicey at times. But one place Borden didn't expect to meet opposition to her ideas was in working for the Playboy channel on cable television. Much to her surprise, she found the Playboy channel had the strictest guidelines about sex. "They had more rules than anywhere else," she explained. "No male erections, no close-ups, no bondage, no S/M." *Love Crimes* and *Let's Talk About Sex* have suffered from similar, but unwritten, rules, what Borden called Hollywood's "fear of the forbidden." The studios will only let her go so far, cutting scenes of female masturbation, male frontal nudity and sadomasochistic fantasy from her films.

"It's very much a censoring of women and women's sexuality," she said with some frustration. "Some of the things I want to show aren't politically correct. I feel very committed to doing films about sexuality, but not just the establishment version."

She disdains what is passing for sex—lesbian, gay and heterosexual—

in movies today. Despite a friendship with gay director Gus Van Sant, Borden was disappointed by the lesbian-themed *Even Cowgirls Get the Blues* (1994). "I wish that the relationships between the women in the film had been as well developed as those in his other films," she said. But she admitted that the lesbian-made independent feature *Claire of the Moon* (1992), directed by Nicole Conn, was also a disappointment. "I mean people just don't *talk* like that," she said. "And *where* is the sex?" Borden said the hunger for lesbian images on screen has made *Claire of the Moon* immensely popular, and leads women to many films that aren't billed as lesbian, like the female western, *Bad Girls* (1994). "When I went to see *Bad Girls,* the audience was full of lesbians," she noted. "Of course, I love Drew Barrymore myself, so who can blame them?"

As for the downsizing of sex in films, Borden said it is symbolic of "a kind of general repression, a narrowing of our culture as a whole. People complained about Bill Clinton because of his sex life, but I was happy to see a president in the White House who *had* a sex life—I thought it was good for the country. Everywhere we look there are articles and news reports about lack of desire, about fear of sex," she lamented. "And I think films are reflecting this. There's a real sanctification of the family in movies today. Even heterosexual sex in the movies is very limited. And that narrows the possibilities for many filmmakers who have sexuality questions they want to address."

Those limitations very much extend to lesbian and gay images in mainstream films, as well as to how women get portrayed on screen. Added Borden, "I guess what I'm waiting for is a *Last Tango in Paris* for gay people." However, that film, noted Borden, isn't likely to be made in Hollywood, because "the studios still look at the audience as male, and the studio executives themselves for the most part are men." What this means, she explained, is "gay men can be hunks but they can't be sexual, and lesbians— forget lesbians. A bisexual woman is an object of curiosity, but a lesbian is an object of revulsion. There isn't a place for the man to come in between two women who are perfectly fine without him." Hollywood films like *Basic Instinct* (1992), *Showgirls* (1995) and *Bound* (1996) only serve to underscore her point; the "lesbian" characters are psychopathological, driven to have sex with men and then kill them. Other films like *Boys on the Side* (1996) show real lesbian characters, like Whoopi Goldberg, but they are alone—there is no actual lesbian relationship in the movie. Films by independent lesbian directors that have gotten mainstream release, such as *Bar Girls* (1994) and Rose Troche's and Guin Turner's *Go Fish* (1994) stint on showing lesbian sexuality up close and personal in the way Donna Deitch's groundbreaking film *Desert Hearts* (1985) did.

Yet most women fantasize about lesbianism, explained Borden, and would very much like to see it on screen. "Women I know who are straight talk about their fantasies about other women all the time, even women who would never, ever act on those fantasies," she said. "But the image of lesbians on screen and in pornography is all about *men* and adding a man to the mix. Like that little thing these women do with their tongues—I've never seen a *real* lesbian do that."

Gay men are more accepted in Hollywood films than lesbians, said Borden, as long as their overt sexuality stays hidden. "In a film like [Jonathan Demme's] *Philadelphia* [1993], which is all about a gay man with AIDS [Tom Hanks] who is in a relationship with Antonio Banderas, there is *no touching,*" she said. "There are all these gay male characters just injected into mainstream films, like the character in *Beverly Hills Cop III* [1994]. But there is no lesbian equivalent. And there is no one right now who can make a lesbian film in Hollywood," she asserted. "Jodie Foster isn't going to do it. Madonna could probably do it if she paid for it herself. And there are all these lesbian executives in the studios, but they can't do anything to get a lesbian movie made either. The climate simply won't allow it. We are really afraid of sex right now."

Borden said that "eventually there is going to be a power dyke movie—with grown-up lesbians in slick clothes and that whole lipstick image. But I think for now we are going to continue to see those 'coded' lesbian movies like *Fried Green Tomatoes* [1991]."

Meanwhile, the director hopes to continue to push the envelope on sexuality in the movies herself. "What I really want to do is show an erection on screen—to actually show a man *getting* an erection. That is something you never see, even in pornography. An erection has been used as an instrument of brutality toward women [in movies]," she explained. "I'd like to turn that around—show it as sexual desire."

These are the kind of ideas that make studio executives shudder, however. "They tell me we won't get an audience, we'll get an NC-17 [no children under seventeen admitted] rating, we won't be able to sell it abroad. As a woman and as a feminist I find it offensive that female frontal nudity is casual and you never see male frontal nudity," she said. To have real sexual equality on screen, Borden asserted, the audience has to see both.

Statements like this may have put Borden over the top in Hollywood, but she has earned a great deal of respect from other women in various areas of the film business who call her "too smart for Hollywood" and call her films "feminist classics" and "serious, risk-taking films about real women."

A new project of Borden's takes more risks, breaks more taboos, involving—once again—issues of female sexuality, desire, danger and power. She's been working on the project for nearly a year and hopes it will be completed soon. "Filmmaking is very different today than it used to be," acknowledged Borden. "Making films ten or twelve years ago was so different—there weren't agents, there was a little more leeway. Most of us [her generation of filmmakers] didn't go to film school—we were artists, designers, writers who became filmmakers and just started making films. You really can't do that today."

What one can do is wait for the right project or hope that the project one has created will work. While Borden waits to complete a project she wants to do, she said she is "writing scripts for features, I'm doing a little TV here and there. I didn't really know about screenwriting—so I've been using this time [between features] to teach myself the things I haven't known before," she admitted. "Part of it is self-protective. The problem with *Love Crimes* was the script was under attack from the outset. Now I realize you gain creative control from a strong script. I'm more likely to be able to do the kind of films I want because I'll have really strong scripts." And, said the director who began her career as a painter after graduating from Wellesley College with a degree in fine arts, "I've been doing figure drawing to keep my eye. But I want to make movies—not television, not cable—but no one will let you. This is not a self-imposed silence I'm going through right now. It's been hard, really difficult. I've been working for the Playboy channel and it feels good to be working again, but part of the whole filmmaking experience for me was traveling with the film, engaging with the audiences."

Borden is committed to filmmaking—her filmmaking. "For me a film is always political, always about a sense of commitment," she asserted. "It has to be an issue or an idea. Other filmmakers are committed to telling a good story—I've always had a different idea."

One of those different ideas remains her feminist consciousness. As is true for many women filmmakers, personal expression and exploration lie at the core of Borden's directorial *ouevre*. Her ardent feminism colored all her early work, particularly *Regrouping* and *Born in Flames*. Her personal exploration of lesbianism in the seventies, as well as her involvement in interracial relationships, led to the writing and making of *Born in Flames*, she said. "I wanted to explore the idea of power between women, but I also wanted to take a close look at how black women and white women might work together." The ideas she developed in *Born in Flames*, she explained, "led to the notion of what *Working Girls* is about—sexuality as a tool, with a specific amount of money attached to it."

The confluence of disparate sexual identities in Borden's work has made it difficult to categorize her work and that has sometimes worked against her. Some consider her a lesbian filmmaker, particularly because *Born in Flames* has become such an iconic work over the years. But others are simply uncomfortable with what seems to be a kind of free-ranging expression of sexuality that remains more reminiscent of the lyrical free-love tone of the sixties sexual revolution than the repressive anti-sex tenor of the nineties. "The irony in my life is I identify so strongly with other women and feel so attached to who women are, but I'm basically heterosexual, even though I continue to like to explore a range of sexual identities in my films," Borden explained. *"Born in Flames* really tagged me as a lesbian filmmaker, which was fine, except I started to feel really disingenuous that people were making assumptions that I was a lesbian when I had started living this rather blatantly heterosexual life. I wasn't copping out—I just felt I should be honest."

How one's personal sexuality is defined both influences how one makes a film, Borden said, as well as how others perceive the filmmaker herself. "Now sexuality isn't overidentified [as much as it was in the eighties]," she noted. "Being called a bisexual makes it seem like I'm out and just pretending I'm not a lesbian, but for me it really refers to what I perceive as my bisexual nature. I've been involved with women and I've been involved with men and all those experiences have really influenced how I make films and how I want to see the sexuality [of the characters] portrayed. So much of my sexuality is related to my work and the other way around."

Love Crimes, Borden's most misunderstood film, was, she said, "about a domain of sexual repression—exploration without catharsis. For me it was never about sexual pleasure. *Born in Flames* was about sexual power and *Working Girls* was about sexual pleasure and power. Those questions I have about sexuality are always there when I do a film: How do you form a relationship with another person? For me it could have been a man or a woman. Sexuality is not the various acts but the ability to conceive of love. And same-sex union is very powerful—just an expansion of one's potential. I believe in a kind of bisexuality or omnisexuality."

Making art is vital to Borden. An element of her cinematic art is her obsession with and passion for observing, a trait numerous directors from Ingmar Bergman to Francois Truffaut to Federico Fellini have admitted to. "I am a voyeur, there's no question," she noted. "And I am certainly political. I don't belong to any political groups—film is where I make my politics known, it's my political tool. My sense has always been more to the left than to the right of any equation, even though it might not be something I would actually *do* myself. *Born in Flames* advocates violence, but I would never do that myself—I would rather make a movie about it."

Borden hopes the repressive sexual climate of the nineties will lead to something more expansive by the time the millenium is reached. "It interests me that on the one hand there is all this new censorship while there is also this burgeoning pansexuality among young girls, who also adamantly reject the label of feminism," she said. "For all of us our sexuality has affected what we do—some in a more direct or indirect way. For me [as a director], I've been drawn by sexuality as a kind of power and my films reflect that. Black lesbians seemed able to risk more, were closer to the edge and that's why I posited them as heroic in *Born in Flames.* In *Working Girls* I left Molly fuller in other ways—didn't overvalue her body. *Love Crimes* was supposed to be about a woman who is so disconnected from herself that she becomes obsessed with women who found a satisfying sexuality with a con man. Originally she was going to rape him, make him feel something that no crinimal justice system could make him feel, but that got edited out of the script. In *Let's Talk About Sex,* it was to show the intimacy that grows between these people through this phone sex experience. So I've tried to show the different thralls sex places on us and how we deal with it."

Hollywood has made Borden wonder if she should return completely to independent filmmaking, but she isn't ready to leave yet. She is still biding her time. "You know, I still haven't really made a real Hollywood movie, yet," she noted with some irony. "Basically I want to do female dramas, films that are about real women," she said. "I know it can happen here [in Hollywood]. I'd just like it to happen now. And I'd like to be the one doing it."

Susan Seidelman

Independent Box Office

Susan Seidelman is one of America's best-known and most successful independent women directors. Her first big box-office hit, *Desperately Seeking Susan* (1985), launched her film career as well as that of pop star Madonna. Her films *She-Devil* (1989), starring Academy Award winner Meryl Streep and Emmy winner Roseanne, and *Cookie* (1989), starring Academy Award winners Peter Falk and Dianne Wiest, garnered mixed reviews and mixed box office, but solidified Seidelman's stature as a director to be reckoned with, one who takes chances with scripts, ideas and casting, and one who maintains her independent profile.

Seidelman completed her first feature, the dark and quirky cult film *Smithereens* (1982), at the age of twenty-eight, soon after graduating from film school. Incredibly low budget, but a resounding critical success, *Smithereens* made the rounds of the most prestigious film festivals, including Cannes, where it was the first independent feature by an American director to be shown in competition. The success—and theatrical

Susan Seidelman (second from left)

release—of the film surprised Seidelman as much as it thrilled her. "I had made the film as a portfolio piece, a movie that I thought would help me get other work when I showed it around," she acknowledged. When the film was the first low-budget American feature to ever be invited into competition at Cannes, she said, "It got a lot of attention and that really got things moving for me as a director."

Smithereens, which Seidelman co-wrote, gave her entrée into Hollywood—and much bigger budgets. She wasted little time acquiring a new project, which she finished quickly. The immediate success of *Desperately Seeking Susan* gave Seidelman a certain cachet—she worked with the largest budgets of any female director in the United States. Her later films, with their elite casts (Streep, Falk and John Malkovich among the stars) and well-known screenwriters (Nora Ephron, for example), have achieved various degrees of success but sustained her position as one of the top women directors in the United States.

Women and women's conflicts are at the core of any Seidelman picture. The films she has made in the nineties have brought her back to the risk-taking that made her first films so impressive. Identity issues are key in Seidelman's *oeuvre,* from the obsessive quest for recognition by the character Wren in *Smithereens* to the dichotomous impulses of Madonna's and Rosanna Arquette's characters in *Desperately Seeking Susan* and Streep's and Roseanne's characters' (literal) face-off in *She-Devil* to the more complex elements of *Confessions of a Suburban Girl* (1991) and *The Dutch Master* (1994).

Born in Philadelphia, Pennsylvania, and raised in the suburb of Abington, a place she recalls as being "like any Steven Spielberg suburbia," Seidelman's early knowledge of film was, she admitted, limited to "what was at the mall." She laughed wryly when she talked about being rejected by the film department of the largest university in the region, Temple—a school whose most famous graduate is comedian and TV star Bill Cosby. She applied to the film school after doing undergraduate work at another Philadelphia school, Drexel University, where she'd gone in the hope of becoming a fashion designer. After realizing she would not be the next Coco Chanel, she took a couple of film courses. While in college she went to films to staunch her boredom and found a whole other level of filmmaking. "That's how I got hooked," she said. "So I decided to apply to film school on a whim."

From her privileged vantage point now, Seidelman said her rejection by Temple was all for the best. "The focus there was more on TV and documentaries, and I was always interested in drama and fiction." She wound up, instead, at New York University. There, three years of hands-on movie-making led to grants from the American Film Institute and the National Endowment for the Arts. She made a series of award-winning short films while at NYU (*And You Act Like One, Too, Deficit* and *Yours Truly, Andrea G. Stern*). Thus began a career that has gone from $60,000 shoestring budgets for independent films to multimillion-dollar budgets for major studios—landing her smack in the middle of a system that has not exactly welcomed women directors with open arms. "It's a good thing I was as naive as I was when I started," Seidelman acknowledged. "I didn't realize how few women directors there were, how hard it was for women to do what men had been doing for years. I didn't know how bad it was, what the statistics were. If I had—well, the good thing for me about the women's movement was I just thought I could do it, just go out and direct."

Although she now spends a significant amount of time traveling to Los Angeles and Hollywood, where most recently she has been directing television drama, Seidelman has not succumbed to moving west. She lives within an hour's drive of where she grew up and where she returned to film *Confessions of a Suburban Girl.* Making her home in Stockton, New Jersey, allows her to visit family in Philadelphia or "be back in Manhattan in an hour," she noted.

An intensely private person, Seidelman keeps her filmmaking and her personal life distinctly separate. Married since the filming of *She-Devil* to producer Jonathan Brett, with whom she has a child, she doesn't talk much about her private life. She also doesn't talk about other people. (Rumors of bad blood with ego-driven actors on her sets, notably Falk and Roseanne,

Films by Susan Seidelman

Smithereens

Desperately Seeking Susan

Making Mr. Right

Cookie

She-Devil

Confessions of a Suburban Girl

The Dutch Master

have splashed across the tabloids, but Seidelman dismisses the tales as "silly.") She has nothing bad to say about anyone she has ever worked with. Some say she's naturally circumspect; others note that unlike many a director who moves in and out of Hollywood, Seidelman knows that the best way to get along with producers, actors and others is to smile and keep working. Seidelman has a well-known reputation for calm and niceness on the set—a far cry from many of her contemporaries.

Despite the box-office successes of women filmmakers like Penny Marshall, Barbra Streisand, Amy Heckerling and action-film director Kathryn Bigelow, money to make movies has traditionally been—and remains—out of reach for women directors, especially as independents. The pattern hasn't changed significantly since Dorothy Arzner was the first woman to direct top stars like Joan Crawford, Katherine Hepburn and Rosalind Russell. When women filmmakers succeed, credit accrues to everyone but the director. (Note the number of films by women directors nominated by the Academy for best picture, among them *Children of a Lesser God* by Randa Haines (1986); *Awakenings* by Penny Marshall (1990); *The Prince of Tides* by Streisand (1991); and *The Piano* by Jane Campion (1993). Yet no woman has ever been nominated in the best director category.) When films directed by women fail, it's the director's fault. Either way, the money continues to flow to male directors.

So it's somehow fitting that Seidelman's budget for her first feature was a mere $60,000. She raised it on her own—"from friends and from my grandmother, who left me $15,000 [when she died]," she said. With it she made *Smithereens,* a tragicomic look at the life of a punk rock groupie who aspires to manage the bands she follows.

"Most of the crew working on the film were friends from film school," said Seidelman. "We'd just gotten out; everyone worked for deferred payment. Everyone got paid from the profits." And there *were* profits; the film became a critical hit and a surprise success at the box office.

Desperately Seeking Susan was another surprise, but for different reasons. Not her project, the film was the brainchild of independent producers Midge Sanford and Sarah Pillsbury. Seidelman was not their first choice for director—the two producers had four big-name male directors in mind before they chose her. But it was Seidelman's idea to cast the then barely known Madonna, from more than two hundred actresses who auditioned, as a rock groupie who swaps identities with a suburban housewife, played by Rosanna Arquette.

"It looked like more fun than it was," Seidelman said. One of the difficulties, said the director, was getting used to a larger budget and the strings that were attached. "*Smithereens* was *my* movie. I didn't have to ask anyone's approval. But on *Susan,*" Seidelman commented wryly, "I was *only* the director. It could have been worse. I was working with two producers I liked and whose tastes were similar to mine. A veteran producer or a male producer without the same instincts would have been hard."

After that success, Seidelman left New York for Florida to work with performance artist Ann Magnuson and actor John Malkovich on *Making Mr. Right* (1987), about a scientist who creates an android and the woman who tries to market it. The film died a quick box-office death. "I didn't understand robots," claimed Seidelman, with a touch of irony. "I was used to working with people." She was also out of her favorite filmmaking element—New York. Flop though it was, she said the film was one of her favorite filmmaking experiences. "There's no correlation at all between what you experience on the set and what can actually happen in a film. I loved making that movie, loved working with everyone on it. It was absolutely a great experience."

Her next film, *Cookie,* didn't replicate the fun of *Making Mr. Right,* but unfortunately did replicate that film's bad box office. The film tells the story of a middle-aged Mafioso (Peter Falk) and his rebellious daughter (Emily Lloyd). Seidelman confesses that with its long shoot and complicated storyline, it was a hard movie to direct. Worse yet, "I was pressured because I was coming off a flop. One failure in this business, and they look at you differently. But I needed the challenge. *Cookie* had characters I'd never worked with before. Many actors were middle-aged—and me a girl director!"

Fortunately, *She-Devil* was well into production when *Cookie* crashed. This blockbuster, based on British novelist Fay Weldon's comic allegory *The Life and Loves of a She-Devil,* concerns a battle between very different women over the same philandering man. It didn't take long for the tabloids to twist that into real-life battles between the film's mega-stars, Streep and Roseanne.

"We laughed," the director said, "because those articles were printed

**Susan
Seidelman**

149

before the two had even been on the set together. If you've read the book, you know that the characters Mary Fisher and Ruth don't really meet till the party, and then again when Mary drops her kids off. In the movie, [Streep and Roseanne] worked together maybe six days out of fifty-five and got along well."

In fact, Seidelman immensely enjoyed working on the film. "It was one of the top two pleasant experiences I've had making a movie—*Mr. Right* being the other—because it all went so smoothly. I've worked on many films where you don't know what scenes are coming next, since the script is still being changed. Actors are having trouble, the plot keeps changing. The great thing about this project was that the backbone of the story and the characters were so strong and distinctive, and it made directing very clear. Hopefully," she added, "that comes out on screen."

As for Streep and Roseanne, it was very enjoyable working with them both, said Seidelman—contrary to the tabloids. "Meryl is incredibly experienced, and Roseanne has wonderful instincts and is *very* funny. And Ed Begley, Jr., who is the male lead, was great. He's really funny and extremely open—willing to take risks and try anything."

Seidelman transplanted characters and story to her favorite venue, New York. But the transposition, she said, wasn't difficult. "The book is like a fable, and the setting is unclear," Seidelman explained. "Fay Weldon came to the set one day, and I asked her about it. She deliberately wrote it in a vague way. I knew it needed a city and a soulless suburb. And it needed a sort of glamorous seaside area. So it could have been set in L.A. with Century City, Malibu and the Valley. Or in New York. I think it needed a place with a sense of glamour—of 'lifestyles of the rich and famous.' To me, transposing it to America meant either California or New York."

Seidelman prefers to shoot in New York. She explained, "I feel comfortable working in New York City—not only because I know the city, but because I've made five union films there and I know the crews. I've found a group that I like. All the grips and gaffers and camera people can make your life easier or absolutely hellish."

Her matter-of-factness makes filmmaking sound easy. But Seidelman acknowledged there can be myriad problems, especially if a film bombs.

"I think the failure of *Mr. Right* was noticed more because I'm a woman. And things can be really difficult. You develop blinders—a sort of tunnel vision. So there are things I choose not to be bothered by. Men may do this too, in other ways, I don't know. But I don't think I've had a lot of the problems other women have mainly because I generate my own projects."

Seidelman, who had been extremely prolific throughout the eighties, seemed to drop out of sight after *She-Devil.* Like other women filmmakers, Seidelman said she used her films to answer questions she had about life—hers and those of other women she knew. One of the struggles women directors (and women in any profession) continually have had to face is the conflict between the personal and professional. Many independent women directors have made their films from a distinctly political perspective—Lizzie Borden, Julie Dash, Barbara Hammer, Pratibha Parmar all cite the importance of film as a political tool for them. Seidelman, while never backing down from her staunch feminist roots, always acknowledged she wasn't a political filmmaker, averring that she was really interested in sociology in her filmmaking, and her incisive views of domestic arrangements and women's place in their own individual lives bolsters that claim.

But making her career work with a personal life was a continually difficult dance. After *She-Devil* (she was pregnant at the time she finished the film) she decided to put directing on the back-burner and put life with her husband and new baby up front. It was a complicated decision, but one she doesn't regret.

"You always have to make choices," Seidelman explained. "That isn't just something women have to do. You see all the divorces and break-ups in Hollywood—it's because it's a hard way to live. You're always in different places, doing different things. It's hard to sustain some kind of daily life that way. There's a lot of energy that goes into being in so many different places and not everyone can do it throughout the length of a career."

Seidelman said she had to make some choices about what she wanted to do. "After *She-Devil* I had a kid, so I decided to take off some time and be a mom for a little while," she explained. "But not being able to just stay in one place, I decided to take on smaller projects, because when you're directing a feature, it's really a full-time job. It's really hard to have another life and be a feature-film director at the same time, while you're in production. I had worked pretty much extensively through all the eighties, and was ready to take a rest."

But taking a much-needed sabbatical and leaving filmmaking were two very separate things. When male directors take time off to recoup after a grueling stint on back-to-back films (Seidelman had made four major films in five years), no one assumes they've given up their craft. But Hollywood double standards disallow women from making the same choices. Rumors get generated and soon a female director is said to be leaving the business because it's too tough to handle. For Seidelman nothing could have been further from the truth. "I still love films and I still want to continue to work," she asserted. "So I started doing some smaller projects, the first of which was something I did in 1991, which is called *Confessions of a Suburban Girl*."

The film took Seidelman back to her roots, cinematically and literally—the film was shot in her hometown and centered on the sociological issues that had first interested her in filmmaking.

"It was about growing up in the sixties in suburbia, and it was done for the BBC, and it was really about what it was like at that time and at that place," she explained. "Basically, I did it around the time I was turning forty, and I brought five of my best girlfriends from high school. Some of them I'd stayed a little bit in touch with, one or two I hadn't seen in fifteen years—some were still living in Abington, one was in San Francisco, one had been living in Japan—and brought them all back to Abington, the little neighborhood we grew up in."

The film's emphasis was on the turns life had taken since the women were growing up together. Seidelman said, "I wanted to talk about what they thought life was going to be like, what life turned out to be like, how their expectations as a woman influenced their lives, how that influenced their goals—what was and what is. It was personal and it was low key, and that's what made it fun, because it wasn't a crew of seventy people—it was intimate. I really liked the way it turned out. I'm glad the BBC allowed me to make it, but I'm also glad for my own personal reasons that I have it in the archives."

Out of the big-budget glare and the constant checking of box-office receipts, Seidelman found herself back where she was in the days when *Smithereens* had debuted to such acclaim—she was once again in charge of her own material and making thoroughly independent decisions for her filmmaking career.

"I was doing projects where people would let me to do what I wanted to do, that didn't have [studio or financial] politics involved," she asserted. "The next thing I did was for a German producer, *The Dutch Master* [1994], which was part of an erotic tales series—a half-hour dramatic short that starred [Academy Award winner] Mira Sorvino. It was one of those situations where the German producer went to different directors around the world and basically said we'll give you the financing to make a film about whatever you think is erotic. There were very vague guidelines—it just had to deal with eroticism in some way. So once she [the producer] agreed on a budget, we went off and wrote the script, she gave us the money, and we delivered her the film."

It was, Seidelman said enthusiastically, "a really nice way to work, having previously done bigger studio movies where there are too many people looking over your back. I was again pleased with the results, because it was nominated for an Academy Award [for Best Short Film] and it was invited to screen at the Cannes Film Festival and about a gazillion other film festivals, so it got shown around quite a bit."

Mira Sorvino in *The Dutch Master*

By 1995, fresh from the successes of *Confessions* and *The Dutch Master* and her child now almost ready for school, Seidelman was eager to try other ventures. "Disney bought ABC, and I had a friend who was a producer at Disney who asked if I would be interested in working for their new family entertainment division," she said. "They were going to remake a lot of their old, classic movies from the sixties, things like *The Parent Trap, The Love Bug*—and asked me if I would be interested in doing a movie for ABC called *The Barefoot Executive,* something I would never have thought I would have been interested in doing. But at that time, having a five-year-old kid, I decided, why not?"

Again, the work was more Seidelman than she would have expected. "It was a satire of the television industry—the original starred Kurt Russell—about a chimpanzee who can pick hit television shows better than any studio executive," she laughed.

"I was now in a period where, when a project came my way, if it was something interesting, I'd say, sure, I'll try it," she acknowledged. "This past summer [1996], I was asked if I'd be interested in doing one of the early original episodes of a new dramatic [television] series that was being developed for CBS, *Early Edition,* a show about a guy who gets a newspaper that's one day in the future and he has the opportunity to change history. So I did the third episode for that."

Her sabbatical from feature filmmaking was both restorative and revitalizing. "You take a hiatus, and then you re-appreciate what it was you were doing. I'm now ready to get back into bigger feature films," said Seidelman. One of those features in development is an adaptation of Barbara Wilson's award-winning mystery novel, *Gaudí Afternoon,* which takes place in Barcelona and features a forty-something female sleuth. (The title refers to famed Barcelona architect Antonio Gaudí, and is a play on the Dorothy L. Sayers title *Gaudy Night.*) The book has the same kind of complexities and dark humor that drew Seidelman to *She-Devil.*

"It's a really fun script," she asserted. "We're talking to some Spanish companies in the hope that we can get the bulk of the financing for it there. I really hope it gets made."

As a female director who has gone from grassroots, penny-pinching independent to small budget pseudo-independent to working as an independent within the studio system with budgets hovering around $20 million and then back to small-scale independent productions again, Seidelman has run the gamut as an independent director. Her work is solid, despite the poor critical reception given to *Making Mr. Right* and *Cookie.* But like many women directors, Seidelman defies easy categorization. Most of her films have had a significant level of popular success—*Smithereens* and *Desperately Seeking Susan* continue to make money in video and repertory distribution and *Smithereens* has found a whole new generation of cult audiences because of its gritty, punk-rock element. But Seidelman has had to struggle back from her few failed features and her brief hiatus from feature filmmaking—something few male directors in similar situations have had to do.

Yet she remains uncompromisingly cheerful and still refuses to speak ill of anyone—studio executives, producers, rumor-mongers. "Hollywood is always about cautionary tales," she asserted. "Everyone has a disastrous story to tell you about what happened to who back when. It can be terrifying or you can simply ignore it and move ahead like you didn't know what could go wrong. That's pretty much what I've always done [as a filmmaker]."

As for what advice Seidelman would give to women starting out in the business, it's much the same—ignore the roadkill that litters the highway to Hollywood or any production studio.

Seidelman said emphatically, "The only words of wisdom I can offer are: Don't listen to the statistics! Just do it! Sometimes it's better not to think about the business angle. In making *Smithereens* I was sort of naive, and I'm glad I was, because I never thought of the end result. I never thought about distribution. In film school we thought: Let's make a movie because we love the story. The kids today are very practical and business-oriented," she explained. "The great thing about being naive is, you only do what you want to do. The best work often comes from your own passion for something, rather than calculating what the response will be."

The director also suggests watching a lot of film all the time—to see what other people are doing, to get a keener sense of what works and what doesn't, to glean new techniques. Seidelman said she is always watching new work and going back to the films she's admired for years—films by Martin Scorcese, Federico Fellini, Billy Wilder and Preston Sturges. She admits to being a "real B-movie addict" who loves old Roger Corman films and drive-in movies. Women directors who have influenced her have all had a specific focus in their directing.

"Mostly I admire the European filmmakers because they have the personal touch," Seidelman explained. "But American directors seem to do generic stuff, so you really can't tell if a man or a woman directed the film. Like *Big*. That's a very good example. I don't think you can tell if a woman or a man directed it. But I liked it a lot, and I think Penny Marshall did a great job. It was a good movie, but there's no particularly feminine touch. I think you can tell that about my films, that a woman made them. I want my films to be distinctive in that way."

In recent years feminist critiques of Seidelman's films have focused on the subject matter of some films in a rather narrow way. Thus the feminist undercurrent and tension of *She-Devil* has gotten lost in critical translation and the film has been slammed as harkening back to pre-feminist on-screen wrangling between women over a man. The actual scope of the film is much broader and much more about women asserting their own individuality. The key element of Seidelman's *ouevre* as a director has always been her focus on female characters and their concerns. There is, ironically, a kind of sexism in the way Seidelman's female characters have been diminished and stereotyped by some feminist critics.

Susan Seidelman

She-Devil, the film by Seidelman that has received the most strident criticism from feminist film historians, is also distinctly feminist in perspective and in its use of female vantage point. The film is about female roles and how those roles are so narrowly defined by patriarchal society. Ruth (played by Roseanne) isn't a stereotype of the overweight, beaten-down pitiful housewife—she *is* that very real woman whose husband (Ed Begley, Jr.) believes he can demand that she stay at home and provide the creature comforts for him while he spends his time and emotional (and sexual) energy on the beautiful romance writer, Mary Fisher (Meryl Streep). The female characters are radically altered by the events within the film while the male character is the only one who doesn't change—is in fact unable to change. It is the stultifying roles these characters have been forced into by society that forces Ruth to fight Mary Fisher for her husband; but it takes tremendous effort for Ruth to do battle with Mary—she has been so beaten down and defeminized by the circumstances of her life.

In *Desperately Seeking Susan,* Rosanna Arquette's Roberta is a distinctly feminist creation: the beleaguered *hausfrau* who goes out and—through quirky accident—finds herself and her true identity. Seidelman readily acknowledges her roots. "I grew up in suburbia right around the corner from the shopping mall," she said. "Of course that influenced me. *Desperately Seeking Susan* was very much about the dual nature of wanting to leave and wanting to stay. My films are very personal in that each of the leading [female] roles has an element of me in them."

One of the strengths of Seidelman's work lies in the individuated female characters that populate her films. Her determination to cast against type and take risks in her films is always apparent in her casting. She was, for example, the first director to cast Streep, a multiple Academy Award nominee and winner for searing dramatic roles in *Sophie's Choice* and *Kramer vs. Kramer,* in a comedic role, to brilliant results. Since Seidelman uncovered Streep's latent talent for the absurd, other (male) directors have cast her in similar roles.

Those who would dismiss Seidelman as anti-feminist or having lost the promise of her early cinematic form miss the essence of her *ouevre.* In the twenty years since Seidelman graduated from film school she has carved a specific niche in independent filmmaking and built a strong foundation for other women directors to follow. Seidelman said she has grown in confidence as a director over two decades and continues to enjoy all the components of filmmaking, especially as an aspect of modern culture.

"I'm really interested in the way culture changes," said Seidelman, "in the way *we* change. I like examining the way those changes take place in modern life. That's my focus—how we act, how we talk, how we think. That's what I want to show in my films—but from *our* point of view as women."

Mira Nair

Exiles, Expatriates and Life on the Margins

Mira Nair (courtesy of Trimark Pictures)

"I can't imagine growing old in America. Some of us must grow old and die where we were born, where we feel at home. Home for me," explained Mira Nair, "will always be India."

Home, what home means and the complexity of issues related to exile, expatriatism and the question of belonging and of experiencing life from the margins of society are all pivotal elements in the work of Mira Nair. Her films delve into the transgressive experience of living in exile, whether self-imposed or imposed by social mores or political struggles. She acknowledges she is drawn to the margins of society: "I'm interested in marginal people—people who are *considered* marginal. I like the prostitutes, cabaret dancers, street kids—real life excites me. I'm interested in capturing the complexity of people and the complexity of life. Why make cinema any less real than life? If I were to find a common thread in my work, it would be these stories of life on the margins, on the edge, outside, people learning a language of being between one group and another, one society or community and another, always dealing with the question: What and where is *home?*"

Nair noted that her cinematic themes mirror her personal interests: "These concerns are, of course, inextricably linked with my personal history as well, since I have spent most of my adult life living between two worlds."

Succinct about her place as an Indian filmmaker in America, Nair perceives herself as neither exile nor expatriate, even though she lived for many years in New York, attended Harvard University, has done much of her work in the United States and currently lives more than half the year in Kampala, Uganda, with her husband, who teaches there full-time, and their young son. Although India is the "home" of her heart, living in several places has made her more appreciative of what home means, Nair said.

"I have a constant desire to go back to India, to be there," she explained. "But I think being in [the United States] has kept me from becoming blind to certain things in India—begging kids, that sort of thing."

An intensely independent woman as well as filmmaker, Nair struggled to make films in her native country but was repeatedly told what she wanted to do was simply not possible. In particular, as she began to scout the shoot for her monumental first feature, *Salaam Bombay!* (1988), she was told her choice to use actual street children and illiterate nonactors and to shoot throughout one of the world's busiest metropolises was unthinkable: No one makes movies in the streets in India. Yet Nair succeeded, incorporating the reality of Bombay's red-light district, turbulent streets and incomparably busy train stations into a starkly emotional film about one young boy's orphan life and the struggle for survival on Bombay's streets.

Salaam Bombay! was not a typical Indian film by any standards. Nair is highly critical of the popular Indian cinema. The majority of Indian films are reminiscent of Hollywood's romantic musical extravaganzas of the 1930s and are extremely popular in India, Pakistan, the Middle East, Russia and Africa. More films per year are made in India than in any other country—about eight hundred, sometimes more—but the film industry is

Films by Mira Nair

Jama Masjid Street Journal

So Far from India

India Cabaret

Children of a Desired Sex

Salaam Bombay!

Mississippi Masala

The Perez Family

Kama Sutra: A Tale of Love

Mira Nair

thoroughly commercialized and remains tightly controlled by the Bombay studios ("Bollywood"), the Asian equivalent of the Hollywood studio system.

The "parallel" or noncommercial cinema, although largely subsidized by the state, remains a predominantly intellectual and avant-garde experience; the films aren't generally seen by mass audiences, even though Indians attend movies more than any other population in the world. And even within the parallel cinema, few women directors have been able to produce their work—Vijaya Mehta, a major film star prior to directing, and Aparna Sen, also an actress, being notable exceptions. So while Nair and her films have become well respected in India, most of her films have not shown there commercially, and financing has come almost exclusively from the United States, the United Kingdom and Europe.

Success has been hard-won for Nair, who explained with some irony, "I had to leave India to make movies about India. Funding is a problem, always, you see."

Problematic in part because Nair has chosen to retain her independent status; after the success of *Salaam Bombay!*, the director was inundated with scripts and projects via Hollywood, but noted with a laugh that the projects "weren't for me. You simply wouldn't believe what I was sent." She thought funding options for other projects would accompany the film's critical success. Instead, she explained, "I almost went broke. Nobody knew what to do with me—all I got were bits about children. Kids from everywhere you could imagine. Because of *Salaam*, and I think, because I'm a woman, it was all they could see me doing."

Instead Nair chose to develop another exploration of life on the margins, *Mississippi Masala* (1992), returning to collaboration with her longtime college friend, Sooni Taraporevala, with whom she had conceived the story for *Salaam Bombay!* and who had written the screenplay for the film.

Despite the recurrent funding problems that plague independents, Nair followed her first film projects—a series of strong and important short documentaries (*Jama Masjid Street Journal*, 1979; *So Far from India*, 1983; *India Cabaret*, 1985; *Children of a Desired Sex*, 1987)—with four major narrative feature films. She has become the best-known Indian director outside India since Satyajit Ray, himself a star of the parallel cinema and of cinematic neorealism, whose films, Nair noted, she never saw in India because "they weren't shown, even though he is India's best filmmaker."

All but one of Nair's films (*The Perez Family*, 1995) places India, Indians and Indian culture at their center. (Still, even *The Perez Family* deals with the Nairian theme of exile and expatriation, as it tells the tale of a Cuban émigré on his way to Florida to be reunited with his family after years in a Cuban prison.) Always at the locus of Nair's films is one or another form of disenfranchisement—personal, political, racial, sexual or social. Yet, despite her cinematic focus and the fact that she lives in several countries, Nair staunchly refuses the title of exile.

"I do not think of myself as an expatriate," explained Nair, "because India will always be my home, my emotional center." Nair grew up in what she calls "the original hick town" of Bhubaneswar, the capital of the Indian state of Orissa. She said, "I had two brothers—so not a lot of attention fell on me, the girl. I was a good student and got to make my own choices." One of those choices was to come to the United States in 1976 to attend Harvard, which had offered her a full scholarship to study drama.

Despite living in the United States and traveling between continents from her late teens through her thirties, Nair has not assimilated into Western culture. "I *feel* Indian, I *am* Indian; I spend more time in India than I do in New York, more time in Kampala than anywhere. I am, really, an *Indian* filmmaker, despite the work I have done in America."

At the heart of most of Nair's films lies India, in all its myriad complexities, to which the filmmaker brings her own prismatic vision. That vision is distinctly different from the view of India most moviegoers have been treated to over the last few decades. Nair's films bear no resemblance to the shot-through-gauze romanticization of British colonial experience in India, like the BBC series *The Jewel in the Crown* (a public television favorite in the United States) or the Ismail Merchant–James Ivory ventures like *Heat and Dust* (1983) or David Lean's epic *A Passage to India* (1984). Even her most recent film, *Kama Sutra: A Tale of Love* (1997), a mythic and dramatically sensual evocation of *The Kama Sutra of Vatsayana*, the classic Indian text of sensual love and sexuality, resists classification as a romantic film about India. Despite its sixteenth century time frame, exquisitely beautiful settings and narrative opulence, the nexus of Nair's film is sexual politics in India and women's roles vis-à-vis class and sexuality. So while *Kama Sutra* may *look* as romantic as the Raj movies, it covers narrative ground common to all of Nair's films.

If Nair's cinematic India has little to do with the colonialist vision Western audiences are most familiar with, neither is it representative of the traditional Indian musical/romance cinema familiar to most Indian audiences, or even the parallel cinema, viewed by a minority of Indians and shown abroad only occasionally. Nair's India is uniquely hers: She presents a wholly different country than the one Western cinematic images (and even images from India itself) have projected—one shot, often literally, from the streets, brothels and cabarets, with the poor and working class as a central focus.

Nair's cinematic gaze is female and thoroughly Indian (white people rarely appear in her work, in part, she explained, because she is more interested in what *doesn't* get seen on screen—"the lives of brown people, like myself.") In her documentaries and in *Salaam Bombay!*, which is docudramatic in style, Nair addresses issues expunged from the highly censored Indian cinema, especially sexuality and the variant roles of women. *Kama Sutra*, despite its basically simple narrative about sex and class, was deemed so problematic to censors because of its explicit sexuality that it was released in the United States un-

Still from *Kama Sutra: A Tale of Love* (courtesy of Trimark Pictures)

rated to avoid the box-office disaster of an NC-17 (no children under seventeen admitted; formerly X) rating. In India the National Censorship Board demanded that the director cut more than ten minutes of the film—ostensibly *all* the explicit sex (in a film titled *Kama Sutra*, no less). After a long battle with the Censorship Board, Nair and the film's producers appealed to the Indian Supreme Court, which agreed to limit the excisions to two minutes. Nair termed the entire censorship battle "archaic."

Nair, well known for exploring sexual politics in her films, was incensed by the censorship. She has been quite vocal over the years about the "perverse sexual portrayals of women" in films in the United States and India, where "rape is an accepted sexual expression, but sensual or spiritual pleasure [in sex] is not." When the edited version of the film was finally released, she argued that sexual mutilations and other extremes of violence against women rarely raised the eyebrows of censors or received more than an R rating (restricted to persons seventeen or older unless accompanied by an adult) from the Motion Picture Association of America (MPAA), while sexual scenes in which women engage in loving, self-affirming, nonviolent sexual experience are branded with the NC-17 rating. Explaining that *Kama Sutra* is about the spiritual element of sensual love, she demanded repeatedly in interviews, "Why is sexual perversion [such as sexual mutilation and violence against women] more palatable to the powers that be than sexual tenderness and love?"

Nair's topics are often controversial, like her documentary *Children of a Desired Sex* (1987), about the prevalence of amniocentesis sex-testing of fetuses in India and what women do when they find they are pregnant with the undesired sex, a female child. The director also faced questions of censorship when she embarked on her documentary *India Cabaret* (1985), about striptease workers in Indian nightclubs—even from her family. Nair's father was appalled that she would even be going to such clubs and speaking with women who performed as sex workers. Nair said he and her mother sat her down, and her father asked her why she was "going to live with *scum.*" Nair said he told her, "I know all about these cabaret girls. They do anything for a quick buck, even sell their flesh." When Nair asked her father how he knew about these women, he explained that a friend of his had offered some of these women to him once. Nair wanted to know how he regarded the friend who had offered the women to him; her father's response was that his friend was "a sophisticated man of the world." The man had, Nair's father reasoned, only offered what was available, not unlike a good cigar or a fine brandy.

That conversation, Nair explained, clarified for her what she wanted to do with *India Cabaret*. "I knew I had a film to make, that there *was* a film to make," she said. "This film would be about the strength of the double standard [in Indian society] and patriarchal values."

Like *Kama Sutra, India Cabaret* was controversial from the outset and continued to create controversy long after its premiere—especially in India. Surprisingly, Indian feminists had some of the strongest criticisms of the film because the dancers are not portrayed as victims but as strong and personally empowered women who are making their own choices, in charge of their own lives. Other audiences felt the way Nair's father had—that the cabaret workers were not simply doing a job to support themselves and their families, but had shamed themselves, lowered themselves because they were publicly sexual in a society where the popular cinema rarely even shows kissing. Then there were those who appreciated the film because of

Mira Nair

the strength of the women dancers in a culture in which women's cinematic roles are almost wholly passive. The response within India was complex, but Nair noted that she had intended that the film be provocative.

"The cabaret involves sexuality and the revealing of the flesh, you understand," explained Nair. "The moment that [sexual element] enters the game, you're a bad woman [in the mores of Indian society], and that is what *India Cabaret* examines. These women don't have a lot of choices—they don't have a lot of skills. It isn't like they could easily be doing something else to survive. They have their bodies, and they use them, and that is uncomfortable for middle-class women to see, especially because, in India, middle-class and upper-class women are very protected, very sheltered. You really don't talk about sexuality, and you don't see it out in the open like this [as in *India Cabaret*]; you don't see this discussion of the two different kinds of Indian women, the two different women men want, the wife and the whore. So it is difficult for an audience to watch this, because we don't ever talk about it, yet it is a reality."

Nair was disturbed by the ire of Indian feminists over the film, particularly because she considers herself a strong feminist and actually approached the film from a clearly feminist perspective. "I think that people have difficulty with ambiguity of any kind, really," she explained. "There is no black and white, no obvious villain [in *India Cabaret*]—it isn't as simple as all the men are bad and all the women are good, or the reverse. Yes, the women are marginalized by a morally corrupt society in which men do apply a double standard, but that doesn't make everything simple. Life is complicated, and that is what you see in *India Cabaret*—that complexity. I like to show ambiguity and contradictions in my films, irony, not just the black and white that you see in a lot of films."

In the United States, *India Cabaret* was very well received critically, winning the best documentary prizes at both the American Film Festival and Global Village Film Festival, and most reviews signaled Nair as a significant emerging director. But some of the Indian controversy carried over to the United States.

Nair noted, "People outside India understood the film and didn't question my intent at all. They liked the film and the women. But even in the United States, there were complaints from Indians living there—so the film was banned in New York [on public television], even though it was being broadcast around the country, because of protests that the film presented

India in a bad light. But it did create a bit of debate, because other people were angry that it *wasn't* airing. It was all very interesting."

Films like *India Cabaret* and *Salaam Bombay!* don't equivocate about women's place in Indian society. Focusing as they do on characters society treats as marginal, they tell a tale of displacement and disenfranchisement. They also shatter simplistic no-

Still from *India Cabaret* (courtesy of Filmakers Library, Inc.)

tions of postcolonial society still held by many Westerners. In fact, Nair's sense of England was irrevocably imprinted on her through the colonial relationship so widely explored in British cinema. Nair declined a scholarship to Cambridge University, avoiding England because of what she termed "a hangover" associated with the ghosts of colonialism.

As a consequence, she learned about film in the United States, at Harvard, where as a theater major she tired of "one more experience of *Oklahoma!* as my opportunity for theater [as a drama student]. I took a film course, which [at Harvard] meant documentaries, and I became a documentarian. I discovered cinema here [in the United States] and I made my first little movie here—and that's the way documentaries are viewed in India—they're not even movies, essentially."

Early in her filmmaking career, well before the debates over *India Cabaret*, Nair understood that making movies in India would be difficult, in part because she was a woman and in part because of the films she wanted to make. The United States offered more opportunities for her to become a director, define her own style and find funding to make her films.

"If I had remained in India and worked with a male director," she explained, "if I had risen very slowly within the system there, it would be quite different. People would see me as an assistant. To direct my own film, then, would be much harder, much more time consuming, much slower and more difficult. Now the way I choose to do it is to return to India on *my*

Mira Nair

terms, which are very different terms—better terms." Although, she added, the particular films she has chosen to make have given her far more recognition as a filmmaker *outside* India. "People [in India] didn't even view me as a real filmmaker before *India Cabaret*."

Nair attributes some of the conflict over her films in India to her choice of subject matter and her style. "Indian cinema doesn't present real-life situations, real-life relationships—it's very constricted. There are tremendous censorship strictures."

Outside of India, Nair's meteoric rise as a filmmaker is due in part to the tremendous success of *Salaam Bombay!*, winner of the coveted Camera d'Or at the Cannes International Film Festival, as well as the Prix du Publique (the prize awarded by the public at Cannes for the most popular film), a 1988 nominee for the Academy Award for best foreign language film and winner of the Jury Prize and Special Ecumenical Jury Prize at the Montreal World Film Festival. A startlingly provocative picture, *Salaam Bombay!* is one of the best narrative films ever made about the hellish lives of street children, comparable to classics such as Hector Babenco's *Pixote* (1981) and Luis Buñuel's *Los Olvidados* (1950).

"I am, in many respects, still a documentarian," said Nair. "Truth *is* stranger than fiction. But what I wanted to do with [*Salaam Bombay!*] was make a story with the strength of reality but the controlled power of fiction."

Nair faced significant problems before, during and even after filming *Salaam Bombay!* She held workshops for three months with street children to find and teach those who played the film's roles, and she worked with a child psychologist as well. But criticisms dogged Nair before she began filming and after the film's critical success. As with *India Cabaret*, she was charged with exploiting her film's subjects: this time, street children.

"Everyone wanted to know, first, why we were using 'real' street children," Nair explained. "No one thought we could or *should* have actors and nonactors together. Then later everyone wanted to know what we were doing for these children. There were very consistent questions about exploitation. I was always very concerned about people calling the film exploitative. I also wanted to be certain that we presented the strengths of these children, not just depression, misery and despair. I hope that people can see the spirit of these children, their will to survive and fight with such humor and strength."

Nair said all the children were well paid for their work and a concerted effort was made to create places for them in schools and work programs after the film wrapped. (The film's young star, Shafiq Syed, who could neither read nor write—Nair and her crew had used cartoons to script parts for the actors who were illiterate—wanted to pursue acting professionally after *Salaam Bombay!*, but continued to hover between the streets and acting.)

Given its epic size and the monumentality of many of the street scenes, *Salaam Bombay!* was made with an incredibly small budget: less than a million dollars, which Nair raised from Channel 4 Television in England; the National Film Development Corporation (NFDC) in India, which funds the art films of the parallel cinema; the Rockefeller Foundation in the United States; and some French grants. Nair said she struggled to get the money, exhausting avenues of grants and foundations in the United States, England and India while she searched for funds to match an initial $150,000 grant from Channel 4 that was based on her low budget—$600,000.

Much of the pressure over getting money for the film was because Nair refused to shoot the film in English instead of Hindi, because "this is a film about class, and while English is widely spoken in India, it isn't spoken on the streets. It's a class issue." But no foreign-language Indian film—even Satyajit Ray's "Apu Trilogy"—had been a commercial success in Europe or the United States, so there was tremendous resistance to Nair's using an Indian language and subtitling for non-Indian markets.

"It was one of those things where you just don't know from moment to moment if you're going to be able to come up with the money," she said. "I didn't think I was going to be able to raise it. You've got the script, everything is lined up, but it will all fall apart if you can't meet the budget. The money from Channel 4 would come through only if I got the rest of it, and my budget—my *low* budget—was for $600,000. I had really determined that I needed $900,000 to do the film properly in 35mm. You can't imagine how you are just holding your breath, hoping that you can get this money; then when it finally comes through, you still have to do the film! It's exciting, but it's difficult work. I think this must be where many [independent] filmmakers just give up, because it's so difficult to come up with this money over and over."

Giving up was never a consideration for Nair, who remains driven to make films that "provoke; I want people to think about something, whatever it is I'm presenting—the cabaret, life on the streets, the [racial and social] conflicts between brown and black."

Yet despite the acclaim that followed *Salaam Bombay!*, as an independent filmmaker and a relative newcomer to the process, Nair still struggled with distribution. "I'm one to continue alliances," she explained. "I go a lot by intuition as well. *Salaam* was sold country by country. There was no magic moment when everything fell into place and happened on its own. You have to go all over with your film, promoting it, selling it, really. I think there are many misconceptions about how filmmaking gets done. The reality is it's very hard work, from beginning to end. This game is so much about persistence."

Despite the hard work, Nair loves filmmaking in all its aspects, except being separated from her husband and young son, Zohran. "I love it, I really do. Even though I have to be separated from him [Zohran] for periods of time, which is the hardest thing, it is just so exciting, never boring, always fresh."

And Nair brings that sense of newness to each project. The films of hers that address the role of women in society, particularly Indian society and Indian culture and other areas where women have been marginalized, aren't didactic feminist tracts, as the controversy over *India Cabaret* elucidates. But they are films in which women are fully developed characters, whether those roles are documentary, as in *India Cabaret*, or fictional, as in *Kama Sutra*.

"I love doing films about women," she said unequivocally. "I want to show on screen people like us, people who are independent, women expressing themselves. I want exciting portrayals—women are fully dimensional in life, so why make cinema any less real than life? This keeps me going as a filmmaker, that there is so much still for us to say. Women have not yet been given the time of day in terms of film."

Nair's feminism extends from content to process in her filmmaking. She always has "as many women as possible" in her film crews because, she said, "I love working with women; it's always a great experience. I've had excellent experiences with women on my crews. A lot of women worked on *Salaam Bombay!* I chose them because they are really good at what they do. It pleases me to work with women. Working with Sooni [Taraporevala], for example, has been a gift. There are always key women I want to work with, try to work with."

In addition to her focus on representing women on screen, Nair has a defining interest in representing people of color. Racial conflicts and issues of exile are at the root of Nair's most compelling narratives, including her early documentary *So Far from India* (1982). In this film, Ashok Sheth is Everyimmigrant: in search of a better life, but finding it elusive. The film explores the clash of cultures: Sheth works as a magazine vendor in the New York subway and lives in a tiny closet of an apartment. Married in a traditionally arranged marriage to a woman he hardly knew, he moved to New York days after the wedding and cannot afford to send for her and his child, whom he's never seen. When he returns to India to see his child, these cultural chasms are exposed.

So Far from India is a film about Indian culture and family, the alienation versus the dreams immigrants must experience. Like the song "America" in the musical *West Side Story*, there is a juxtaposition of expectations and desires. India remains beloved—beautiful and bucolic while America is stark and uncomfortable. Yet the immigration experience holds promise—for those who come to the United States, as well as for those who remain, like Ashok Sheth's wife, Hansa, at home, waiting.

Although they are fictional narratives, rather than documentaries, *Mississippi Masala* and *The Perez Family* echo these themes of exile and expatriation. *Mississippi Masala*, said Nair, was a film "I carried around in my head for a long time. I had been thinking for a long time what it meant to be a brown person in America, ever since I was a student, because there you are, in between white and black. When you aren't either, you move between both, rather comfortably. But there is this sense of dislocation, too, because you don't belong to either [group]."

In this film, set in Mississippi and Uganda, Nair really synthesizes her thematic foundation. An upper-class Indian family, the Lohas, flees Uganda when Idi Amin purges the country of its huge Asian population in 1972. The Lohas settle in Greenwood, Mississippi, where they operate a cheap motel off the highway and are the poor relations of their cousins—even though the father was a lawyer in Uganda. The main story revolves around the romance of the Lohas' daughter, Mina (beautifully played in her first acting role by Sarita Choudhury, who also stars in *Kama Sutra*), with a working-class black man, Demetrius (Denzel Washington), who cleans the motel's carpets, and the conflicts this interracial and interclass relationship creates. Mina's father, Jaymini (Roshan Seth), wants desperately to repatriate to Uganda after Amin is deposed and is suing the government for return of his property and violation of his human rights, because, as he explains, it is his country, too. Jaymini has put all of his hopes for the future—and his concomitant expectations—on his daughter.

As in *So Far from India*, the Nairian theme of exile in *Mississippi Masala* differs from the standard portrayal in American films of immigrant life in which the émigré is terribly grateful for a new life and new identity in a new country. Nair's immigrants are often—like Sheth, Jaymini and the Perez patriarch—reluctant or confused immigrants, either driven by external forces to emigrate or discovering that the new country isn't the dream country they had expected.

A huge film—shot in two countries (Uganda and the United States) with seventy-nine speaking parts, a budget over ten times that of *Salaam Bombay!*, and stars like Oscar-winner Washington and Shakespearan actor Seth, *Mississippi Masala* represented another major step for Nair as a filmmaker.

"*Masala* is an Indian word—it means hot and spicy, a mixing of spices," explained Nair. "The film is about the mixing of black, brown, white— *masala*. I think this kind of mixing is what we are coming to see all over— here [New York] you see it everywhere."

Nair wanted to address what has rapidly become a noteworthy racial conflict in the United States—the struggles between African-Americans and Asian immigrants, although those conflicts weren't as dramatic in 1989 and 1990, when she began making the film, as they are now. Nair uses the expulsion of Asians from the predominantly black country of Uganda as a parallel to the American conflict in which Asians are often perceived as taking middle-class jobs away from African Americans. There is added irony in that it is the Asian immigrant, the Indian Jaymini, who dreams of a return to Africa, not the African-American Demetrius. Nair explained, "It is a melding of these two groups, these Indians who have never been to India, who are really Africans, but who have been expelled from the country because they are not black, and these African Americans who were born in America and know nothing of Africa. So you have that exploration of what home is, of personal and cultural dislocation."

Nair said, "I wanted to explore what happens when you cross the color line from one community to another. We've seen films deal with that on the white–black level, but not this color-to-color. But the film is also about exile and dislocation—how [Jaymini's] memories of Uganda, of *home*, are nostalgic to the point that he can't live in the present, he can live only in the past or in a future that he hopes will happen."

A defining directorial and personal experience for Nair, *Mississippi Masala* introduced her to the American South, which she found "has a much more subtle racism than I expected, but where I was very welcomed by blacks; they were very warm to me. I felt very comfortable with blacks." But Nair noted, "There really isn't any of that mixing, that *masala* going on. You don't see blacks in the restaurants; and these aren't expensive restaurants, but small cafes. So there is that separation, that racism."

Mississippi Masala also introduced Nair to her second husband, Mahmoud Mamdani, whom she met in Uganda during her research for the film; he had written about the Asian purge from Uganda. Nair now lives part of the year in Kampala, where her husband teaches at the university.

Nair said making films about "black and brown people for black and brown people" is another of her interests. But those interests then necessitate a wholly different cinematographic perspective. Filming darker skin tones—the browns and blacks of Nair's casts—poses unique lighting questions and remains a peripheral concern in film schools or technical discussions about filmmaking. Lighting techniques having been built around pale skin tones. In *A Dry White Season* (1989), for example, black director Euzhan Palcy chose to use amber lenses to minimize the skin tone changes between her white and black characters. Nair explained that lighting for her films requires a significant amount of work beforehand by the cinematographers so that the actual skin tones come across on the screen, rather than a diffusion of the darker colors.

Producers were initially nervous about the dearth of white characters in *Mississippi Masala*, but Nair explained that white characters weren't essential to creating an audience for the film, that there would be an audience for a film without white characters. "It's just like what they say about films in which women are the main characters—they ask, 'Where are the men?' as if there are no films in which men are central to the story and women are peripheral. We have stories to tell [as directors of color] that are important, and there are audiences for those stories, and, I think, those audiences will continue to include white people as well as people of color because we tell stories that different people want to see, want to experience."

Delving into areas that have rarely been addressed by traditional

Mira Nair

narrative cinema is one of Nair's passions. "I want to create the unpredictability of life, that gray area that makes us all what we are and not just the black-and-white/good-and-bad that cinema is always relegated to, but that very real life that we all live. That is my passion."

Marleen Gorris

Uncompromisingly Feminist

In 1996, Dutch director Marleen Gorris did what no female American film director has yet done: She won an Academy Award. Admittedly, Gorris did not win in the Best Director category, but for Best Foreign Language Film for 1995's *Antonia's Line*.

Marleen Gorris

Most Americans had never heard of Gorris, and even fewer had seen *Antonia's Line*. But those who were familiar with Gorris's work weren't surprised that her epic story about a Dutch matriarch won the Oscar.

Gorris's career began with the 1982 film *A Question of Silence*. Gorris read a newspaper account of a woman arrested for shoplifting and wrote a screenplay based on the account. Because she had no experience as a filmmaker, she approached veteran Belgian director Chantal Akerman with the screenplay. "She [Akerman] said

Films by Marleeen Gorris

A Question of Silence

Broken Mirrors

The Last Island

Antonia's Line

that she was overcommitted to her own projects—so why didn't I just do it myself," said Gorris. "She told me, 'Directing isn't all that difficult.' Chantal was both right and wrong. The nuts and bolts of directing aren't all that difficult. However, making a worthy film that people will remember is."

The Dutch government contributed two-thirds of the money required to produce *A Question of Silence*. Gorris had expanded her story from the original news item: Instead of one woman arrested for shoplifting, three are arrested for the murder of a male shopkeeper after he catches one of them shoplifting. To further confuse matters, the three women are all strangers to each other, brought together in the same shop and by the same moment of feminist rage. A woman psychiatrist is brought in by the court to determine what actually happened and if the women are sane. After extensive interviews with the three women—a waitress, a secretary and a housewife—the psychiatrist comes to the conclusion that all three are sane and perhaps even justified. Unfortunately, she cannot make herself heard in court above the arguments of the male lawyers.

A Question of Silence was the first salvo in Gorris's career as a feminist filmmaker. The film generated considerable controversy, in part because the film ends before justice—men's justice—is meted out to the three defendants, in part because it argued that the oppression women suffer can lead to rage and violence against men. It also set the stage for all of Gorris's later films, which are told from a female vantage point and point out the inequities between the sexes.

Gorris's second film, *Broken Mirrors*, was released in 1984. In it, Gorris follows two narrative threads: that of the lives of the prostitutes who work in an Amsterdam brothel, and that of a male serial killer who kidnaps, imprisons, tortures and then kills women. The brothel and even the personal lives of the prostitutes are marred by violence, whereas violence is the serial killer's response to the passivity of his victims. Although the two stories seem completely separate for the length of the film, in its final minutes they converge, providing a chilling knowledge for the viewer, if not the characters.

Because *Broken Mirrors* dealt with prostitutes, their customers and a serial killer—what many viewed as characters of a different social class— it did not generate the controversy that *A Question of Silence* did, even though it also pointed out the injustices of gender when it comes to economic and social status. Many critics found the violence in *Broken Mirrors* too overwhelming and preferred *A Question of Silence* for its examination of the oppression of "ordinary" women.

In 1990, Gorris released her only English-language film, *The Last Island*. Frequently compared to William Golding's novel *Lord of the Flies, The Last Island* is the story of the seven survivors of a plane crash: five men and two women. At first, all seven survivors work together to provide for the necessities: finding food, constructing shelter and building a raft. But soon the men regress to competition and violence, with rape, mutilation and murder becoming the new order. Gorris was quite clear in her commentary that *man* cannot be trusted: Two of the five men are gay, but they also revert to a primitive state on the island. Only the essential natures of the two women are unchanged.

With *Antonia's Line*, Gorris decided to take on gender inequity on a much larger scale. The film chronicles four generations of women in the same matriarchical family and the different paths they must take as women in the world: Antonia, the family matriarch, who returns to her

Willeke van Ammelrooy and Els Dottermans as Antonia and Danielle in *Antonia's Line*

Dutch village at the end of World War II; Danielle, her grown daughter, who returns with her; Therese, Danielle's daughter; and finally Sarah, Therese's daughter, slated to carry on Antonia's line. Antonia returns to her village to visit her mother on her deathbed; when her mother dies, Antonia inherits the family farm, which she and Danielle run with the help of two village misfits, whom they shelter from ridicule and abuse. When Danielle decides she wants to have a child but not a husband, she and Antonia go to the city in search of good genetic material. They go to a home for unwed

Marleen Gorris

mothers, where one of the pregnant women there introduces them to her brother, who in turn fathers Therese. Therese grows up to be a mathematical scholar, marries her childhood sweetheart, Simon, and bears Sarah.

Interspersed with the idylls of country life is the unrelenting violence man brings with him: When Danielle catches Pitte, the son of a neighboring farmer, raping his mentally handicapped sister DeeDee, she skewers him with a pitchfork. Pitte leaves the village to join the military, but returns years later to rape an adolescent Therese. Shotgun in hand, Antonia tracks him down and tells him to leave the village. When he goes home to bid farewell to his family, Pitte is drowned by his brother in the family well.

Gorris wrote the screenplay for *Antonia's Line* in 1988, and described it as "a family chronicle. It deals with birth, death, love, hatred, childhood and the flowering of each new generation. It is also a film about women's independence. The women in the film are thoroughly themselves and not defined through their roles as wife, mother or daughter. Of course, the film is a fairy tale."

Dutch producer Hans de Weers, who produced *The Last Island*, also produced *Antonia's Line*, pulling in funding from sources in the Netherlands, Belgium and England. The film was actually shot in Belgium with a primarily Dutch cast. "The possibilities in preproduction were mind-boggling," noted Gorris of casting the film. "English? English cast? An English lead dubbed into Dutch? A double shoot, Dutch and English? I understood that a leading English name would considerably enhance the film's international potential. I'm relieved to say that in the end we made the film in the language I wrote it in—Dutch."

Even though *Antonia's Line* was Gorris's fourth feature film, she noted, "It was hard to get the film off the ground. The struggle to finance a film is soul-sapping—you have to experience it to believe it. But the real challenge, as is true of all my films, is to give shape to my vision, to shoot the film as it exists in my head. That's not to say that the vision doesn't change during the filming, but all things considered, the realization of the vision is the biggest challenge.

"I am a feminist, both by temperament and intellect, and my films are shaped by my outlook on life. Otherwise they would not be mine. However, I don't put political or moral lessons in my films."

In addition to the Oscar, *Antonia's Line* garnered a slew of awards: Best Picture at the Toronto Film Festival, Best Screenplay at the Chicago International Film Festival, and Best Director and first runner-up for Best Picture at the Hamptons International Film Festival. It also won Golden Calf Awards—Dutch cinema awards—for Best Director and Best Actress.

With the film's overwhelming success, Gorris came out about her lesbianism and her relationship with her lover Maria Uitdehaag, who served as the first assistant director on *Antonia's Line*. "I hardly ever discuss it," Gorris said. "Everyone knows it, but I'm not in the film business because I'm gay. It just so happens I'm gay. And occasionally that seeps through in what I make, but it's not something I set out to do." Gorris's lesbianism seems to have seeped into the character Danielle, who grows up to be an artist and falls in love with her daughter's tutor, Lara, a relationship that receives Antonia's blessing.

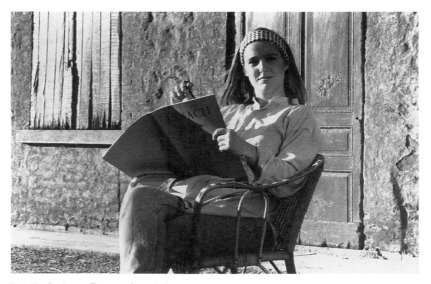

Veerle Van Overloop as Therese in *Antonia's Line*

De Weers was joined on the film's production team by British producer Judy Counihan, who served as one of the film's co-producers. "I really got caught by Marleen's intelligent exploration of that inexplicable thing that unites women, the bond that exists between mothers and daughters, and women in general," said Counihan. "I'm so tired of seeing American 'women's pictures' such as *Steel Magnolias*, which deal with women's lives in a pat, sentimental manner. *Antonia's Line* is a much more sympathetic and celebratory approach to who women are. Marleen does not separate women from men in this film. The women aren't competitive, but protective. The film overflows with love. People who know Marleen's work will be surprised by the change."

Of the place *Antonia's Line* holds in the continuum of Gorris's work, Counihan added, "Women are allowed to change. This is a mellower side to Marleen, but it's in no way a compromise of her politics. It's feminism for the nineties. *A Question of Silence* was harder and more didactic. This is gentler, funnier, and reflects the changes that the intervening decade has brought."

Jane Campion

A Girl's Own Story

When Jane Campion's student film *Peel* (1982) won the Palme d'Or for best short film at the Cannes International Film Festival in 1986, few realized that within four short years, the thirty-two-year-old New Zealander who

Still from *Peel* (courtesy of Women Make Movies)

had studied at the Australian Film and Television School would become a major force in independent film. In many ways, *Peel* offered the public a glimpse of things to come: The

Films by Jane Campion

Peel

Passionless Moments

A Girl's Own Story

After Hours

Two Friends

Sweetie

An Angel at My Table

The Piano

Portrait of a Lady

nine-minute film is a study in claustrophobia, family relations gone wrong and the perils of family road trips, themes Campion has examined and reexamined in her films.

But for many years, Campion was a well-kept secret of devotees to independent cinema. Her second feature film, 1989's *Sweetie*, was released in the United States in 1990; the three-part *An Angel at My Table* (1990), originally produced for New Zealand television, was given an art-house release before moving to video. And then Campion scored big: Her fourth feature film, 1993's *The Piano*, won Academy Awards for Best Screenplay (Campion), Best Actress (Holly Hunter) and Best Supporting Actress (Anna Paquin), as well as the Palme d'Or for Best Film at Cannes.

The Piano, a costume drama set in New Zealand in the mid-1800s, captured audiences of women because it seemed like a parable for our time, a story of self-reliance, much as Australian director Gillian Armstrong's costume drama *My Brilliant Career* had entranced female audiences when it was released in 1979.

Campion followed *The Piano* with another costume drama, a film adaptation of the Henry James novel *Portrait of a Lady* (1996). But viewers who enjoyed *The Piano* and *Portrait of a Lady* may be in for a shock if they rent Campion's earlier work on video.

Purists might consider Campion's filmmaking career as beginning when her father gave her a Super 8mm movie camera in the early 1960s, which she used to shoot home movies; she later learned to edit and splice them. She studied anthropology as an undergraduate in Wellington, New Zealand, and later enrolled in the Chelsea School of Arts in London, England. After a year in London, she moved to Sydney, Australia, where she finished her art degree at the College of Fine Arts.

While she was living in Sydney in 1977, Campion attended the Sydney Film Festival and decided she wanted to make films. The Super 8mm *Tissues*, a dark comedy about a family in which the father has been arrested for child molestation, was her first effort, and Campion would haul her projector out of her car to show the film to interested viewers. Campion noted: "I was absolutely thrilled by every inch of it. Then one day somebody said to me, 'You don't have any wide shots in the film.' And I said, 'Wide shots? What are they?' I realized that I didn't have any idea of what I was up to."[1]

Campion enrolled in the Australian Film and Television School in 1981 and there met cinematographer Sally Bongers, who shot *Sweetie* for Campion and thus became the first woman to shoot a 35mm feature in Australia. Campion's student films are now available as a compilation video, and they give a strong indication of the directions in which Campion was moving. The black-and-white study *Passionless Moments* (1983) captured vignettes of daily life in Australia, but is perhaps more notable for Campion's wry commentary in the film's end credits of who did—and didn't—do

Still from *A Girl's Own Story* (courtesy of Women Make Movies)

what. *Peel* showed, in living color, a red-headed family's argument on a car trip. The black-and-white *A Girl's Own Story* (1983) captured childhood as it teeters on the edge of adolescence, growing up with Beatlemania and a father who thinks it is a good idea to take his daughter and his mistress out to dinner—together. *A Girl's Own Story* foreshadows all of Campion's longer work, with its themes of seeing the truth versus stating the truth, longing to belong and the oppression of children by their families.

Campion's first feature film was *Two Friends*, which was made in 1986, but only released in the United States in 1996. Shot in Sydney, Australia, in 1985, *Two Friends* goes backward in time, much as does Harold Pinter's play—and filmed screenplay—*Betrayal*. The two friends of the title are Louise and Kelly, both fifteen years old. Louise is a conservative, serious high school student who lives with her divorced mother. Kelly is a punk rocker with bleached blonde hair who lives at the beach and is experimenting with sex and drugs. But as the movie goes back in time, we learn that Kelly was once very like Louise, and we see the places where their paths diverged.

Two Friends might have been an auspicious beginning for Campion's feature film career if it had received widespread release, but it wasn't until *Two Friends* was re-released, after the success of *The Piano*, that many people realized that *Sweetie* wasn't Campion's first feature. Recognition for Campion instead had to wait for the underground success of *Sweetie*, which she co-wrote with Gerard Lee, a film that captured the attention of distributors through the sheer bizarreness of the title character. Sweetie is the spoiled, younger sister of the film's protagonist, whose mere presence is enough to metaphorically curdle milk. In a capsule review listing *Sweetie* as one of the best films of 1990, *The Village Voice* opined, "Imagine David Lynch disgorged, disemboweled, and at last, denied. The family romance as monster movie, but fiercely, willfully feminist."[2] What the *Voice* didn't say is that *Sweetie* is the story of sibling rivalry between two sisters gone mad, and that Sweetie is the monster of the movie, intent on possessing everything and everyone in her sister's life. Although *Sweetie* gained an underground art-house following, it was not universally liked. When it had its premiere at the 1990 Cannes International Film Festival, the site of Campion's earlier triumph with *Peel*, half of the audience walked out before the film was over, and many of those who stayed to watch the entire film booed Campion at the end of it.

Edith Armstrong and Jane Campion in *The Audition* (courtesy of Women Make Movies)

Before one draws the conclusion that art reflects the artist's life, we should stop to consider a student film by Campion's younger sister, Anna. *The Audition* is a Campion family documentary: Jane, working on preproduction for *An Angel at My Table*, has returned home to audition their mother, former stage actress Edith Armstrong, for a role in the film. Anna captures the love-hate relationship that Jane and Edith share, including the silent disapproval Edith has of Jane's work and Jane's grudging admiration for her mother's talents. Anna—unlike Jane's Sweetie—is absent from the film, present only as an observer, ostensibly ignored by the film's two subjects. (And yes, Armstrong was given a small part in Campion's film, although *The Audition* ends before this determination is made.)

The staccato quirkiness of *Sweetie* was the perfect calling card for Campion's next project: *An Angel at My Table*, based on the autobiography of New Zealand writer Janet Frame, whose own quirkiness led to her being misdiagnosed as schizophrenic and subsequently hospitalized in a mental institution for eight years. *An Angel at My Table* may easily be considered the feature-length version of Campion's *A Girl's Own Story:* Once again the themes of isolation, the need to fit in and the cruelty of families are explored. Winner of the Silver Lion at the prestigious Venice Film Festival in 1990, *An Angel at My Table* did better business at the video store than at American cinemas (in part because of its length), but received critical raves from film reviewers, who had found *Sweetie* too over the top. Campion impressed reviewers with her truthful rendering of Frame's life, at times stark, at times lush, and always filled with a frenetic vibrancy.

The critical success of *An Angel at My Table* gave Campion important cachet when it came to her next project, *The Piano*. She was able to attract three major stars—Holly Hunter, Sam Neill and Harvey Keitel—which in turn bolstered the film's chances of box-office success. But now Campion was up against a different stumbling block: creative control. *Sweetie* and *An Angel at My Table* were funded with government grants, which allowed Campion to have full creative control, including the final cut of her films. American investors were interested in financing *The Piano*, but wanted to have the Hollywood prerogative of final control. Instead, Campion received her funding from a French production firm that was willing to give her creative control.

With *The Piano*, the themes in Campion's previous works come to lush fruition. *The Piano* begins with the arrival of Ada (Hunter), a mute Scottish woman, and her ten-year-old daughter, Flora (Paquin), in New Zealand. Ada has come to New Zealand to be the wife of a wealthy local landowner, Stewart (Neill), in an arranged marriage. As a mute, Ada communicates in only two ways: through her daughter, and through her piano playing. Ada, by her marriage, becomes trapped in the social confines of Stewart's stiff world. Stewart gives Ada's piano to Baines (Keitel), a European with strong ties to the indigenous Maori, in exchange for land and tells Ada that she is to give piano lessons to Baines. But Baines is not interested in playing the piano—he is interested, instead, in having Ada play it for him. Through his appreciation of her, Ada falls in love with Baines and, with him and Flora, leaves Stewart and New Zealand.

Jane Campion

The Piano was hailed as a feminist masterpiece because it drove home the point that women are not adjuncts to their husbands and because it showed the heroine getting what she wanted—true love, as an equal.

In *Portrait of a Lady,* Campion once again returns to the nineteenth century and a story about a woman's fight for—and, this time, ultimate loss of—independence from the men around her. Like *The Piano, Portrait of a Lady* is a parable for modern women, telling them to guard the independence that was so hard won and so easily lost. Though Campion was able to rack up a stellar cast—including Nicole Kidman, Barbara Hershey, John Gielgud, John Malkovich, Shelley Duvall and Martin Donovan—the film's cast and Campion's reputation weren't enough to guarantee *Portrait of a Lady* either critical acclaim or box-office success.

Despite the obvious feminist politics that underlie her films, Campion denies a political agenda: "I think it's quite clear in my work that my orientation isn't political or doesn't come out of modern politics. The ability to be honest about what's really happening is the most important thing I've got."[3] Campion also tends to downplay her talents: "I'm not a deep intellectual, I just have my ideas. I reckon I'm really lucky to be able to just dream up my own ideas and that someone's prepared to pay for them."[4]

Campion is not an artist who secludes herself from the rest of the world. When she's not at work, she prefers to "go to the beach and calm right down—I love being with friends, laughing and making jokes about life, talking about what's happening, clothes, makeup, animals, wondering where you can get a good haircut."[5] All of which finds its way into her films, a backdrop to Campion's recurrent themes of independence and belonging.

Notes

1. Ashley Hay and Michael Duffy, "Girl's Own Stories," *The Independent* (Australia), June 1996, 67.
2. "Our Favorites: *Voice* Critics Pick the Best, the Eclectic, the Overlooked," *The Village Voice,* Jan. 8, 1991.
3. Hay and Duffy, 67.
4. Ibid, 68.
5. Ibid.

Allison Anders

Woman Alone

In the world of feature films, a first feature is a calling card that can get a director a distribution deal or production financing for a second feature. What the public and the film industry like, however, can be quirky: After *Born in Flames*, Lizzie Borden had to raise the money for *Working Girls* herself, whereas Susan Seidelman was tapped to direct *Desperately Seeking Susan* after the release of *Smithereens*. Allison Anders's first feature, *Gas Food Lodging* (1992), garnered critical acclaim; her second feature, *Mi Vida Loca* (1994), received mixed reviews but was trendy enough to buy her a spot in the otherwise all-male anthology film *Four Rooms* (1995). Then came *Grace of My Heart* (1996), Anders's tribute to sixties pop music, which most critics hated and the public didn't go to see. In an industry whose primary concern is box-office dollars, Anders's only apparent mistake has been to make films that center on the struggles of female characters. "It seems I always have a woman alone at the end of the movie,"[1] Anders has said of her work.

Films by Allison Anders

Gas Food Lodging

Mi Vida Loca

Four Rooms

Grace of My Heart

"When I started, I had no idea it would be as hard as it is," the single mother of three recalled. "I was in a fool's paradise thinking that it doesn't matter that I'm a woman. But when I came back from shooting *Gas Food Lodging*, I read an article in the *L.A. Times* that said two hundred-some films had been made that year and eleven were directed by women, which was 'a good number.' I freaked out because I realized I was one of those eleven, and it is hard for us."[2]

Gas Food Lodging—based on the classic young adult novel *Don't Look and It Won't Hurt* by Richard Peck—is the story of a teenage girl, her waitress mother and her wild older sister. The older sister becomes pregnant after a one-night stand and opts to go to a home for unwed mothers and put her baby up for adoption. Anders was able to attract major talent for her first film, with Brooke Adams playing the mother, Ione Skye as the older sister and James Brolin as the absentee father. Hugh Grant had originally agreed to play the part of the English geologist who captures the older sister's heart, but backed out of the deal.

Gas Food Lodging put Anders on the map of women to watch and scored a major success for Cineville, the independent company that produced the film. The film is frequently cited as a good example of low-budget filmmaking, and it established Anders as a director of films about women.

After the success of *Gas Food Lodging*, Anders turned to a subject literally outside her door: girl gangs in the Los Angeles Latino neighborhood of Echo Park. "I'd walk around and I'd see these girls," said Anders. "They were so intense: their attitude, their hair, their makeup, their clothes. I had to get to know them. It was a long process. Once I finally got them to meet with me and know that I was serious and persistent, then they opened up and it was fine. It was definitely a long process, and even when we were starting preproduction, there was still one boy who was convinced I was a cop."[3]

Mi Vida Loca—*My Crazy Life* is Anders's fictional version of the stories the Latina girl gang members told her about their lives—their men, their children, drugs, tattoos, turf and drive-by shootings. The film received mixed reviews and showed primarily on the art-house theater circuit, but solidified Anders's place in the independent film community.

Anders was the only woman to contribute to *Four Rooms*. The other directors included Quentin Tarantino (*Reservoir Dogs*, *Pulp Fiction*), Robert Rodriguez (*El Mariachi*), and Alexandre Rockwell (*In the Soup*)—all of whom, like Anders, are writer-directors with low-budget hits under their belts. The segments of the film take place in four different rooms in the same hotel. The segments by the three Generation X male directors

Angel Aviles and Seidy Lopez in *Mi Vida Loca*

were universally excoriated by the critics as slipshod, self-indulgent work. Only Anders's segment was singled out for praise, and her contribution—the opening segment, in which a coven of witches, played by Madonna, Lili Taylor, Sammi Davis, Valeria Golino, Alicia Witt and Ione Skye, attempt to resurrect a 1950s stripper—wasn't strong enough to carry the remainder of the film.

Anders has commented: "The problem with *Four Rooms* was that the script was never worked on. We had done only one draft of the script when we were green-lit. We didn't have much time for rewriting."[4] *Four Rooms* ended up being edited and re-edited. "At the point we were making radical cuts, we were kind of tired of it and very disillusioned with the whole process. We originally started with very humble and sincere desires to make a film together and not have any big stars. But I don't regret having big stars. I will go to my grave thrilled that I got to work with Madonna, Valeria Golino, Lili Taylor and all the wonderful women whom I worked with. Still, it was always intended to be a much simpler project than it ended up being. I feel now that if you don't have the script ready, you can't fix it later. Just like you can't edit what you haven't shot, and you can't shoot what you haven't written."[5]

After the disaster of *Four Rooms*, Anders started work on *Grace of My Heart*, her tribute to the women songwriters of the 1960s. In *Grace*, songwriter Denise Waverly, played by Illeana Douglas, composes hit songs for others, but really wants to record the songs herself. Interwoven with her musical career is the story of a string of failed relationships with men in the music industry (played by Eric Stoltz, Matt Dillon and Bruce Davison). Unlike Anders's previous two feature films, *Grace* had a larger budget, solid star presence and a mentor—veteran director Martin Scorsese.

Anders said of her mentor: "It's been a phenomenally good experience just working with him. I mean, I was scared to death at first. It was like, 'Oh my God, Martin Scorsese!' I was so nervous. And we'd have these funny conversations, and he knew that I was scared stiff, and he'd say, 'Well, what are you doing right now? What are you up to?' And when I was finished talking about some editing problem or something, he'd say, 'Yeah, I know, I remember on *Raging Bull* blah blah blah blah . . .' and I'm like 'Oh my God, this is Martin Scorsese!' I was petrified all over again. I couldn't call him Marty for a very long time. I couldn't call him anything . . . and I still don't really call him Marty to his face. I can't quite do that, although he keeps saying that I can. But he doesn't understand that I can't."[6]

Scorsese was most helpful when it came to editing *Grace*. Anders first cut the film herself, but wasn't happy with the result, so Scorsese suggested that Anders come to New York City, where Thelma Schoonmaker, who had edited many of Scorsese's films, would edit *Grace*. Anders decided to take Scorsese up on his offer.

Anders wrote of the editing process in *Premiere:* "While doing this one scene, where we had earlier agreed to rearrange material for greater clarity and emotional connection, she [Schoonmaker] went even further, crosscutting within the scene with complete grace. If any other editor did this, it would be jarring. But the way Thelma has done it, it's like turning over in your sleep into the arms of your favorite warm body. That's what her cuts are like."[7]

The reviews of *Grace* were so poor that the film seemed to make only an overnight appearance at cinemas before being released on video. Despite the cast, Schoonmaker's editing, Martin Scorsese, good response to preview showings and a strong publicity campaign, the public didn't seem interested in *Grace*.

But Anders continues to write screenplays that interest her. One of her latest screenplay projects, *Boxcar Children*, is based on the series of classic 1940s children's books. Anders also continues to write her screenplays her way: "To me, the three-act structure format [the classic Hollywood structure for writing screenplays] is a very patriarchal structure for telling a story. It has this intention, these plot points, this climax and this falling action, and then you turn over and go to sleep. If you're telling a very masculine story as a woman, that structure will work for you, but if you're trying to tell a woman's story, that might not be the best model."[8]

Telling women's stories is what Anders has been doing all along. "What shocked me was that I hadn't realized I was writing anything any differently. I was just telling stories the only way I knew how. What surprised me was that people kept saying, 'You have such strong female characters,' and I didn't understand what that meant. I was just telling the story the way I needed to tell it. Then later I started to realize I did do things differently. That, of course, was when I failed to get any work in the industry."[9]

Later, when she was working in the industry, her woman's sensibility led to clashes with the studio over the end titles to *Grace of My Heart*. She wrote to a friend, "The end titles are being held up, 'cause the studio is reluctant to allow me to credit my child-care providers. I missed my son's kindergarten year so I could edit this film in N.Y.—a tremendous sacrifice for both of us—so it is extremely important to me that this is acknowledged."[10] In an interview, Anders noted, "Universal says, 'We've never done that before.' So I had to draft a letter saying, 'I know you've never done this before, but you probably haven't had many single moms directing films for you, either.'"[11]

Notes

1. Steven Rea, "For *Mi Vida Loca* Director, Female Self-Reliance Is the Theme," *Philadelphia Inquirer*, Aug. 28, 1994, G2.

2. Anthony C. Ferrante, "Allison Anders Telling Her Own Story," *scr(i)pt*, Sept./ Oct. 1996, 29.

3. Rea, G2.

4. Ferrante, 32.

5. Ibid.

6. Rea, G2.

7. Allison Anders, "Director's Diary: Cut to the *Grace*,*Premiere*, Oct. 1996, 49.

8. Ferrante, 30.

9. Ibid.

10. Anders, 55.

11. Ferrante, 32.

**Allison
Anders**

Julie Dash

Someone Always Says No

Julie Dash in *The Cinematic Jazz of Julie Dash*, a film by Yvonne Welbon (courtesy of Women Make Movies)

Julie Dash doesn't equivocate on the status of black women filmmakers. "You have to build confidence in your work on your own because there are no precedents," she explained. "Getting a 'name' hasn't happened for black women yet—can you name a black woman director? If you can't, you certainly aren't alone. I think many [white] women filmmakers have been taken under someone's wing. That has not happened with black women filmmakers. No one has gone out there and opened any doors. And it is difficult to know how to open the doors yourself when there are no precedents, no models to follow."

Since the release of Dash's critically acclaimed film *Illusions* in 1983, much has changed for African-American filmmakers. Spike Lee, a contemporary of Dash's, is now one of the most well-known independent directors in the United States. Other African-American directors like John Singleton, Robert Townsend, Mario Van Peebles, Forest Whitaker and Tim Reid have had critical success as independents *and* in Hollywood, where films by blacks have traditionally been considered unmarketable. In the last decade Hollywood has taken note of a fact long denied, that there is indeed such a thing as black box office.

But the influence of black box office on the Hollywood studios has barely extended to black actresses, let alone black women directors. Even stars like Whoopi Goldberg, the highest-paid actress in Hollywood, complain there are few quality roles for black women in Hollywood. Black actresses argue that until there are more black directors and producers, the dearth of roles will continue. And as white actresses have discovered, women are more likely to find quality roles, particularly if they are over thirty-five, in movies directed and/or produced by women.

Black women have not ridden in on the wave of the New Black Cinema, said Dash, and there haven't been any signs that they will, despite Hollywood's wooing of Dash after the critical success of her first feature film, *Daughters of the Dust* (1991). That romance, however, has stopped short of her being offered a feature film to direct; thus far she has been offered only television directing, which she has done consistently, predominantly for cable television venues.

The color barrier has yet to be formally crossed by black women directors in Hollywood—though not for lack of trying on the part of the filmmakers themselves. But serious impediments obtain for women directors across the board, in Hollywood and as independents. For women of color, the struggle to achieve in spite of institutionalized sexism *and* racism within the film industry is incredibly tough. "We still haven't seen that many films by white women filmmakers—that's still considered 'new' to an extent—and women [directors] get treated very differently in Hollywood [from men]," noted Dash. "There aren't *any* [Hollywood studio] films by Asian or Chicana women—that's an area where only a few men have broken in. So it isn't really surprising that there aren't films by black women filmmakers, either. When people ask me what advice I have for women who want to make films, I tell them, be tough and don't let anyone else tell you what film to make, because if you have a different vision, a woman's vision, something we don't see in every movie or on every television program, then you are going to face obstacles and people are going to tell you you can't do the film you want to make."

Dash explained the reason for those obstacles: "Trying to present images

Films by Julie Dash

Four Women

Diary of an African Nun

Illusions

Praise House

Daughters of the Dust

**Julie
Dash**

Roseann Katon and Julie Dash on the set of *Illusions* (courtesy of Geechee Girls)

on the screen that *I* want to see as a black woman is essential to me as a filmmaker, but it may be at odds with what Hollywood wants to present."

The paradoxical and dichotomous nature of Hollywood images of black women is the central metaphor in Dash's film *Illusions*. Set in the year after Pearl Harbor at a prototypical Hollywood studio, *Illusions* tells the intricate story of Mignon Dupree, a black woman studio executive who is presumed to be and passes for white, and Ester Jeeter, a black torch singer who dubs the singing for a major white Hollywood star. As the title suggests, the film delineates the illusory world of Hollywood mythmaking and details the myths held by Hollywood—and white male studio executives—about who and what black women are.

Beautifully shot in stark black and white, *Illusions* has, like all Dash's work, a lush and lyric quality despite the shoestring budget of less than $30,000. "One of the things I try to do in my films is create images of black women that other black women will recognize," explained Dash. "I want to redefine images of black women [in cinema] because the *images* I grew up with [in movies and television] weren't the black women I knew."

Long before a film like Forest Whitaker's version of the best-selling Terry McMillan novel *Waiting to Exhale* became a box-office smash in 1996, Dash had been "dreaming of a film in which all the main characters are black women." That film, *Daughters of the Dust*, was seventeen years in the making. It received extraordinary critical attention at film festivals in the United States and abroad. The film was so successful, in fact, that Dash claims the discomfiting distinction of being the first black woman director in the United States to have a feature film in major theatrical distribution. *Daughters of the Dust* then appeared on American public television as part of the *American Playhouse* series.

While the success of Dash's film has certainly pleased the director, her calm demeanor belies a simmering anger evident in her discussion of *why* it took a century of American cinema for the theatrical release of a film by a black woman.

"I want to make a certain kind of film," Dash asserted. "I'm addressing a different audience, with a different voice and a different perspective from what white men are used to seeing on screen. And I do have to emphasize the fact that decisions about *what* gets seen and *how* it gets seen are still made by white males. They are generally in the position of privilege, because they are producing the films. The story is *from* their point of view *for* their point of view. Most films are made for this [white male] audience." She added, "This isn't an issue of political correctness, it's about what's out there. I want to make something different."

When Dash speaks of what is out there and available to audiences, she includes a class of films that typically depict African-American women in very restricted—and white-stereotyped—roles. In these portrayals of black women in films made by white men, the women are most often portrayed as highly sexualized; the black female character is either a prostitute or her role in the storyline devolves from a white male's eroticization of her so-called exotic sexuality. Dash said she would like to change that image of black women on screen.

"I want to depict black women as sexual beings," she said, "but I don't want to duplicate the vehicles that have been used in the past."

Black women also find themselves in what some feminist critics have termed "the sexless Mammy role," traditionally played in Hollywood films in the 1940s through the 1970s by actresses like the superb Hattie McDaniel (the first black woman to win an Academy Award, for her supporting role as Mammy in Victor Fleming's *Gone with the Wind* [1939]) or the great Ethel Waters, in Fred Zinnemann's *The Member of the Wedding* (1952). These roles portray the black woman as the mother-protector of, almost invariably, white children (Julie Harris in *The Member of the Wedding*) or young white women (Vivien Leigh's Scarlett O'Hara in *Gone with the Wind*). As in the sexual roles, the black woman is defined by a quality—sage wisdom—that is explicated as intrinsically and thus exotically black, utterly separate from anything experienced by the white characters.

Whoopi Goldberg has frequently played a modern variation on this nonsexual protector role in the 1980s and 1990s, portraying a range of

**Julie
Dash**

nonsexual women who further the goals of young white women. (Goldberg won the second Academy Award given to a black woman for just this type of role in Jerry Zucker's *Ghost* [1990], where she played a medium attempting to help the young, white heroine [Demi Moore] reunite with her dead lover [Patrick Swayze].)

Critiques of the restrictive roles for black women in Hollywood films (as well as many independent films, including those made by African-American men like Spike Lee) have only served to impel directors like Dash, who states unequivocally that the dearth of images of black women on screen has inspired her as a filmmaker and underscored her desire to make movies in which black women not only appear but dominate the screen, shifting the power dynamic to which black women have traditionally been subjugated. In Dash's films, black women are central, never peripheral, and the filmmaker's gaze is always distinctly female and definingly black.

"My films are from the culture of women," Dash asserts, "so I think a lot of white men don't understand them. My films seem foreign to them, because they never see this experience of life, the expression of this experience. Authentic lives of African-American women don't get very much play [on screen]."

Dash also explains that her influences weren't so much white filmmakers as black women writers. "I was influenced so by black women novelists— Alice Walker, Toni Morrison, Toni Cade Bambara," she recalled. Dash said when she read their books in college she wanted to see films that were like those novels. "I thought, why don't I make films like this? I recognized these [characters]. I'd never seen [these characters] on television or in films. It made me feel so cheated, to know those people were there. I wanted to see those people on screen."

Born in New York, Dash was raised in the Queensridge Projects, surrounded by "real" black women and men. She notes that not seeing black women she could relate to on screen later compelled her to create realistic and diverse images of black women in her own films. But she also acknowledges that as a young girl she had no idea that *she* could make films because mainstream images of blacks were so limited that she "didn't even know blacks *made* movies."

Dash's initiation into filmmaking began when, as a high school student in the late sixties, she attended an after-school workshop at the Studio Museum of Harlem in New York. Like many of Dash's experiences as a filmmaker, it was fraught with an undercurrent of racist politics. The workshop, Dash explained, was part of a government program established after the Harlem riots in 1966 to keep black youth in check.

"They pumped a lot of money into black communities for after-school programs to keep students off the streets [after the riots]," she recalled. "It was a place to go to be with my friends."

Like many women filmmakers, Dash initially hadn't been drawn to film-making. But the experience was so formative that she went on to study film at New York's City College, where she began making short films. She also studied at the American Film Institute (AFI) in Los Angeles and at the University of California at Los Angeles (UCLA). At AFI she made *Four Women* (1977), a lyric dance film Dash calls a "choreopoem" based on the powerful Nina Simone ballad of the same title about historical stereotypes of black women. The experimental film won several awards.

During the same period Dash also made a film of Alice Walker's short story *Diary of an African Nun* (1978). Both films incorporate Dash's love of lyric visual imagery that is most acutely rendered in *Daughters of the Dust*, Dash's eleventh film. These moving early pieces were followed by the far more linear and dramatically powerful *Illusions*, which firmly established Dash as an important and compelling cinematic voice. *Illusions* proves Dash's strengths go beyond the technical and lyric; like *Daughters of the Dust*, the film is historical fiction that illuminates Dash's ability as a storyteller. The viewer knows these are fictional narratives, but the explication is so compelling, the coalescence of history and fiction so smooth, the characterizations so stunning that the audience is swept away by Dash's vision.

Illusions, like Dash's more experimental earlier films and her later documentary *Praise House* (1991), incorporates layers of text and subtext. The principal tale is of Mignon Dupree and her high-profile role within the studio system during World War II when women—because so many men were fighting abroad—were given brief access to power. But the drama of Mignon's role goes beyond her position as a female Hollywood mini-mogul; Mignon is also a black woman whose light skin allows her to pass for white.

(Interestingly, the role of Mignon is played by Lonette McKee, who has said that she has had a great deal of difficulty getting roles throughout her career because of her light complexion and Caucasian features: too black, she asserted, to play white roles, but not dark enough to play black roles. She was, she said, in the bizarre position of being a black woman criticized for her skin tone by other blacks because of the internalization of the negativism attached to skin color; she was, in essence, penalized for her lighter skin by both races. As a consequence she found herself particularly drawn to the role in *Illusions*.

Several years after she worked with Dash on *Illusions*, McKee got a major role in Donna Deitch's *The Women of Brewster Place* [1989], based on the novel by African-American novelist Gloria Naylor. She was asked by interviewers if playing a lesbian in *The Women of Brewster Place* concerned her, if she worried about what people might say about her taking what some considered to be an unsavory role. McKee, who had frequently been relegated to mulatto-stereotype roles, was

Roseann Katon as Ester Jeeter in *Illusions*

incensed. She said, "For years people have thought there was nothing lower than playing a black woman [on screen]. Why would it bother me to play a lesbian? I feel grateful to be offered such a good role in which I play a *black woman*.")

The overlay of issues Dash addresses in *Illusions* delineates the complexity of her filmmaking and storytelling. Mignon *knows* she is black, and other blacks around her either intuit or are sure she is black. That puts her in the complicated position of defending her passing to those who cannot pass because their skin is too dark. But she also sees how these darker blacks are treated by the same whites who treat *her* with respect, and thus must deal with the internal ethical conflict passing poses. As a Hollywood executive, she is also in some sense in charge of perpetuating other myths of passing and, hence, of discrimination; Ester Jeeter is darker skinned than Mignon—obviously black, so she cannot be shown on screen. But her voice *does* get on screen—coming out of the mouth of a white actress.

Dash explores all the variant elements of Hollywood "illusions," as the film's title suggests. Other blacks see whites treating Mignon as white; they share the "joke" on the white power structure. But the obverse of Mignon's assumed power is the tragedy of Ester's tremendous talent going unremarked because she is black. Dash resolves the conflicts in the only way possible; Mignon must stand up for herself as a black woman in order to empower herself and other blacks.

Illusions is indicative of Dash's interest in making films that reflect her concerns as an African-American woman and her complex relationship to the subject of her films. *Daughters of the Dust* is Dash's dream movie; that is, it is the film she always dreamed of making, a film starring only black women in a range of colors and roles (here the light-skinned woman, Yellow Mary, has a place in which there is no racial subterfuge because she is living in a black society). The film, a period piece set at the turn of the century, follows a family in the Gullah Sea Islands off South Carolina as they prepare to move to the mainland. Former slaves, the Gullah, or Geechee, people have maintained their rich West African cultural heritage, and the film weaves the complicated tale of their past, present and future lives together.

The geographical element was important to the story as well as the historical background of the film, Dash explained, because the Sea Islands were "where African captives were first dropped off [in the Colonies] before they were sold into slavery." She added that the lives of the Gullah are an intrinsic part of African-American history because of their pivotal role in the development of a black culture in America.

The desire to make the film suffused Dash for close to two decades before she was finally able to raise enough money. To do that she had to first make a short trailer to show to prospective funding sources. The critical success of her earlier work, especially *Illusions*, helped sell *Daughters of the Dust*, but she was raising money throughout the entire project—in addition to all the other roles she filled in the making of the film. Even after the shooting was complete, Dash said, money still had to be raised for postproduction costs. In addition, she later had to cut the film down from an original length of just over four hours to a release length of two hours.

Dash spent years conducting historical research for the film. As in her other films, all of which have been meticulously researched, every aspect of *Daughters of the Dust* is historically accurate. Dash started her research by gathering oral histories from members of her family and the families of friends. She also pored through data in the Smithsonian Institution and the National Archives, in Washington, D.C., and collected other information at museums in and around the Gullah Sea Islands. She noted that she was not alone in conducting this research; the Gullah have become fascinating to scholars of African-American cultural history. The islands, in part because they are separate from the mainland and are overwhelmingly populated by African-American descendants of the original inhabitants, have retained much of the original culture those women and men brought with them from West Africa. The power of this historical and cultural heritage forms the foundation for Dash's film.

Daughters of the Dust blends this essential history into Dash's script in a complex, dreamy, nonlinear narrative reminiscent and resonant of Toni Morrison's novelistic style. The setting is extraordinarily beautiful, as are the costumes, while the performances are as strong as they are demanding.

The film has a twofold impact. There is, of course, the beauty of the story, a tale of leaving home (throughout the course of the film the family is preparing to leave the island for the mainland), knowing that home will probably never be seen again, while also acknowledging the necessity of retaining the cultural heritage inextricably connected to that home. Dash, who also wrote the screenplay, crafts the story with great subtlety. But the film also marks another debut of sorts—an historical feature film about blacks in which the narrative is told from a wholly black vantage point, a strikingly black gaze—*and* a female gaze as well.

This aspect of the filmmaking was also important for Dash, again because of the Hollywood treatment of blacks on screen and behind the camera. When the television miniseries based on Gloria Naylor's critically acclaimed novel *The Women of Brewster Place* was proposed, and Oprah Winfrey signed on to the project as an executive producer, Dash hoped to be offered the job of director. The miniseries seemed perfect for her: a project about a diverse group of black women and their lives over a period of several decades written by an African-American novelist. But director Donna Deitch, fresh from the success of her feature debut, the lesbian film *Desert Hearts* (1985), got the job.

"I guess this is the kind of thing you're not supposed to talk about," Dash admitted, "but the movie was about black women—lots of different black women, not just the lesbian characters. It was stereotyping all around. [Deitch] was hired because she'd just made a film about lesbians and there were lesbians in this project, and I wasn't hired because I had only made films about black women that weren't features." She added, "This is why the influence of black producers is so important. And I think the black producers on this project could have pushed for a black woman director." (Nor was Dash ever asked to direct any episodes of the television series that spun off from the miniseries.)

Daughters of the Dust was more than vindication for the *Brewster Place* debacle. Myriad films have been made about the period in American history between the Civil War and the Great Migration, films in which black characters appear and may even play major roles, but, like *The Women of Brewster Place*, they haven't been directed by African Americans. (For example, Edward Zwick directed the brilliant, award-winning 1989 film *Glory*, about a battlion of blacks in the American Civil War. The cast starred many of the finest African-American actors in Hollywood, including Morgan Freeman and Denzel Washington, both of whom made cinema history by being nominated for Academy Awards. Washington became the first black male actor to win an Academy Award for best supporting actor.)

The significance of Dash's watershed film (since followed by other historical pieces like John Singleton's haunting *Rosewood* [1997] and Tim Reid's moving *Once Upon a Time . . . When We Were Colored* [1996]) cannot be underestimated, especially because so few feature films by African-American directors prior to the release of *Daughters of the Dust* (notably films by Charles Burnett and Spike Lee, all situated in an historical present) have received either critical or crossover audience attention. Dash's film is maverick in this regard and impact, similar to plays by Langston Hughes and Lorraine Hansberry: written specifically for a black audience with black characters and a wholly black plot, but also garnering white audience interest without diluting the subject matter to accommodate the white viewer. Dash embarked on *Daughters of the Dust* hoping only to make the film she had always dreamed of making; white critical success never played a part in what she sought for the film. "I needed this film to be the film *I* wanted to make," she asserted. "If I worried about what a white male audience response might be, how could I ever have made a film like this?"

Yet despite Dash's achievement with *Daughters of the Dust*, she noted that many white male viewers didn't understand the film because it was, she

Julie Dash

said, "almost foreign to them," a fact underscored by some of the commentary about the film. For example, popular film critic Leonard Maltin, in his comprehensive *1997 Movie and Video Guide,* writes, "The material is fascinating, and some of the imagery is stunning, but too much of the historical background remains unexplained, and the slow pace weighs it down." He gives the film two and a half stars out of a possible four-star rating and does call the film "poetic," but there is an obvious lack of comprehension of Dash's black, female style—which differs distinctively from that of a white or male director. And there is a presumption in Maltin's comments that white viewers must be led into black narrative, though no comparable assessment would ever be made about a white film for black audiences.

That is one of the issues Dash addresses in her work—the singularity of the black, female cinematic gaze and how her films "focus on African-American women and speak to African-American women."

This reflects another iconoclastic element of Dash's *oeuvre;* her films are *all* about the lives of black women—historically, personally, professionally and culturally. She isn't looking to make a so-called crossover film that is scripted and cast with a white audience in mind. She has continued to make shorts because she doesn't want to wait around to do features, either because she's waiting for funding or waiting for a producer or studio. For years when she lived and worked in Atlanta, Dash made what she described as "bread-and-butter films," documentaries for various organizations. "I made a lot of films for money," she explained, "because as a filmmaker you also have to make a living unless you have some other source of income, which I don't. And I have a child."

But, she asserts, those working films don't have to be infomercials or other work that makes one cringe. "I did documentaries for the National Black Women's Health Project," she said. "And my first film was a training film for Morehouse [College in Atlanta]. I also did a reproductive rights film, a film on teenage pregnancy in the black community. Sometimes," she added, "you barter services, because you need a lot of money to make your films and you have to invest a lot of money in an individual project." She has also done public service shorts for the Southern Christian Leadership Conference, the American Civil Liberties Union and the National Association for the Advancement of Colored People (NAACP).

"What's important is that you are working, that you are making films you feel good about," she explained. "I've never thought you were any less of a filmmaker if you work in shorts instead of features. I've done shorts for many years. And I tell people, if your shorts are successful, you can do a feature if you want to, because you'll be able to raise the money to make a feature film. That's how I made *Daughters of the Dust*."

But funding remains a complicated issue, particularly for black women directors who often have far less access to sources of big money than other filmmakers do. Dash noted wryly, "As a black woman I don't generally work with people who do venture capital and so forth."

Since Dash made *Daughters of the Dust*, there has been no groundswell of features by other black women directors. There has been no Spike Lee–style surge; she maintains her singular status. And her relationship to Hollywood continues to elicit a complicated response. "There's always an obstacle they throw at you," she said. "There isn't a great desire to see people succeed at something new, and I am doing something new [in Hollywood] because I am not presenting traditional, white, male roles."

The role blacks have most frequently played in cinema, especially since the 1970s, explained Dash, is that of the person who impedes the white protagonist or is the bearer of bad news. "In films and television, you see it all the time," she said. "In an effort to put blacks in nontraditional roles in [white] films—that is, not domestics—you see blacks as judges, police officers, doctors, lawyers—some role in which they basically come up to the white character and say, 'No, you can't do that,' or keep the main character from doing something important; or they are telling the main character or some other sympathetic white character bad news—about a death or something else that will impact on them in some terrible way." She added, "It's very ironic, of course, because in real life we don't exactly keep white men from doing what they want to do, but this is who we are in films."

Dash knows that changing the screen roles of black women and men is no simple task and that getting black women into feature directing roles may be the hardest of all. "I know it's going to be a long process," she said. "Black women have to work in development with story ideas and implementation." As for her own work, even though she is now living in Los Angeles and working in Hollywood, she is unequivocal about what she *won't* direct. "I don't want to duplicate the Hollywood popcorn fodder," Dash asserted. "The thing is, there is always going to be someone here [in Hollywood] who is going to tell you you can't do the kind of film you want

Julie Dash

to make. People told me that about *Daughters of the Dust;* now they tell me that about [other projects] I want to do. I know what films I want to make, my life isn't determined by people in Hollywood—I can't let it be."

What does determine Dash's directorial *oeuvre* remains her own desire. "I'd like to see us [black women and men] in different roles," she said. "I [continue to] want to see the women I have always known on screen. It doesn't seem like a lot to hope for. It certainly seems like the right goal to pursue."

Patricia Rozema

I've Heard the Mermaids Singing

In 1987, the independent film world was taken by storm when Patricia Rozema's first feature film, *I've Heard the Mermaids Singing*, was released. *Mermaids* quickly became a case study for low-budget feature filmmaking: It cost $400,000 (Canadian) to make, and worldwide receipts grossed $10 million (Canadian). Rozema was only twenty-nine years old.

Mermaids—which takes its title from the final lines of T. S. Eliot's "The Love Song of J. Alfred Prufrock"—is about art, authorship and interpretation. In it, Polly, an erstwhile "Person Friday" is hired by a small art gallery to do clerical work. She discovers that the gallery's curator, Gabrielle, has a burning desire to be a painter. Polly, a photographer, anonymously sends her boss some of her photos, only to have them rejected by Gabrielle. But then Gabrielle's lover, Mary, makes

Patricia Rozema

Films by Patricia Rozema

I've Heard the Mermaids Singing

White Room

When Night Is Falling

Polly see her own art in a different light, and Polly discovers the secret that Mary and Gabrielle are keeping.

The pivotal role of Polly is played by Sheila McCarthy. Rozema noted, "I auditioned two hundred other actresses before Sheila came in. It really was a case of 'Of course, this is it. She looks great. *Please* let her be able to act.' She sat down, she started. She was funny. She was touching. It was perfect: a very immediate feeling she was right. A very fine line between being too pathetic or too shaky, or too old, too young, too beautiful, too ugly. It was really different. She makes you feel wonderful as a writer, too, because everything you write sounds completely improvised and spontaneous from her mouth. I have to say I felt fairly comfortable with the voice of Polly. I wrote thousands of pages for Polly. That was fun stuff. What was hard was eliminating from that. So both of us were comfortable with Polly's voice. That was easy. But she inhabited it. It was spectacular. She's really good."

Mermaids took Rozema "eighteen months from first draft to first print. It was actually very, very quick. I had the entire concept of the character, the situation with the general tone simultaneously and pretty spontaneously. It was really fast and unlabored.

"There's nothing more guaranteed, I realize now, to engage the sympathy of the viewer than injustice," explains Rozema of *Mermaids*. "Polly suffers at the hands of the authorities and that makes us flock to her. There's also an unquantifiable element in her as written and in her as played, which is something called charm. She's just a charming human being. And there's something appealing in someone who acknowledges her own weaknesses, which she does immediately, this 'organizationally impaired' thing. And I think that I introduce people to a world of a woman who knows another woman in a very innocent, unaggressive way. People like to have a world opened to them, sort of a new vision. I give an audience a fairly easy position, which is they can see it all through the eyes of Polly, an innocent. They're not expected to identify. I think it's a film that is very honest, and that it has a lot of love for things, for the world and for its characters. Like when you have a conversation with someone you know wasn't sincere, and you know that they're filled with rancor; so it is with a film. Its intentions were very pure, and people respond to that, and it's not something that can be manufactured."

Rozema also points to the film's structure as being a key to its success: "It has a classical narrative structure, with some very unusual elements plugged into that structure. It's not disturbing in its structure, in that we [don't] get information before we know what to do with it or that we shift gears quickly in the middle of the story. It's easy to follow; it has a familiar storytelling tempo. I don't think every film needs to be that way. I'd like to venture further in storytelling techniques. But the one I used in *Mermaids* was quite comforting for audiences. And it's funny, and people love to laugh—it's just basic to human nature. It's a physical need."

Kate Nelligan and Maurice Godin in *White Room*

The success of *Mermaids*, said Rozema, "brought me a lot of opportunity and freedom. It brought me the opportunity to make a film that isn't an obvious crowd-pleaser."

That film—the one that's not an obvious crowd-pleaser—was Rozema's second feature, 1990's *White Room*. "The genesis of the original image is that of a white room," explained Rozema. "A white room is very, very simply the interior space, the scene, the mysterious place of honesty that has been dealt with in history in various forms, religiously, as a holy of holies. And so I gave that space a physical incarnation as a white room, and I wanted the film to be very simply related to it; thematically it revolves around this white room, and the plot revolves around this white room. The mystery of the story is: What is in this white room? What happens in there? Why is it so significant? That's the whole plot.

"The general structure of the story is of a Grimm's fairy tale," continued Rozema. "The main character, through whom I speak, is a young man named Norman Gentle [played by Maurice Godin]. Norman goes on a journey. It's set up ironically by a third-person omniscient female narrator, voiceover, and Norman sets out on his journey toward knowledge, truth and, of course, love. On his journey, he encounters three women. One is Zelda, a self-absorbed, hungry, kind of scattered debutante street performer, played by Sheila McCarthy. Another is a woman he spies on in the night, purely in his mind, in an attempt to get inspiration for his story writing; that's Madeline X, played by Margot Kidder. She's a famous singer in the story. At the funeral of Madeline X, he meets Jane, the third woman, played by Kate Nelligan. Norman follows Jane home and finds that she lives com-

Godin and Nelligan in *White Room*

pletely alone in this very rough, uncared-for house completely overgrown by foliage, and he convinces her to hire him as her gardener. She has, in the back of her house, this white room that she disappears into every night, and he doesn't know why. She never lets him inside the house. A love story develops between them, but she never lets him inside the house. And then Norman hears through Zelda and other sources that Madeline X is rumored never to have sung herself, to have always brought in the tracks already recorded and never toured live. She only did the celebrity shtick. So suddenly the question opens about Jane and this white room. There are two endings, one very grim and one very fairy-tale-like. The grim one is reality, and the fairy tale one is the story that Norman finally writes after all his incompetent, inarticulate muddling throughout the movie. It's sort of a disturbing ending because reality is definitely not as we would have hoped it to be, and the fairy tale is so euphoric it's impossible."

White Room gave Rozema the opportunity to work with world-class actresses Kate Nelligan and Margot Kidder. "She [Nelligan] is really a remarkable woman. It was a professional high point for me to be able to work with her. We got along like a house on fire. She says, not quite publicly, that this was one of her best professional experiences," said Rozema, noting that "I have very little need to be the boss or to show myself to be the boss. So there's no power-play stuff going on. I wrote it, so I know what I want, and I'll deal with any actors the way they need to be dealt with to work well. So she respected that, I guess."

Rozema also enjoyed working with Kidder. "Margot is one hell of a party girl," she said. "She's quite serious about her work, but she laughs very hard and very loud. It was perfect for the character because the character was a professional celebrity, and Margot is, to some extent, a professional celebrity. So it pleased me to take someone, a real-life celebrity, and adapt that to my fictional needs."

White Room had a significantly larger budget than *Mermaids:* $2.5 million (Canadian). Rozema estimates that the film took two years to make, from start to finish. She wrote the screenplay and then shot the film in thirty-five days in Toronto. "Shooting is a minor, minor part of the whole thing. The plan was to do it the way we did *Mermaids*, which was to finish the thing and then sell it," she said. "I'm afraid of interference. I jealously guard my control."

White Room suffered the fate of many second films—it received only a limited release and not only never showed theatrically in the United States, but has not been released on video as well.

Rozema's third feature film, 1994's *When Night Is Falling*, was a foray into a world of crossed boundaries. In the film, Camille, an academic at a Christian college, gives in to her attraction for the African-Canadian Petra, a circus performer. Camille's life then becomes multiple choice when Petra prepares to leave town with the circus: Should Camille go with Petra, or stay with her boyfriend? Chuck in her career? Convince Petra to stay?

The American theatrical run of *When Night Is Falling* was limited by an NC-17 rating (no children under seventeen admitted; formerly X) from the Motion Picture Association of America (MPAA). The MPAA has repeatedly given films that portray explicit lesbian sex or male frontal nudity— such as Lance Young's *Bliss* (1997) and Philip Kaufman's *Henry and June* (1990)—the NC-17 rating, which is shunned by many "family-oriented" chains of cinemas and video stores. Nevertheless, *When Night Is Falling* has continued to rack up serious home video sales, many of them through mail-order, due in large part to its erotic lesbian love scene.

Patricia Rozema

Rozema's success has made her a "poster child" for independent Canadian filmmaking. "I'm not very fond of nationalism, which is one of the things I dislike about America: It is a nationalist country," she said. "People identify with political and geographical—arbitrary—realities. But not being very nationalistic is a completely Canadian characteristic. You rarely find a Canadian who brags wildly about the country. You often find a Canadian who will criticize other countries, but you won't often find one who says Canada is the best country in the world. I'm really attracted to this lack of nationalism. I'm attracted to being able to be in a place and take from the world what I want to. It's a country of immigrants, as opposed to America, which has an image as a melting pot. We have the image of a mosaic. So we're separate. Cultures are maintained. I'm a first-generation immigrant myself. My parents are from Holland. That's more a part of my identity than being Canadian. A Dutch, Calvinist background, and I went to Dutch, Calvinist school from grade school through college. I went to Calvin College in Grand Rapids, Michigan, for several years.

"But suddenly, when you have success, you're thrust from the margins out to the world as some kind of ambassador. And I have *post facto* become a representative of the country. So if you ask, 'Is *Mermaids* a Canadian film?'—it has *become* one. It has become a means whereby people characterize Canadian film. I think in the creation of *Mermaids*, I did see it in political terms. I thought of the underdog. Canada is not a superpower by any means. It's very quietly, comfortably democratic, but it's plagued by a sense of inferiority. There's a bit of hostility here. A combination of hostility and inferiority because the Americans are so big and loud.

"It's 25 million people spread all over the second largest territory in the world," she noted. "So it's a tiny country. I find it slightly more civilized and less self-promotional. That's appealing to me. I've had quite a lot of offers to go work with studios, but it wasn't my idea of fun to go and work for corporations, essentially, when this [Toronto] is a really big film center. Per capita in North America, more people see films in Toronto than anywhere else in North America. So that interest from an audience is there and the filmmaking mechanics are there. I hate representing anything. Because unless *everything* that I am can be represented, I don't want to represent any *one* thing. I don't want to represent just Canadian film, or just Dutch Calvinist immigrant film, or females or pink, fair-haired people. Unless all of it can be taken together, I'm not interested in being a symbol for anything."

But being a Canadian filmmaker does have its advantages. Rozema noted: "Somehow I'm never too worried about money—maybe that's absurd—but I always figure that there's *so* much money in the world and I need such a small fraction of it, that I'll find it." Most of her funding comes from the Canadian government "and a private station—[British television station] Channel 4. But one of the joys of a more socialist-leaning country, which is in danger of being overwhelmed by the American culture, is that we have money for Canadian films here. If your film is wholly Canadian, you can receive a fairly large portion of your financing. We also got money from the Canadian distributor Alliance.

"I really do believe that I can find the money to do what I want to do," said Rozema. "I might have to scale down my project. I might have to adapt to the lack of people throwing money at me. If my films are successful, it won't be a problem. But *all* you need to make a film is a camera and film, really, and persuasive powers!"

Rozema did not originally start out as a filmmaker. "I always think of myself as a writer, and that's how I thought I would make a living: telling stories," she noted. "I come from a world so in love with *facts*, that I couldn't imagine making a living with *fiction*. So I went into journalism. I felt frustrated there, because I felt I was *observing*, not *doing*. And as soon as I started *doing*, I felt I was violating the main principle of journalism, which is to let the subject speak. So, through a strange combination of circumstances, I became involved in television, and worked in brief internships in Chicago and New York at NBC stations there, and that got me a job back here at CBC [the Canadian Broadcasting Corporation] for a program called *The Journal*. I was doing research and low-level producing about short items or whatever was current. I discovered that I enjoyed technology while I was out there. I have no technophobia—I'm able to see the logic in technology. But I still was frustrated with how quickly one had to do everything and how superficially. I had to write around holes in my knowledge rather than be completely informed about a subject before I'd have to write copy for it.

"At some point I had come up with this little theory that it's good to learn facts first before you venture out into fiction—to learn how real people react in crisis and how they change, and then do your fictional characters based on that knowledge. So in the summer I was always writing stories. Of course, you can't make a film in a summer, so eventually I just spent full time on it [my writing] and got some jobs as an assistant [film] director, which meant I was hanging around film sets learning how long it takes to set up, knowing the protocol of the set, knowing who does what, learning from the group what these various pieces of equipment are called. Then I took a five-week night course in filmmaking and learned which end of the camera to stand behind and the differences in lenses and loading, et cetera. And then I made shorts that got longer. So it was a fairly gradual process over a number of years. I didn't make my first film until I was twenty-seven, which I quite regret. I wish I had been making my first mistakes when I was eighteen or nineteen."

Rozema noted that her parents are "happy to see me do well, but they don't quite understand what it is I'm doing. My parents are really quite enlightened human beings, but they do come from pretty strict-minded farming communities in northern Holland, where filmmaking is not one of the career options. It *never* crossed my mind. We didn't see film as a matter of course. It was totally outside of my experience.

"I'd say a much greater influence than journalism and television—which was more of a detour than anything else—was just reading fiction," explained Rozema. "It's all the creation of possible worlds, right? The difference between writing fiction and writing and making a feature film is really quantitative rather than qualitative, I think. The creation of fictional people in fictional worlds is the same process.

"I don't think you need to be particularly technically gifted to be a film-maker, either. I do enjoy that, but the gift you *need* is to be able to close your eyes, imagine something and describe it well. If you can't describe it well, you're stuck; if you can't imagine it well, you're stuck."

Film plays an important role in Rozema's world view: "I really do believe that we come to films for the same reason we go to religion: We want stories that tell us there *is* order. Although there's conflict, we come out okay in the end. Go ahead, leave the theater, it's worth it to keep trying. That's really what we want, again and again, on a sophisticated or a simple level. Whether or not that's always *given* by the artist is another question. *If* you want to make money, yes, do that. *If* you want to make people feel really good in their skins, yes, do that. And I did that with *Mermaids.*"

Rozema is critical of those who claim that her work is anti-feminist. "There's a strain of feminism that seems to suggest that you can only create heroic female characters. And that is the death of fiction," she explained.

"All I can do is react to my environment. I'm not a polemicist or a moralist. I don't promote certain behaviors. I look and write in reaction. My job is to feel as acutely as I can and hopefully transform that into a form that seems to serve some purpose, either pleasurable or painful or somewhere in between, for the viewer. I could never write a film where people would say, 'My films *assume* feminist principles.' It's so clear to me that there have been major injustices against women for centuries. That *has* to be changed, *is* changing and hasn't been changed enough. That's feminism. That's all."

**Patricia
Rozema**

Lourdes Portillo

You Can Only Make a Good Film If You Look Inward

Lourdes Portillo directing an actor in *After the Earthquake*

If you were to ask Lourdes Portillo for the short version of her life, she might say, as she said in 1989, "I was born in Mexico, and when I was thirteen years old, my whole family immigrated to Los Angeles. I lived in Los Angeles until I was twenty-one years old, and that's when I began getting into film. I had a friend whose father was a screenwriter for television, and she started making films and hired me; I worked with her making educational films. Then I went to Mexico and worked there for one year with another friend of mine who was an actress—this was at the time of *The Wild Bunch*, Sam Peckinpah and all that—and then I came back to the United States and started studying film. And I've studied film at different places, but I have my degree from San Francisco Art Institute."

Portillo then worked in feature-length films, where she was trained as a camera assistant through the union NABET [National Association of Broadcast Employees and Technicians]. "I worked on one of the first independent feature films in San Francisco, which was called *Over, Under, Sideways, Down*," she remembered. "It was put together by a group of Marxist filmmakers called Cinemanifest—Rob Nelson belonged to it, John Hanson, [cinematographer] Judy Irola. So that was the beginning of working as part of a crew. Then I made an application to the American Film Institute [AFI] with my friend Nina Serrano, who is a poet and a writer; we asked for money to make a film that had something to do with the Nicaraguan insurrection—at the time, the Sandinistas had not won, and we wanted to make something that was very realistic, not so much didactic and revolutionary in the sense of spouting a lot of the stuff that was happening at that time in the Nicaraguan communities. We got the money from the AFI and we started making this film—we wrote the film and we di-

Vilma Coronado in *After the Earthquake*

rected it [*After the Earthquake*, 1979]. That was first film that I made that really got out there—not in a big way, but it got a prize in Poland at the shorts film festival in Kraków."

After the Earthquake is the story of a woman who emigrates to San Francisco from Nicaragua after the 1976 earthquake. There, she works as a housekeeper and finds herself torn between the traditions of her homeland and the new world she discovers in the United States. Those conflicts become foremost in her life when her boyfriend comes to visit from Nicaragua; Portillo ends the film with the couple's conflicts unresolved. *After the Earthquake* was cutting edge in portraying Latina characters who, depending on their age and how long they had been in the United States, understood only Spanish, some both Spanish and English, and some only English.

After the success of *After the Earthquake*, Portillo decided to collaborate

Lourdes Portillo

213

Films by Lourdes Portillo

After the Earthquake

Las Madres: The Mothers of Plaza de Mayo

La Ofrenda

Columbus on Trial

The Devil Never Sleeps

on a documentary film about the group of Argentinian mothers who have been demanding information from the government on the sons and daughters who have "disappeared." "I got together with another friend of mine, Susana Muñoz," she recalled. "She was from Argentina, and we started doing our research and we went to Argentina and we started making connections with the mothers in order to make this film." Portillo and Muñoz began work on *Las Madres: The Mothers of Plaza de Mayo* in 1983, finishing the film in 1985. *Las Madres* was powerful enough to earn Portillo and Muñoz an Academy Award nomination for best documentary the year it was released.

Las Madres cost a paltry $167,000 to make. "We didn't pay ourselves any money; that saves a lot of money," noted Portillo. "We figured that we needed to make the film, we needed to hurry up and do it; it was important to do it in a certain amount of time. We couldn't get paid. So we had to struggle. If you really want to do something, you have to make sacrifices, unless you're terribly wealthy."

The success of *Las Madres* "affected our [Portillo's and Muñoz's] relationship as partners," said Portillo. "It made it very hard, because as soon as you have a little bit of acclaim, then there are things that one could receive that the other one doesn't receive; there is jealousy. I think it also spoils it for a filmmaker to have a very successful film and then make a more humble film after that. The audience is expecting more dynamite. But you have to grow as a filmmaker, and you can't be making *Las Madres* I, II and III."

Portillo and Muñoz also collaborated on the 1989 documentary *La Ofrenda* [*The Offering*], a study of the celebration of the Day of the Dead both in Mexico and by Mexican Americans in the United States. Although *La Ofrenda* did not receive the acclaim that Portillo and Muñoz's earlier collaboration had, it can still be seen in repertory cinemas and on public television almost every Halloween. "It's so different from *Las Madres*," noted Portillo. "It's about culture; it has nothing to do with injustice. I think people expected us to come up with a film about injustice and inequality. That's a sensationalistic way of looking at film. But there are other things in the Latin-American culture that have to be explored in order to round us off as human beings—we can't always be relating to the American public as victims.

"Stylistically, I think all three films [*After the Earthquake, Las Madres, La Ofrenda*] are very different," commented Portillo. "The very first film that I made was not documentary, but dramatic. I had never directed a dramatic film, but I just went into it and did it. I loved it."

In 1993, Portillo made the short video *Columbus on Trial.* To mark the five hundredth anniversary of Columbus's arrival in America, Portillo brings the explorer back from the dead and into a courtroom, where he must stand trial for the atrocities committed against the native peoples of the New World, including the rape of native women. Columbus is cross-examined on the stand by members of the Latino comedy group Culture Clash. With the video, Portillo offered two views on colonialism.

"I'm a Latin American," she explained, "I'm a Mexican, so I feel that being who I am—and in making films, you have to make films that really touch you, that really are a part of you in some way, and you can only make a good film if you look inward—so I am very interested, to put it in a superficial way, in making films about Latin Americans, but as I say, it has to do with my inner self and how close I feel to the subject. There are people who have dedicated their lives to making, say, Chicano films. I don't feel that way. I feel that I am a little bit broader in that respect. I'm interested in a lot of things: I'm interested in Brazilian music, I'm interested in the life of immigrants—deeply interested in that, because I am one.

"I think there is a big lagoon of ignorance on my part," she added, "about why I really make films, but also I have the idea that when I came to this country, people did not understand me or the culture that I came from; they had a lot of preconceived notions about who I was. I think that film is the way that I have found of rounding off characters, exploring the inner life of people, the different aspects of human drama, filling in all the elements that make a human being, and in making a human being, having that human being be understood and not be seen as a stereotype. I think that was the greatest impetus for making films, and to this day, when I think about a film, that's what I want to do—I want people to understand who I am and who the people I come from are."

Although Portillo's focus may consciously be on Latin Americans, other aspects of her experience also wend their way into her work. "I've made things unconsciously," she remarked. "I've made things that were close to me, that I was familiar with—if you're going to portray someone in film, you want to be able to do it in an honest and true way, so you do what you know most. I never consciously said, 'I'm going to make films about women's issues'; I just thought these stories were interesting, and they happened to be about women."

Financing, as it is for many women directors, has been a struggle. "Most of the films that I've made have been given grants," Portillo noted, "and I've made films for very little money. I don't think I could exist as a filmmaker if I had not made films for very little money, if I had not gotten grants, and if I did depend on filmmaking for my livelihood. *Las Madres* made some money, and we could probably live on that money for one year—and that's a whole lot of money for [an independent] film, for two people. I don't really expect to make money on filmmaking—I'm not in it to be supported by my work; it's more like a labor of love and sacrifice. I happen to have an income from something else, but that's the only reason I exist—as a filmmaker. Otherwise, I'm sure that I would not be making films as often as I do. It's like anything else, like writing—if you don't have a steady income, you cannot make it as a writer; you certainly cannot be writing all the time, you have to make a living.

"As women, we are more accustomed to disappointment, and we also are more accustomed to persevering," she noted. "I don't think it's any easier for men [in independent film] than it is for women—if anything, we can take the punches a little better, because we're used to it.

"I don't think that people [in the film industry] have as much confidence in women. In Hollywood, they'll give a film to a twenty-five-year-old guy to direct—no sweat. There could be a woman who's been working, trying to get a feature for the last ten years, who is capable, can do a beautiful film—she won't get the job. It comes from the top: It comes from the producers, it comes from the distributors, it comes from their decisions how far a filmmaker can get. Basically, it's the producers or the big studios. If they decide that you're going to make money for them, they're going to push you. You can be a Martian; it doesn't matter. But somehow the issues that women deal with are not interesting to those men, and not interesting enough to promote. Our issues are irrelevant in the world of Hollywood cinema. To compromise, in this regard, never gets you anywhere. Sometimes you have to compromise as a filmmaker because everything goes wrong. But in making a film, if you want to make a lot of money, then you make trash. If you want to continue, if you want to be an artist, and you want to pursue your career and develop as an artist, then you have to be pretty uncompromising; you have to retain your ethics. There's no other way."

Portillo does point to differences in being a Latina working in the American film industry. "I think it's going to be much more difficult for me to make a dramatic film, a feature-length film, than it would have been for Susan Seidelman or for Lizzie Borden; I think I'm going to come up against some real, heavy-duty problems," she noted in 1989. "I don't know of what sort, but I think, first of all, that culturally I'm different than they are—I relate to people in a different way. There's a certain aggressiveness that you need in film in order to get your way. I have a hard time being very aggressive and very assertive even though I know what I

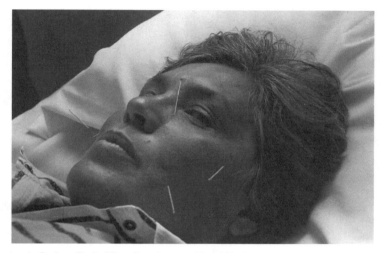

Lourdes Portillo in *The Devil Never Sleeps* (courtesy of Xochitl Films)

want. It's a cultural difference. I have to remain with my integrity intact and try to do the things that I want to do. I'll just get a son-of-a-bitch for a producer."

Portillo noted that directing a dramatic film is easier than directing a documentary. "I've made short dramatic films—if I'd gone on shooting for five or six more days, I would have had a feature," she laughed. "You have more control over everything [with a dramatic film]. You can repeat things, whereas in documentary, you just catch what you can."

Portillo mixed fact and fiction, documentary and drama, in her 1995 film *The Devil Never Sleeps*. Ostensibly about the mysterious circumstances surrounding her uncle's death in Mexico, *The Devil Never Sleeps* also studies Portillo's own connections with Mexico and Mexican culture. The film received funding from the Independent Television Service (ITVS) and the National Latino Communications Center, and was broadcast on public television in addition to its film festival screenings.

Portillo has three adolescent sons—"It's like being in production all the time," she joked. "They see the films, usually before anyone else; they come when I'm working and I show it to them. They're very harsh, so I have to laugh, or something. I actually admire what they have to say, but it's so harsh sometimes.

"I think there is a very hungry audience for things that are different, for things that they have never seen in film," said Portillo. "I don't make offensive films—I try to make films that illuminate upon the human experience. That is my goal in life—to make those types of films."

Zeinabu irene Davis

A Powerful Thang

African-American film-maker Zeinabu irene Davis is now reaching a much larger audience. Her most recent film, 1995's *Mother of the River*, was funded by the Independent Television Service (ITVS) for public television broadcast, which must seem like a triumph to Davis, whose 1991 video *A Period Piece* was rejected by Black Entertainment Television (BET)—"they said the production values weren't up to their standards," noted Davis, eyebrow raised.

Zeinabu irene Davis (photograph by Matthew Gilson; courtesy of Women Make Movies)

Davis, who originally hails from Philadelphia, Pennsylvania, went to the University of California at Los Angeles (UCLA) to study film. "UCLA is a public institution, so that made a big difference in terms of being able to finance my [own] education," said Davis. "And [there] you did get to see the belly of the beast; you did get to see up close and personal what the Hollywood thing is really all about, and whether or not you want to participate in it. Unfortunately, when I was there, there was a drought of people of color. It isn't so bad now, but in the mid-1980s there were very few students of color and, in particular, no black women in the program. Out of a few hundred students, we were lucky if there were five of us at any given time.

Still from *Cycles* (courtesy of Women Make Movies)

"I wouldn't say that many of the teachers were not supportive—there *were* teachers who certainly were supportive—but you did have to be a fairly strong person to get through that system. I had particular battles with a screenwriting professor who said that I couldn't write, my work was shit—he made it look like it was okay to use this language to a student. You develop a certain armor that you know will help you after you finish graduate school. I learned a lot from the filmmakers who had gone to UCLA just before me, particularly Julie Dash [*Daughters of the Dust*, 1991] and Charles Burnett [*To Sleep with Anger*, 1990; *The Glass Shield*, 1995]. Those were the folks who really helped me develop an aesthetic sensibility and practical production techniques that were not necessarily being taught in the classroom."

Davis's own work focuses more on her humor than her anger, with a highly developed sense of irony. Her 1989 black-and-white film *Cycles* is about a woman's attempt to control her life through her belief in the spiritual. The main character, Rasheeda, prays for her period. She cleans her house, cleans herself and prepares other offerings to the spirit to "fix" the problem. *A Period Piece* (1991) is a hilarious rap video about menstruation and what the culture tells women about "confidence" and "security." Two women (one the filmmaker) rap about confidence, using tampons as microphones, as women of various races are shown getting their periods at the wrong moment.

A Powerful Thang (1991), Davis's first longer work, has the same feminist power and drive as her short pieces, as well as a cohesive story line that addresses all parts of the African-American community—including feminists and lesbians. The story of an emerging relationship between a writer and a saxophonist, *A Powerful Thang* is about emotional and sexual intimacy. Safe sex is also an issue in the film, very neatly tied into the plot (as is the lesbianism, which is treated as nothing out of the ordinary). The film also boasts performances by Edwina Lee Tyler, the lesbian drummer, who is the first black woman in the United States to play African drums (traditionally a male preserve).

Davis's latest film, *Mother of the River*, tells the story of a young girl who meets an injured woman in the woods. The tale, which is found throughout Africa and the African diaspora, is a parable about independence, honor, humility and respect for others. Davis resets the story in the antebellum South, with a young slave girl meeting Mother of the River, who has been injured by a bullet.

Although conceived of as a children's film, *Mother of the River*, with its atmospheric use of black-and-white film, is also captivating

Joy Vandervort, Adrienne M. Coleman and Michael L. Nesbitt in *Mother of the River* (photo by Timothy D. Harper; courtesy of Women Make Movies)

for adults. Davis was initially criticized for using black and white and was told that kids wouldn't like a black-and-white film. Davis noted that just the opposite was true, with *Mother of the River* winning awards for children's programming, "so I felt vindicated."

Davis funds her films with a combination of grants and her salary from a teaching post at Northwestern University in Evanston, Illinois. For *A Powerful Thang*, Davis sold T-shirts with the film's logo on them to help raise money for the film. She also has sold videotapes of previous

Zeinabu irene Davis

221

Films by Zeinabu irene Davis

Crocodile Conspiracy

Cycles

A Period Piece

A Powerful Thang

Mother of the River

works—"you name it, we've tried it," she noted.

Davis is committed to filmmaking from the African diaspora—blacks descended from the peoples of Africa, the Caribbean and various other points who now live in the United States. "I take my culture from all over the world—West Africa, Haiti, Kenya, the former U.S.S.R. My films are informed by that culture." Davis noted, "Our history as African-American women has been obscured, but we didn't just start making movies." She said one reason black women weren't represented in Hollywood films was because they weren't part of the "system." "Black women in particular aren't going to be incorporated into this system because we don't have [family] in Hollywood to give us jobs. So we come out of the film school experience, like myself."

Davis also points to the differences between films made by African-American men and those made by African-American women. "Black women tend to choose documentaries as a forum because we are re-creating those images we haven't seen of ourselves—heroes, role models, whatever you want to call them. You'll see lots of issues of identity in black women's films because we are still struggling with our identity and not having seen our history on film." When asked what black male filmmakers like Spike Lee and Robert Townsend are doing to help black women filmmakers, Davis said, "Spike doesn't have much to do with black women filmmakers, and Robert Townsend—well, he has his own agenda, he's not much interested in anyone else."

Davis said that while black male filmmakers were getting a lot of attention in the mainstream, particularly television, directors such as Julie Dash were unable to find distribution for their feature-length work. "Finding distribution is a big issue for black women," she noted. The same problem is true, however, for black male filmmakers who are working on alternative styles of filmmaking, like Charles Burnett, who has been a strong supporter of black women filmmakers, including Davis and Dash.

Davis points to the inequalities that black women filmmakers suffer: "When a Julie Dash or a Darnell Martin [*I Like It Like That*, 1994] gets to go to Sundance [Film Festival] and win awards for her work, it's not like you then have people banging down the door and offering to give her money to do the next film, whereas you've got people like Tom Noonan

[*What Happened Was . . .* , 1994] who relatively immediately get sucked into the system and offered an opportunity to continue to do their work. We don't see that kind of thing happening with African-American women or pretty much anybody of color, maybe with the exception of some African-American men."

Davis, who is known for including lesbian characters in her films, stated that there have been more films by black lesbians in the past six years, but also noted that there have been more films overall by lesbians. "Filmmaker Cheryl Dunye [*The Watermelon Woman*, 1995] spoke to a lot of voices that were not visible before, and I think in this particular community, once her work started to get out and other people saw it and accepted it, then there was a lot of other work that became more prominent. I don't think it wasn't being done before; it was, but it wasn't being exhibited to the degree that it is now."

To Davis, mainstream films made for black female audiences can be dangerous. "*Waiting to Exhale* [1995] is a particularly dangerous film in a lot of ways," said Davis, "because the film, to me, promoted the idea that black women had an 'enemy,' and the enemy was, more often than not, in the film, labeled as the white woman, which is totally ridiculous, stupid, divisive, asinine. It also had this thing that black women should be striving for men, and that pissed me off, too. A lot of people, including myself, fed into that kind of hope for this film, that this was going to finally be a story that could somehow reflect African-American women's lives. Certainly, we've now seen that it doesn't matter whether there are black people in positions of relative power in Hollywood or not—a Hollywood film is going to be a Hollywood film."

Davis is currently at work on another longer, black-and-white film, titled *Compensation*, a love story based on a poem by Paul Laurence Dunbar and featuring a black deaf woman as one of the leads. "I'm a little frustrated," Davis noted, "because I shot this film before I started *Mother of the River*. I tried to edit both of them at the same time, but it got too crazy, and I had to concentrate on finishing up one."

Davis is working in black and white, which, though cheaper than color film, is not without its disadvantages: "The major problem is that there are so few black-and-white labs left," noted Davis. "I had to send my film out [to the west coast] for processing—it was kind of painful to have to wait that long to make sure you have an image on the film." When Davis first began shooting *Compensation* in 1993, there was a Detroit laboratory that processed black-and-white film, but "that lab has since left. It's been frustrating to lose some of the resources I had, but I get the work done."

Davis said she chooses black and white "because *Mother of the River* and *Compensation* are stories that have a connection to specific time periods, which are not contemporary; I think that shooting in black and white aesthetically gives you a sense of timelessness. I think that's more powerful for the kind of stories I wanted to tell."

Donna Deitch

Desert Hearts and Beyond

Donna Deitch will probably go down in film history for being the first woman to direct a mainstream lesbian feature film. That film—1985's *Desert Hearts*—was Deitch's first feature and is perhaps the piece she is best known for.

Desert Hearts, based on a novel by Canadian writer Jane Rule, was the first mainstream film about a lesbian relation-

Donna Deitch

ship in which neither woman is killed, commits suicide or runs off with a man. In *Desert Hearts*, the two women actually end up together, a first for mainstream cinema.

Films by Donna Deitch

Desert Hearts

The Women of Brewster Place

"Esperanza"

Deitch began her career as a painter. A native San Franciscan, she attended the University of California at Berkeley during the pivotal 1960s. She moved from painting to still photography and then began doing photographs in a series. Her first films were experimental. "When I was in film school [at the University of California, Los Angeles]," Deitch said, "I said to this friend of mine who was a boy inventor, 'Let's make an optical printer—let's build one.' And he said, 'What's that?'

And six months later, it was built. We used to produce all these [optical] effects, we even had a little business going called Latent Image. We would do special effects consulting for student films and industrial films. It was all about manipulating images. That was all very fun, but you had to be very clean to do it, because any dust was a menace to the film. So eventually we had to get out of that, because we couldn't handle all the dust, and I started making documentaries."

Deitch made a short documentary on the free speech movement at People's Park in Berkeley, and then made several short films on women's lives, women "who are finding out things about their own lives."

Of her first feature, *Desert Hearts*, Deitch said: "I made it for myself—it was a film I wanted to see. A film had not been made about a positive lesbian relationship—there had been no positive cinematic roles for lesbians. I bought the rights to Jane Rule's book [*Desert of the Heart*] in 1979. It took two and a half years to raise the money; the shooting took six weeks. Then I had to raise more money to finish it. It was cut in twelve weeks and then I had to take it around to sell it. It took about five years in all from beginning to end. And while I'd do other independent projects again, I wouldn't want to have to raise money that way again."

The money for the film came primarily from independent investors. When Deitch took the finished film to different studios to find a distributor, she didn't encounter any problems over the lesbian theme. "In fact, I found myself in the middle of a bidding war over the film," she said. Samuel Goldwyn Studios, who later released Rose Troche's and Guinevere Turner's *Go Fish* in 1994, won.

Of the explosion of lesbian-themed films that were released starting with *Go Fish*, Deitch said, "*Desert Hearts* was definitely ahead of its time in the sense that had I made that movie now, I think that it would have crossed over or attracted even a much wider audience, and in every way been more 'mainstream.' Somebody gave me this book—one of those books you get in an airport or a drugstore—something like *101 Ways to be Romantic*. It had a list of ten or twelve movies to stay at home and rent, and *Desert Hearts* was on that list, which was so astonishing to me because, really, it was one of those books you'd pick up in an airport. So that was a pretty mainstream spot to be."

Chemistry, Deitch noted, is important when a film is a love story. "Casting is such an important part of a love story." Of filming the love scenes in *Desert Hearts*, Deitch recalled, "The actresses [Helen Shaver and Patricia Charbonneau] were wonderful. Helen had had some bad experiences filming heterosexual love scenes, and this was Patricia's first [love] scene. She says that it was easier with a woman, and I think that Helen felt that way, too. And, of course, there was a closed set. But I think it works because the scene is part of the plot of the film. In fact, we filmed the big scene before we filmed the scene of the kiss in the rain and I had to say, hey, slow down, this is your first kiss, remember? In so many films, the sex scenes seem dropped in, gratuitous. They were a full part of this plot line and I think it worked because of that."

Helen Shaver and Patricia Charbonneau in *Desert Hearts*

Deitch's second mainstream directing effort was *The Women of Brewster Place*, made in 1989 as a miniseries for ABC. Based on Gloria Naylor's novel about seven black women, including a lesbian couple, *Brewster Place* was twice as long as *Desert Hearts* and twice as controversial. Some black women directors were critical of the choice of Deitch as director, saying that a black woman should have been chosen. One black woman director thought Deitch was chosen for the assignment because of the lesbian element in *Brewster Place*, commenting "Maybe they thought she'd be more sensitive to lesbian themes."

Deitch thinks she was chosen because she's a good director and *Desert Hearts* had been a success. "I think the final reason I was chosen for the project was because the producers thought I had an ability to bring humor

Donna Deitch

Donna Deitch directing Oprah Winfrey in *The Women of Brewster Place*

to the surface in a nonhumorous situation. At that time, there hadn't been a black woman director on a TV miniseries or for a major feature and, though I think my not being black was an issue, there were black producers, including Oprah Winfrey, on the project, and I had a good script and great actors. So I felt the project would work."

Deitch sums up the controversy with a story about a trip to New York City just after *Brewster Place* aired: "I was in a cab and I asked my driver, a black woman, if she had seen it. She rather sarcastically said that every black woman in America had seen it. Then I told her it was my film, and she pulled the cab over and wouldn't stop talking about it. She loved it, and she didn't want to let me out of her cab."

Deitch ignored the reviews of *Brewster Place*, which were uniformly poor. She said that reviews and criticism are subjective—"everybody has their own opinion." She believes a director basically makes a film for herself and then the audience follows.

"The more controversial a project is, the more you're likely to find extreme reactions," she said. "People hate it or really love it. When you're making a movie, everybody has an opinion—the people in your crew, everybody. But you're still the one making the film."

Brewster Place's poor reviews didn't keep Deitch out of television. In 1991, she was hired by Home Box Office (HBO) to direct a segment of *Prison Stories: Women on the Inside*, a feature-length trilogy. Penelope Spheeris (*Wayne's World*, *The Beverly Hillbillies*) and Joan Micklin Silver (*Crossing Delancey*) each directed another segment. Deitch's segment appears in the middle of the film, even though it was shot first. "They strung them all together," said Deitch. "It was three stories about life in a women's prison. We all used the same set. Because I did the first one, I was rather involved in the putting up of the set—the first one on sort of has more say about that, only because you have to be there. It was low budget, so naturally we all shot in the same place. They were supposed to take place in the same prison—the stories were just about different people."

In addition to having up-and-coming women directors, *Prison Stories* also featured up-and-coming women actors: Deitch's segment, "Esperanza," starred Rachel Ticotin, who later garnered the female lead in Paul Verhoeven's *Total Recall* (1990), while Spheeris's and Silver's segments featured Rae Dawn Chong and Lolita Davidovich, respectively.

Deitch currently directs television dramas: You'll find her name under the "directed by" title of episodes of *NYPD Blue*, *ER* and *Murder One*. She's also directed series pilot episodes for shows such as *Second Noah*. "I was an independent filmmaker—I like to the think of myself as that," said Deitch, "but in that world there's something of a difficult transition into any more bureaucratic structure, whether television or studio filmmaking, coming out of that independent world." Although she would happily go back to independent films again, Deitch added, "I don't know that I would go back to it in the way I did *Desert Hearts*. I don't want to go back to spending vast amounts of my time raising money. I love the process of making independent films, but I don't like the business of raising money."

Deitch, tired of the male vision of women's lives on the screen, thinks it is essential that women get their own visions of their lives into film and that more women direct films: "Women don't have equal access to do what men do. The opportunities for women are mirrored in society at large. There are more women directors now than there were ten or even five years ago. But this is a society run by men, so it isn't surprising that they are in control of the film industry as well." Deitch believes women directors have a responsibility to employ other women on their films and portray women responsibly on screen.

Deitch is developing some feature projects and working on final postproduction of a documentary. Titled *The Angel on My Shoulder*, the feature-length film is, she said, "about my best friend, Gwen Welles, who was an actress, who was in *Nashville* and a bunch of Henry Jaglom movies and some Robert Altman films. Gwen lived in my back cottage. She got cancer. And we decided to document her time with cancer. It was a free-flowing sort of enterprise, which we would shoot on Hi8 video when we felt like it. Gwen died in 1993, and the footage sat around, and then I finally cut it, and then it sat around for another year because I had to write a voiceover narration for it, and I never knew what to say. So it sat around while I figured that out. Now all I actually have to do is mix it. Gwen was extremely forthright—she was very funny, and brilliant, and very beautiful—all the elements that are wonderful to have as a major character in a movie. It's very intense. I shot the whole thing myself. It was the quintessential low-budget independent film."

Deitch noted that "documentarians are always traveling off—like that brilliant job Barbara Kopple did with the coal miners [*Harlan County, U.S.A.*, which won an Academy Award for best feature-length documentary in 1976]—she spent years down there. That was far from home. And that's what documentarians often have to do, they have to move into somebody's town or house or country. And here, with *The Angel on My Shoulder*, all this took place in my backyard, and we [Welles and Deitch] had a preexisting relationship. It was an obvious thing to do. I feel pretty good about the film. It had been so many years since I'd done an independent film, it was really wonderful to get back to that."

Radha Bharadwaj

Coming Out of Closet Land

Not all critical acclaim propels a woman filmmaker to directorial stardom. When women directors choose to break ground, the result can be devastating controversy. Radha Bharadwaj found out just how complicated the impact of the female gaze can be when her feature film, *Closet Land* (1991), debuted. A powerful and frightening neorealistic foray into the realms of torture and sexual abuse and how they intersect, *Closet Land* is a singularly political film, from a distinctly female vantage point. The director's experience after the film premiered was torturous in its own right— Bharadwaj found herself assailed for both the film's succinct anti-torture politics and the stylized manner in which she presented her narrative.

After having won a highly coveted and prestigious Nicholl Screenwriting Fellowship sponsored by the Academy of Motion Picture Arts and Sciences in 1989 for her *Closet Land* script, Bharadwaj also had her screenplay chosen for study by the 1990 Sundance Institute screenwriting lab. That auspicious preproduction experience did not carry over post-premiere. *Closet Land* received mixed reviews in the United States, some of them searingly misogynistic and vitriolic. Bharadwaj, who had been hailed as a rising star in the United States and abroad, described her experience as "a complete bashing," which she found sexist and racist at its core.

The first feature film about political torture directed by a woman, *Closet Land* was definitely pathbreaking. But unlike previous films addressing the issue of political torture, like Constantin Costa-Gavras's *Z* (1969) or Richard Bugajski's *Interrogation* (1982, which was considered so subversive by the Polish government that it was banned and had to be smuggled out of the country for distribution), Bharadwaj's film received wide theatrical release beyond art-house and repertory cinemas, in part because it was co-produced by director Ron Howard and distributed by his company, Imagine Films Entertainment. However, mainstream audiences found the graphic nature of the film disturbing and critics seemed to understand neither the film's narrative nor its politics.

"They just didn't get it," Bharadwaj said succinctly of the film's critics.

Although *Closet Land* was her first feature film, Bharadwaj already had a strong background in film, television and theater prior to her American debut. A native of Madras, India, Bharadwaj worked in various capacities in documentary and industrial filmmaking in India and was a freelance playwright for Madras Television. Her award-winning work in India included a radio play, *Kuralkal,* which won the National Award in 1983. Her teleplay *Ammavukku Theriyakodathu* was rated one of the best ever previewed by a 1983 audience survey—the same year Bharadwaj won the Tamil Nadu Award for best playwright and best director.

She lived in Madras until moving to the United States in 1982 to study film at Temple University in Philadelphia. After receiving a master's degree from Temple, Bharadwaj taught film and film theory at Villanova University in suburban Philadelphia. In Philadelphia she met and married attorney David Barrett Cohen, whose work with Amnesty International provided the impetus for writing *Closet Land*. She explained, "David had always wanted to do something that would take the commitment to human rights further. I responded to his suggestion immediately and wrote the script."

Closet Land was not Bharadwaj's first script and certainly won't be her last, although to date it is her only film. She spent years writing screenplays and, since *Closet Land*, has returned to screenwriting for feature films as a full-time occupation. Her experience with *Closet Land* was a perilous debut, due to the risky nature of her subject matter, her femaleness and her

youth—she was merely thirty when the film premiered. Yet in the intervening years since the film's initial release, *Closet Land* has garnered a strong independent audience and has been used for course instruction in numerous film classes, under-

Radha Bharadwaj directing Alan Rickman in *Closet Land*

scoring the groundbreaking nature of the film. In addition, Bharadwaj has received a great deal of response from survivors of torture.

"A number of torture victims have told me that *Closet Land* truly captures the psychological reality of their experience," Bharadwaj said. "If *Closet Land* had been as pretentious as some of these reviewers claimed it was, the former victims who so strongly identify with the film would have been able to smell it a mile away. And they would certainly never have responded to a movie that degraded their harrowing life experience to the level of 'porno chic,' a fashionably flippant characterization of [some of the film's critics]."

Closet Land is disturbingly and stunningly beautiful, a purposeful juxtaposition with its grim subject built into Bharadwaj's vision. She wanted the interrogation chamber (which is the sole set in the film) in the unnamed place of the story to act as a third character in the two-character confrontation. "I wanted the film to be as monochromatic as possible," said Bharadwaj. "I didn't want any color unless it was used for a specific reason. A few drops of blood then become a vivid statement."

Radha Bharadwaj

233

The complex and eerily claustrophobic sets were designed by world-renowned Japanese artist Eiko Ishioka, who was nominated for two Tony awards for her sets for Broadway's *M. Butterfly*, for which she received several other design awards. Her production designs for Paul Schrader's *Mishima* (1985) were so dazzling they won her an award for Artistic Contribution at the Cannes International Film Festival in 1985. Bharadwaj added another heavyweight for the score—minimalist composer Phillip Glass.

The film is also powerfully acted by its two-person cast of the ethereal but tenacious Madeleine Stowe and Alan Rickman at his most villainous. But it was the film's concept that caused the controversy.

The director believes the response to her film not only focused on her gender, but also on her race. "I think many people are afraid of the film," she explained. "They don't know how to categorize the film, and they think that as an Indian woman I should be making films about Third World poverty, films that they can distance themselves from and that they can feel comfortable with—that they can feel superior toward; films that reaffirm their stereotypical ideas about what kinds of films a woman of color would direct. They think I'm a little brown woman who should be making little brown films. They would have liked me to set the film squarely in the Third World so they could say, once again, 'Look how terrible *those* people are,' and distance themselves completely from the issues in the film." Bharadwaj adds that *Closet Land*—its politics as well as her direction—"flies in the face of their preconceptions." She explained how the film "provoked a predictably polarized response—people either love it or hate it. But where many people have missed the point is in not understanding that this film doesn't attempt to *literally* depict the physical reality of political interrogation. I'm more intrigued by the psychological experience—the disorientation, the absurdity, the terror. That's why *Closet Land* unfolds in a Kafka-esque environment grounded more in nightmare logic than gritty reality."

Criticism of the film often degenerated into criticism of the filmmaker, a problem women directors frequently face. *Village Voice* reviewer Amy Taubin stated the film had only been made because the producers wanted to assuage their white guilt by making a film directed by a woman of color. Well-known film critic Roger Ebert, who reviews film for the *Chicago Sun-Times* as well as for the syndicated TV program *Siskel and Ebert*, alleged the film's premise was based in the realm of fantasy—because women were not political prisoners. (The United Nations annual report on the status of women contradicts that fallacy; women represent close to seventy percent of all political prisoners worldwide.) Ebert also termed the film "sexism in reverse" because the film focuses on a female protagonist and a villainous male torturer. *Los Angeles Times* critic Kevin Thomas's review reiterated the complaints of many reviewers. He wrote, " . . . surely anyone with the slightest degree of awareness of what's going on in the world knows of the horrible plight of political prisoners subjected to unspeakable torture. Consequently, why should anyone subject himself or herself to this pretentious and contrived two-person drama which punishes the audience rather than enlightens it?"

Such sexist and racist critiques repeat within the mainstream, as evidenced by Leonard Maltin's comments on the film in *Leonard Maltin's 1997 Movie and Video Guide*. Maltin, the most-read film critic in the United States, writes scathingly of *Closet Land*, calling it, "Among the oddest of early '90s films: a two-character drama about the political interrogation of an allegedly subversive children's author by one of a totalitarian society's finest. Like a bad play that never went beyond workshop status, though no one can accuse the filmmakers [sic] of taking the easy way out. Well performed, under the circumstances. Co-produced by Ron Howard." Maltin gives it a "worst" rating—one tenuous step up from "bomb." Maltin's "bad play" comment is certainly belied by the Nicholl Fellowship Bharadwaj won, while the mention of Howard's role appears to validate Taubin's criticism.

Key in these critiques of the film is how reviewers have misunderstood Bharadwaj's intent and how hard she worked to get the film made. She believes that such criticism minimized to tokenism her struggle to find financial backing for the film and reduced the film "to a feminist tract." It also misses the point of the film overall. Bharadwaj adds that "the bad reviews all focused on what each critic thought I couldn't do as a director— but none focused on what I *did* do."

What Bharadwaj did was make a first film that was released as a major feature in mainstream theaters—a feat few male directors have pulled off. And Bharadwaj had never actually made a film before *Closet Land*. "I managed to graduate from film school with a script as my thesis, without ever having made a scrap of film," she admitted. As for those castigating the film's stylized production values, the director noted simply, "We made the picture in twenty days. I brought it in on time and under budget. And I don't believe a picture has to be poorly made and look grainy and ugly to be important and serious."

The budget for *Closet Land* is part of the dramatic history of the film and received a great deal of press. Bharadwaj had been writing scripts on speculation since she completed her film degree at Temple in 1985. Her husband, David Barrett Cohen, read an article on African-American director Robert Townsend that said he made *Hollywood Shuffle* (1987) on money borrowed from his credit cards. Cohen suggested Bharadwaj make a film on money from *his* credit cards—a total budget of $40,000. He told her if it took place in one room, with only two characters, it would be feasible. Taking the initial idea, Bharadwaj wrote the script for *Closet Land* in two months and began trying to sell the idea to producers. She had five offers to buy the script or to co-direct with a more experienced director, but Bharadwaj wanted to make the film her way and on her terms. "I figured if no one would give me money then I'd just take David's money and make the film the way I wanted on the $40,000," she said.

The film *was* made on a small budget—by film standards ($1.8 million). But it was produced by director Ron Howard (*Apollo 13*) and Brian Grazer of Imagine Films Entertainment, who were alerted to the script by Jack Healey, then executive director of Amnesty International in the United States. Grazer acknowledged the controversial elements of the film, noting "*Closet Land* was an extreme departure from our more mainstream films," but that it attracted him because "it's really a celebration of life." As for the decision to allow first-time director Bharadwaj to direct her own script, Grazer's explanation was succinct. "Radha is definite, decisive and absolute—everything a good director must be. Her passion for directing the film was so seductive, her writing so detailed and specific, that I knew she would be quite capable."

Closet Land is about a woman (played by Madeleine Stowe), a children's book author, who is arrested in the middle of the night for alleged subversive activities. A man (played by Alan Rickman) questions her, torturing her emotionally, psychologically and physically. Interwoven in the theme of political torture is the parallel theme of sexual abuse of children and women and the complicity of both victim and torturer in the degradation of both acts. As *Closet Land* unfolds, the viewer begins to see how traumatic experiences in the life of the author (which have made her books vivid enough to gain the attention of the State) are also what allow her to survive this current experience of torture. A complicated relationship develops between torturer and victim, blurring the lines between captor and captive. It is a harrowing and complex film, with stellar performances from both actors. The film, which takes place in one room, has a set fitted with exquisite furnishings and gadgets. Bharadwaj said that some people complained the film is too beautiful, to which she countered, "I wanted to remind people of the mentality, so clearly evoked by the Nazis, that yearned for, was striving for, physical beauty and perfection—the mentality of people who can play chamber music on violins by night and gas six million [people] by day."

It is just this sort of uncompromising vision that makes *Closet Land* such a disturbing and compelling film, and Bharadwaj such a figure of controversy. In India she began writing and directing plays at the age of twelve. She repeatedly dealt with controversial or taboo subjects, including one play about two men who were lovers. "Homosexuality isn't discussed in India, so this was very radical," she noted.

She was led to film by her interest in filmmakers such as Jean Renoir, Ingmar Bergman and Federico Fellini and by her desire for perfection as a director of plays. "As I stood backstage I would always think, why can't I preserve what's best in each performance?" she explained.

Closet Land certainly ranks as a performance worthy of notice for a debuting director, and Bharadwaj was angry that so many critics misread the film, fearing the negative criticism would kill the film's sales and distribution. "I think it's important that people see that these issues exist within the context of our own experience, not just in some gulag somewhere, or some dank Latin American prison," Bharadwaj noted. "This film is about how any one of us could cross over the line and become either torturer or victim—because there are only fine lines separating them. It's about how one form of torture, of inhumanity to another person, can lead to others. People have said, 'Oh, we know all about this.' But if we know all about it, why does it keep happening?"

Another problem Bharadwaj believes critics had with the film was the importance she placed on the sexual abuse of women and children. "There is a real resistance," she asserted, "to discussing this [sexual abuse of women and children] as torture, yet that is what it is. So I think many people—women too—were very resistant to the parallels I was drawing in the film.

Radha Bharadwaj

237

Closet Land springs from my belief that all forms of aggression are organically linked. Most who have grown up in the sheltered West have no direct experience with the pathology of political abuse and consider it alien. By likening political abuse to something more accessible to Westerners—child abuse—I can give people a better feel for the paternalistic power dynamics of political abuse." And, Bharadwaj added, there's a larger point. "Though the Western democracy is the antithesis of the police state, Western society harbors psychological pathologies that, under the wrong circumstances, can form the basis of a police state."

But that concept underlies the main political message within the film and acts as a metaphor for the personal nature of the political. Bharadwaj said *Closet Land* "likens large-scale political oppression to the conditions in one's own heart. The biggest thing that you can do is make people look into themselves and question their own violence—whether they are the abusers or the victims—and wonder why."

Bharadwaj said her desire is for the film's message to strike a blow against apathy. "We become apathetic both politically and personally," she asserted. "We pretend that we're not seeing what we're seeing. As George Bernard Shaw says, in order to fight evil, you have to confront it. You have to stare it in the face, look at it, accept its existence—and only then can you fight it."

Bharadwaj explained she wants to make the kind of films that make people think. She also wants her experience of directing *Closet Land* to make people think. "I hoped that other young women would look at my film and at how I did it and take heart, that they could do it too," she explained. "I still think they can do that. But what also must be seen is that directing is still the preserve of the white male, and women and people of color have not been accepted yet. There is room in Hollywood for a woman of color directing big, important, serious films that are not stereotypical. I don't want to start playing safe. I don't intend to."

Jan Oxenberg

Scowling Jan

Imagine Woody Allen reincarnated as a lesbian, and you have some idea of what Jan Oxenberg, filmmaker and screenwriter, is all about.

Like Allen, Oxenberg is very, very funny. Sometimes it's that side-splitting kind of humor that makes us laugh until we cry, but more often it's the subtle kind of irony that takes everyday life and transforms it into satiric metaphor. Like Allen, Oxenberg is New York Jewish through and through, serving bagels and lox (with "two-cents plain" seltzer, of course) to her luncheon guests. Like Allen, Oxenberg is a superb filmmaker, a chronicler of her own life on the big screen. And like Allen, Oxenberg takes the intensely personal parts of her life and transforms them into pieces that anyone can identify with. As Allen

Jan Oxenberg (photo by Kelly Linvil; courtesy of *Curve* magazine)

Films by Jan Oxenberg

Home Movie

I'm Not One of Them

A Comedy in Six Unnatural Acts

Thank You and Good Night

is Kleinman or Everyman, Oxenberg is Everydyke. Her films evoke the range of lesbian experience in the last gasping decades of the twentieth century: a compelling and moving vision that is also very, very funny.

Oxenberg has made a series of films, done work for the Public Broadcasting System (PBS) and cable television and, since the resounding success of her film *Thank You and Good Night* (1991), has turned her considerable talents to writing for film and television. Oxenberg is one of the writers who penned the short-lived but applauded television series *relativity*, and is credited with making an openly lesbian character part of the show.

Oxenberg was only twenty-one when she made her first film, *Home Movie* (1972), a groundbreaking short about coming out. The film, like the director's later work, is autobiographical, thoughtful and intensely satirical. The film intercuts home movies from the director's childhood with scenes from her adult life. Oxenberg juxtaposes these images nicely—home movies of her days as a high school cheerleader vie with scenes of a lesbian football game. Oxenberg gives an ironic voiceover description of the counterposed images, uncovering the dichotomy of who she was versus who and what she perceived herself to be. Lesbianism, therefore, is always in the wings of Oxenberg's early, seemingly "normal" and "heterosexual" childhood and adolescence; *Home Movie* expresses how the filmmaker was clearly directed by an internalized lesbian sensibility, despite her appearance of conformity with heterosexuality.

Home Movie was the first independent short on the lesbian coming-out process to be shown widely in theaters and at festivals, repertories and other public screenings. The film was followed by another short, *I'm Not One of Them* (1974), in which Oxenberg once again explores the dichotomy of lesbianism and perceived lesbianism, using the vehicle of a woman attending that lesbian-encoded icon of seventies exhibitionism, the roller derby. (The roller derby film *Kansas City Bomber* starring Raquel Welch was a box-office smash the year *I'm Not One of Them* was released. Today, golf tournaments like the Dinah Shore Classic have replaced the roller derby as lesbian events, but no lesbian director has yet attempted to juxtapose the golf circuit groupies with the closeted lesbian element of the game itself.)

A pioneer of lesbian filmmaking, Oxenberg addresses lesbian life from

Narrative Film

240

the inside—these are films in which the lesbian is not the "Other" but the affirmed protagonist, films in which lesbian life is not hidden or marginalized but explored using accessible and readily identifiable images. In *A Comedy in Six Unnatural Acts* (1975), a searingly funny and smartly ironic take on lesbian stereotypes, Oxenberg examines how straight society and lesbians themselves view the "lesbian lifestyle." A film very much ahead of its time, *A Comedy in Six Unnatural Acts* is an extremely clever parody of homophobia and anti-lesbian bias reminiscent of films like the now-classic "exposé" *Reefer Madness* (1936), expressed as it is in the mode of a well-articulated "documentary" of the "evil" lesbian. Early showings of the film, however, aroused protests from activists who felt the film was too subtle to be understood as parody by nonlesbian audiences. But in the seventies Oxenberg tended to show her early films to women-only and lesbian-only audiences and stated clearly to interviewers that her films were made specifically for lesbian audiences.

After a long hiatus from filmmaking in which she worked on scriptwriting and raised money for her own film projects, Oxenberg completed her first feature-length film, *Thank You and Good Night* (1991), which was distributed theatrically and later shown nationally in the United States on PBS.

"It's been wonderful and very, very gratifying to see the response [*Thank You and Good Night*] has gotten—both critically and from audiences," said Oxenberg. "I think that the film deals with a subject—death—that most people want to avoid. I read a book by Ernest Becker where he refutes Freud, saying that the underlying human motivation is not sex, but denial of death. Sex, he says, just *reminds* people of death. But if we avoid the emotions that are called up by confronting death, then we shut off access to a whole range of emotions within ourselves. So I think we have to face death as part of life." Oxenberg added, with her characteristic dry humor, "I mean, I don't think about death every minute of every day—like right now I'm more worried about the plumbing problems I'm having in my apartment—but it is very definitely something I think about. It's a part of my life and who I am."

Thank You and Good Night is an autobiographical montage—both hilarious and gut-wrenching—about the death of Oxenberg's grandmother, an integral person in her life. The film combines documentary and fictional narrative and is compelling as well as innovative filmmaking. The film deals not only with the loss of Oxenberg's grandmother, but also with the death of Oxenberg's younger sister, Judy, who died of cancer when Oxenberg was eleven and Judy was seven. Oxenberg sometimes features stand-ins in her films—objects functioning as characters, anthropomorphized, in a sense, because of the key role they play in the narrative structure of the film (in *Six Unnatural Acts*, for example, a comb and "butch wax" hair treatment are exemplified because the role they play in lesbian life is so significant).

Thus in *Thank You and Good Night* Oxenberg peoples her narrative with a central character, Scowling Jan, a cardboard cutout of the five-year-old Oxenberg who appears in different clothes and different situations. Scowling Jan, always silent, provides a bridge between the documentary and narrative portions of the film.

"The film has been a success with a wide range of audiences," said Oxenberg. "Michael Lumpkin saw it at Sundance [Film Festival, where the film had its premiere in January 1991] and told me he wanted to show it at the San Francisco Lesbian and Gay Film Festival. He said that it was an important film for our community because we have had to learn to deal with death because of AIDS and cancer in our community. He showed it with *Home Movie*, my film about coming out, and it was my very favorite screening of the film. There it was, at the Castro Theater, and it was packed and the audience loved it—it won the audience award for the entire festival."

After being shown at a series of festivals and getting rave reviews, *Thank You and Good Night* was picked up for theatrical release by Aries Film Releasing. "It was really brave of them to take the financial risk with a lesbian director's film about death. I mean, it's a tough one to sell at the box office," noted the filmmaker wryly.

The film did modest but critically solid business as it moved around the country, opening first in New York and Los Angeles. Reviews were consistently positive. "I think the film is successful with audiences because it is very cathartic—it's laughing in the face of death, it's an irreverent and defiant approach to death, and I think it's not just the gay community who needs that kind of catharsis. My film is about living with death as a fact of life," she said.

Oxenberg points out that when it comes to the big screen, "Denial of death doesn't extend to an abhorrence of seeing people blown away in sadistic and horrific ways. Imagine a film like *Die Hard*, if every time there was a death, the family and friends came out to mourn the victim. Denial of death makes killing possible, it makes war possible, it excuses a lot of violence."

Unlike the films she made throughout the seventies, *Thank You and Good Night* isn't about lesbianism. "The *fact* of my lesbianism wasn't organic enough to fit into the film without sticking it in with a shoe horn," she said, and added that her personal narrative style of filmmaking isn't necessarily a lesbian aesthetic either. But she acknowledged that all the film work she does is colored by the fact that she is an open lesbian. "I'm not about to go back in the closet on my way to Hollywood," she said, but is also realistic about what a lesbian director might find in Tinseltown.

"I still consider myself an independent filmmaker—so whatever films I make, whether I work with someone as talented and feminist as [actress] Geena Davis or I work on something that is my own personal idea, a lesbian idea, I am still going to retain that independence. And that means I am not going back in the closet."

Oxenberg is very much aware, particularly considering the media hype attending the public coming out of celebrities like Chastity Bono, Ellen DeGeneres, Amanda Bearse, Melissa Etheridge and her actress partner, Julie Cypher, that "the subject of being out or not in Hollywood is certainly in the news these days. There are lots of lesbians and gay men in Hollywood and an equal number of people know who they are. But being 'out' to the general public *is* a different issue entirely, and I think the lesbian and gay community needs to be a little more realistic about what that means. I have the greatest respect for Martina Navratilova—who is really our only openly gay celebrity megastar, out for years and unapologetic about it. But, really, did her coming out change the world?"

What is more important than urging Hollywood notables like director-actress Jodie Foster to come out, said Oxenberg, is "for the gay community to create an atmosphere in Hollywood where lesbian and gay films get made, where lesbian and gay actors and directors *can* come out without destroying their careers."

Implementing that process, said Oxenberg, will include using different strategies. "Take [the film] *Fried Green Tomatoes* [1991] as an example. We should be celebrating the fact that a movie about a lesbian relationship is so popular with the general public. Maybe get people outside theaters with signs saying something like 'If you like this movie, you like lesbians.' Instead

Jan Oxenberg

of getting angry about the 'L' word being left *out*, remind people that this is *still*—'L' word or not—a lesbian movie. Otherwise the gay community is just colluding with the straight society that says this *isn't* a lesbian movie. Instead they should be saying, 'You enjoyed the reality [of lesbianism], and this is what it's called.'"

Oxenberg dedicated *Thank You and Good Night* to gay film historian Vito Russo, author of the groundbreaking book *The Celluloid Closet*. She noted, "Vito was always pointing out what Hollywood was saying about us. We can't tell gay filmmakers and actors that they *have* to play these kinds of roles and they *have* to make these kinds of movies. That will only be an impediment to getting people to come out. As a community we can do what blacks have done, what women are trying to do—we can create our own changes at the box office. We have to show we are a financially viable commercial audience. We have a lot of power, a strong voice. We just have to learn how to use it to get what we want."

Oxenberg's filmmaking elicits powerful audience response, in part because she is a skilled director whose ideas are well crafted into her films, and in part because she addresses issues central to lesbian (and female) experience. Although she admits that her open lesbianism has often stood in the way of financing larger projects and made it more difficult for her to achieve some of her goals as a filmmaker, she notes that the struggle is worthwhile and important.

"We need to have more gay and lesbian films, more gay and lesbian directors, more gay and lesbian images," she noted, "but that process takes time and hard work and a certain amount of effort from outside the film world. But it can happen—it *is* happening." Oxenberg, who has been scriptwriting for several actresses in Hollywood, added, "As much as I want to see lesbian images on screen, I also want to see feminist images on screen, images of strong women, a variety of images of women. It's all part of a larger struggle. A lot of it happens at the box office. We *can* control what we see. We just have to say what it is we want a little louder."

Vijaya Mehta

Women, Work and Parallel Cinema

If artists and their craft are products of their environment, then Vijaya Mehta's films have definitely evolved from this director's extensive (and intensive) experience: as an actress, theater director and producer, but just as definingly as an Indian woman—wife and mother—from an era before women were allowed a strong voice in either Indian culture or politics.

India, as the filmmaking capital of the world, produces nearly one thousand films each year in the sixteen different languages native to the country. In addition, it has the world's largest film-going population, with an insatiable appetite for popular movies (people go to the cinema on a nearly daily basis). But, as in the United States, the majority of Indian films are made through the studio system. These mainstream films—musicals, romances and comedies—are the most popular and best financed. About five percent of Indian films are produced outside the studio system by the "parallel" or independent cinema (the phalanx of Indian cinema that spawned the brilliant classic neorealist Indian director, Satyajit

Films by Vijaya Mehta

Smiriti Chitre (Memory Pictures)

Rao Saheb

Pestonjee

Ray), which is subsidized by the National Film Development Corporation (NFDC). Because of the NFDC, Mehta explained, filmmakers like herself are able to make films about subjects of more social and political import than the mainstream cinema does.

Like many women directors, Mehta came to filmmaking by way of another career, but unlike many women filmmakers, she came to her filmmaking career later in life, when she was over fifty years old. For over thirty-five years she was an extremely popular and highly regarded stage actress and theater director. Then she discovered film, more by happenstance than any actual urge to make movies. "I glided into film," she said simply. "I am basically a theater person, but I have been directing in the theater since I was twenty-one, so directing itself was hardly new to me. The shift from theater to films was not difficult, but there are differences such as time and space. A live performance has certain restrictions, but then so does a filmed [performance]. The differences create the excitement and tension."

Mehta's filmmaking career began in 1981, when she read a story she wanted to adapt for the stage and was approached by Bombay television to do a film version of the tale. She wrote the screenplay and then ended up directing and editing the film as well. "I was just bringing to life the scenes," she noted. "I had no one to do the editing, so I just did it—and the mixing and dubbing. It was a crash course in filmmaking." The film, *Smiriti Chitre* (*Memory Pictures*), a probing look at Brahmin traditions in India, won the National Award, the Indian equivalent of an Academy Award, for Best Picture in 1983. "*Memory Pictures* is about who the Indian woman really is," she said, "a story of perseverance, struggle and strength during a period of tremendous social change and contradiction."

Mehta's "crash course" in filmmaking took root amazingly fast. She learned film language and skills quickly and moved forward almost immediately into her next project and her alliance with the parallel cinema. "There are some limitations with the NFDC," Mehta acknowledged. "Money is tight, so resources are limited. Low budget is essential, so there's not much allowance for experimentation. They [NFDC] use locations, and I believe in that, but you can use any theater or studio [for sets]. You have to shoot in 16mm and blow it up [to 35mm]. So it isn't always ideal."

And there are other, more pervasive drawbacks with films made through the NFDC, such as distribution. "These films are viewed as art movies," explained Mehta. "So you don't get the big audiences you get for a musical or a comedy. Quite a lot of the parallel cinema becomes ineffectual because you reach out to a limited audience in a limited venue. The parallel cinema is for people who want to be changed in their sensibility." Many Indian directors working in India, Europe, Canada and the United States argue that films made for the parallel cinema get seen by more foreign audiences—particularly in the United Kingdom, Canada and the United States—than Indian audiences.

Directors like Mehta who stay in India and work solely within the parallel cinema aren't deterred by the limitations, however, anymore than American independent filmmakers are deterred by the financial constrictions placed on them by working outside Hollywood. "You have to understand," Mehta explained, "Indian cinema is two very different things, the independent and the commercial. Commercial cinema is a ritual, it is for fantasy, it is a totally different world that appeals to any viewer who wants to escape life's miseries. The middle-class intellectual minds are who I want to share my ideas with."

Because she is so deeply involved with the parallel cinema, Mehta is extremely concerned about its progress and survival; producer may very well be her next role. She has already produced plays, including a show that ran in New York and Bombay based on the letters from Jawaharlal Nehru to his daughter, Indira Gandhi.

"Becoming a filmmaker has turned me into a businesswoman," she explained. "I've been going to women's seminars on management training. Financial viability is the key to the survival of parallel cinema. We *must* make it, and very low-budget [filmmaking] is the answer to viability. Television has begun to play a part in all of this—the parallel cinema will become more popular through our films being viewed on television."

There is also a strong film society movement developing in India, Mehta noted, which will also help the process of getting films from the parallel cinema known. "We are working toward building small theaters for parallel cinema to get around the issues of distribution [which in India is also controlled by the studio system]. If one NFDC film does well, it means others can be made."

Mehta's films, by parallel cinema standards, have certainly done well. Her second film, *Rao Saheb* (1985), deals with the roles of women in Indian culture, juxtaposing inherited customs and traditional life with a more modern view of the progressive social reform sweeping the nation at the turn of the century. It too was greeted with critical and audience acclaim and won Indian film awards.

But it is *Pestonjee* (1988) that is Mehta's favorite film, one she feels required a great deal of personal drive to make and to which she feels a deep emotional connection. Mehta's third film tells the story of the tiny Parsee community of Bombay, an elite group of intellectuals and professionals descended from Persians who migrated to India in the eighth century to escape religious persecution for their devotion to Zoroaster. Though *Pestonjee*

Still from *Pestonjee*

is a far less politically significant film from a Western standpoint than Mehta's other work, it received wide acclaim as the first film to tackle the issues of the Parsee community, which have been largely ignored in mainstream Indian culture.

A bittersweet tale of human frailties, *Pestonjee* is set in the Parsee community of the 1950s. Piroisha (played hauntingly by Naseeruddin Shah) focuses much of his attention on the lives of those around him, particularly his best friend, Pestonjee (Anupam Kher).

Busy being the conscience of Pestonjee, Piroisha loses the woman he loves, Jeroo (Shabana Azmi), to him. The three remain friends, however, and it is only at Pestonjee's death that painful secrets are revealed.

The success of *Pestonjee* is indicative of the problems inherent with the parallel cinema and NFDC productions. Mehta said, "*Pestonjee* got an award and then Channel 4 [an English television station that also broadcasts in India] bought it. So now it has made money, because it didn't make money in the theaters."

One reason *Pestonjee* may not have enjoyed a financially viable theatrical release is because the subject matter is deeply emotional and the characters are from the extremely isolated Parsee community: a typical independent film in any country. But Mehta feels the tale has a universality to it, and many film critics have agreed with the director's assessment of her film. "It is a tender story, highly tender," said Mehta. "It's a first-person narrative about relationships and the definition of friendship—is one willing to accept surprises?"

Mehta doesn't seem surprised by her new success as a filmmaker, taking it in stride as simply another aspect of a remarkably successful life. Even though there are only a handful of women filmmakers in India and many women, including India's best-known woman director, Mira Nair, have left the country in order to make films, Mehta insisted it hasn't been difficult for her to break into the male bastion of Indian cinema and believes it is "more difficult for a woman to be a filmmaker in the United States than in India. I haven't had a problem as a woman film director. It was more of a problem [for me] in the theater—everyone loved me when I was twenty-one, but then I got older and I felt uncomfortable. Now I feel I am accepted as a director and filmmaker."

Mehta does acknowledge that her experience is unique, however. "Historically and socially I come from an area where women are more accepted," she said. "Women are educated in the middle class, the woman's role outside the home is accepted. India is really very matriarchal." Thus, she explained, when she lived in England for a few years, she felt "no different from other women. I was accepted as a working woman, after a time, but I already had a husband and children, so I was ordinary in that sense—and I continued to work, which was unusual in the middle class. But if one wants to do something *real* bad, one does it, one doesn't get held back by society."

Striking that balance and addressing those issues of family and work are at the core of Mehta's *oeuvre*. Film critics have interpreted her films as political *and* feminist, but the director herself denies any political construct in her movies, stating that her politics do not enter her films, even though the NFDC focus is primarily on political films. Mehta also resists labels, bristling at suggestions of a feminist nexus in her work. "I am," she stated unequivocally, "a humanist. That is how I see the world. I don't do things for political statements or cause. This sort of commentary doesn't create a revolution. Films and theater haven't created a revolution. They've *documented* revolution, they've made people see the need for revolution,

Vijaya Mehta

but they can't *create* a revolution."

An unusual woman, particularly for her age and caste, Mehta doesn't fit the model of the older Indian woman. Beautiful and dramatic, she retains much of her stage presence. As she speaks about breaking into the parallel cinema and about the role of women there, she explains that first and foremost she is an actress, theater is in her blood, her deep and long-lasting involvement in the theater made it easier for her to break into film and her most important perspective on film is as a humanist. "I look for the human story," she said. "Sometimes that is about women and sometimes it is about men, but mostly I want to do films that explore the realms of Indian culture and society through the human story." Making films about diverse aspects of Indian life is equally important to the filmmaker. "Your ethnicity gives you your identity," she stated unequivocally. "You can discard that identity later, if you want to, but you need to establish it initially to know who you are. You must know where you are from to get where you are going."

Mehta's experience runs contrary to the majority of Indian women of most castes—she has always worked outside the home; in addition, she has had the support of the men in her life (two husbands and three sons) to pursue her various careers. Her personal philosophy is any woman can do that, if she wants to, even in a country as sexist as India is perceived internationally.

"Often women feel they have to choose between home or career," Mehta said. "I've had both, I've enjoyed both. I became an actress early and soon after became a director as well. I then married and had my son. My first husband died and I married again. But I have always worked, and the reason why I work is because human beings and human minds fascinate me. I love the journeys, I love the conflicts. I think many women want to work, but they aren't sure what it is they want to do."

In *Rao Saheb*, in which Mehta played the lead, in addition to directing the film, she noted, "I play a woman who is trapped in the kitchen, a widow with a clean-shaven head. I had to get inside her and understand where she found joy in order to make her a powerful character that the audience could relate to as well."

In *Pestonjee*, the director said, "I explore the roles of women and these choices. Some women choose only to be housewives, and they [spend] their lives that way, waiting for the babies to grow up before they can live for themselves. I don't like that kind of woman very much," she admitted. "Then there are also women who feel they have to sacrifice their personal lives for career. I don't think that's essential at all."

The female characters in *Pestonjee* were received with some controversy by Indian members of audiences at screenings in the United States in Philadelphia, and in the United Kingdom in London; both cities have very large Indian communities. Several people suggested that the women in the film were portrayed as shallow and grasping: the wife as cold and dependent, the mistress as a woman who would do anything to further her own career. To that criticism, Mehta replied that these were examples of Indian women, somewhat traditional but definitely real. "The Indian woman has different functions than men," she acknowledged, "but I don't feel there's a need to compete."

Mehta spoke at length about the much-discussed sexism of Indian society and explained that its level depended on the social status of the people involved. She explained, for example, that dowry deaths, the infamous practice of burning a new bride to death because her dowry is too small, happens in predominantly lower-middle-class and rural families where money and position are extremely important, and that the practice is limited mostly to that group. In the lower classes, Mehta asserted, women and men are on a more equal footing because they are both clawing for money and survival. And in the upper classes from which Mehta comes, women are given equal chances at education and career.

But Mehta agreed that the role of woman in India is often viewed as that of second-class citizen and that the image is hard to contradict because of dowry deaths and other examples of sexism within the culture. Women directors breaking into the parallel cinema are important to show the impact of these changes, Mehta believes, because they give an entirely new perspective on the role of both men and women in the society.

"My input as a filmmaker is that of a woman," Mehta explained. "My women become very strong when I act them and when I direct them, but my men are strong, too. If you make a character weak, then you have sentimentality and sentimentality is the weakest form of human emotion."

The influence of the parallel cinema can be seen through films like Mehta's. "I think my films show people in a different light because I'm a woman and therefore I am perceiving both the women and the men with a level of sensitivity that comes from my being a woman," Mehta stated.

Vijaya Mehta

"There are now five or six women directors working in the parallel cinema, and they are making quite a stir because their films deal with controversial subjects. We are winning awards, and the community that sees our films is noticing this."

Marta Balletbò-Coll

Costa Brava

Future filmmakers may well use Marta Balletbò-Coll's first feature film, *Costa Brava*, as a textbook example of how to make a low-budget movie. *Costa Brava* was shot in Barcelona, Spain, over the course of fourteen days, on 35mm film, for a total production cost of $180,000. In 1995,

Marta Balletbò-Coll in *Costa Brava*. Balletbò-Coll directed and appeared in the film. (courtesy of Northern Arts/Naiad Press Video)

the year of its theatrical release, *Costa Brava* won the Audience Award for Best Picture at the Los Angeles Gay and Lesbian Film Festival and the Audience Award for Best Lesbian Picture

Films by Marta Balletbò-Coll

Harlequin Exterminator

Intrepidissima

Costa Brava

at the prestigious San Francisco International Lesbian and Gay Film Festival.

Luck had very little to do with *Costa Brava*'s success. Instead, a creative screenplay, good business sense and advance targeting of potential audiences and venues led to a low-budget hit.

Balletbò-Coll was born in Barcelona in 1960. Although she majored in chemistry at the University of Barcelona, she wrote for television sit-coms and worked as a radio and newspaper reporter. In 1986, she received a Fulbright Scholarship and enrolled in film studies at New York City's Columbia University. In 1991, she earned her master of fine arts degree with the short thesis film *Harlequin Exterminator*.

Harlequin Exterminator was Balletbò-Coll's first brush with Anna Giralt-Romaguera, the main character of *Costa Brava*. As with the feature film, Balletbò-Coll played Giralt-Romaguera in *Harlequin Exterminator*, which she described as "a bittersweet comedy about lies, obsessions and roaches [that] shows Anna in New York City, coming to terms with her sexual orientation." Balletbò-Coll noted that the film was shown at a number of festivals, including the Toronto Film Festival, where it was suggested to her that she attend all the *specifically* gay and lesbian film festivals in the world. She was reluctant at first and entered festivals like the San Francisco International Film Festival, where the short received a Golden Gate Special Jury Award. But when she was turned down for the prestigious London, Cannes and Berlin film festivals, she decided to try all the gay and lesbian festivals she could.

Balletbò-Coll returned to Barcelona in 1991, and in 1992 she directed and produced the short film *Intrepidissima*. "Something straight, I said to myself," Balletbò-Coll recalled, "something suitable for a general audience." In *Intrepidissima*, a hysterical young mother—played by Balletbò-Coll—goes shopping with her twelve-year-old daughter. The catalogue for the 1993 San Francisco International Lesbian and Gay Film Festival, where *Intrepidissima* won the Audience Award for Best Lesbian Short Film, described it as "a cathartic triumph for every little tomboy ever pushed to go out shopping for dresses." The film also screened at the New York Lesbian and Gay Film Festival where, Balletbò-Coll said, "Friend and filmmaker Francine Rzeznick pointed out how much people loved the red fingernails

Narrative Film

254

of the 'mother from hell' character I was playing. I took very good note of it. Desi del Valle, then the distribution assistant of Frameline [the organization that produces the San Francisco International Lesbian and Gay Film Festival and distributes *Intrepidissima*], kept me posted about the enthusiasm the short brought about in the audience. She also wrote a comment about her being an actress besides her distribution job. Again, I took very good note of it."

1993 was spent in Barcelona with a part-time job stuffing envelopes. Balletbò-Coll tried to get grants for a Catalan-language comedy about two women falling in love, but, she noted, "It seemed as if the grants were never for people like me. I started suspecting being discriminated against [because of] the subject matter of my comedies. I had a hard time in every possible way. The San Francisco audience and the people at Frameline were crucial to keep me going. Otherwise, alone in Barcelona, I would have given up."

Instead, Balletbò-Coll made up her mind to go for broke. Taking the $30,000 U.S. she had received in awards and grants for *Intrepidissima*, Balletbò-Coll decided to make a film in English for an American market: "My plan," said Balletbò-Coll, "was to put all that money back into preproducing, shooting and editing—just the offline edit—a long feature film." Balletbò-Coll would once again play Anna Giralt-Romaguera and she would ask Desi del Valle—who has an extensive résumé as an actress in underground theater—to play opposite her.

But before Balletbò-Coll could shoot the film, she had to write it. "I met Ana Simón Cerezo [her lover] just when I was lucky enough to have at least one area of my life in a gayer tone than the rest," she punned. "Ana invited me to write the script at her place, and she ended up being the co-writer. Ana goes a lot to the movies. She is the kind of person who knows 'who dunit' after two minutes. She's just what I needed. In terms of working on my character, I remembered how popular the red flashy fingernails of 'mother from hell' in *Intrepidissima* were. I thought it was a sure bet, and I used it again."

In the script, Anna Giralt-Romaguera is back in Barcelona, working as a tour guide and honing her skills as a playwright. She has written a monologue, "Love Thy Neighbor," which she is videotaping and sending to a San Francisco theater company. Then she meets and falls in love with the closeted Montserrat Ehrzman-Rosas, a Jewish seismic engineer from the United

Marta Balletbò-Coll

Desi del Valle and Marta Balletbò-Coll in *Costa Brava* (courtesy of Northern Arts/Naiad Press Video)

States, played by del Valle. *Costa Brava* follows their tumultuous relationship, punctuated with moments of hilarity and despair.

Balletbò-Coll began pre-production knowing she couldn't afford anything. "We needed people who knew how to work without a big budget. We decided to shoot at Ana's place. If a potential art director happened to mention, 'Oh no problem, we'll paint these walls,' she or he was immediately crossed out. Directors of photography who needed 'a minimum of $50,000 U.S. to start with' were disconsidered. Numerous locations had to be crossed out because of budget restraints."

One of the reasons Balletbò-Coll was able to shoot *Costa Brava* in fourteen days was because she rehearsed with her actors before the cameras rolled. She also saved money by not buying film stock: "Josep Amoros [the film's production manager] and I would go through all the production companies in Barcelona, Madrid and Basque country asking for heads and tails of 35mm stock left over from their shoots. We ended up with all our 35mm film stock for free. Spanish people are very generous."

Cerezo proved to be key to the film's production. "Ana is like God," Balletbò-Coll remarked, "she's everywhere. She's the kind of person who, in moments of big crisis, starts her sentence with 'I don't know anything about filmmaking, but . . .' and generally she hits home."

Balletbò-Coll and her editors cut the film and sound on videotape at an offline studio that was loaned to them, free of charge, when advertising clients weren't using it. It took Balletbò-Coll close to a year to complete the final cut. But at that point, she had run out of money.

"Francine Rzeznick and Desi del Valle had told me about this very American thing, fundraising parties," said Balletbò-Coll. "Honestly, I've never asked for money from anybody. I didn't like the idea at first and I thought it was too American to work in penny-pinching Catalonia. But we set up some meetings where we showed the offline edit of the film in

English to a Catalan audience who didn't understand English. Then we would ask them for money. And it worked. We used to call them 'Tupperware meetings,' showing the film instead of the plastic pottery. This has been the most spiritual experience I have ever had. People I didn't know, friends of friends, would give us money, up to a maximum of $1200 U.S.— we declined bigger contributions." Cerezo also put up $30,000 U.S., but, Balletbò-Coll noted, "the rest, up to $90,000 U.S., was obtained at the Tupperware meetings, from mostly women, a vast majority of whom were high school teachers. We would pay labs and sound studios on a cash-on-delivery basis, something never heard of in the Spanish film industry, and we got important discounts in exchange."

Costa Brava opened in Barcelona at a women's film festival; shortly thereafter, it opened commercially at a cinema in Barcelona and ran for three months. Meanwhile, it was showing at American lesbian and gay film festivals to great reviews. The film was bought for American distribution by Northern Arts/Naiad Press Video and has been sold to Brazil, South Africa and Belgium, and has toured in Japan and Australia. In November 1995, *Costa Brava* was invited to be screened at the London International Film Festival, one of the festivals that had turned down *Harlequin Exterminator*.

In 1996, Naiad Press published the book version of the movie, which continues to rack up sales. Balletbò-Coll and Cerezo are at work in Barcelona on their second feature film, which they are calling *Honey, I've Sent the Men to the Moon!* And once again, they've asked Desi del Valle to be one of the lead actors.

Beyond the Director's Chair

Debra Zimmerman

Women Make Movies

Women Make Movies—the world's largest nonprofit distributor of films and videos made exclusively by women—was founded in 1972 with a collection of thirty films. At its twenty-fifth anniversary, Women Make Movies had over four hundred films and videotapes for rental or purchase. Debra Zimmerman, the organization's executive director, noted, "In 1972, there were just a handful of women making films in Hollywood and the independent film movement was just beginning. The name 'Women Make Movies' was a novel statement—in 1996 it is a reality." At times, the fortysomething Zimmerman seems less like an individual and more like a force. A tireless advocate of films by women, Zimmerman has traveled the world watching and talking about films by women.

"In 1975, there was a conference of feminist film organizations," Zimmerman recalled, "and there were seventy-five people at the conference, representing between fifty and seventy-five groups. It is just extraordinary when you think that

Debra Zimmerman (photo by Pat Thompson; courtesy of Women Make Movies)

we're really the only one left in this country. The ones that have managed to survive are the film festivals and the distributors. All the production groups seem to have been folded into the larger associations, like AIVF [Association of Independent Video and Filmmakers] or all the media arts centers that were set up around the country. I think it's very easy to understand why, when you look at the patterns of funding."

Funding women film- and videomakers has been a long-standing mission for Women Make Movies. In addition to its work as a distributor, the organization serves as a fiscal sponsor for filmmakers who receive grants from nonprofit organizations and hosts workshops on all aspects of film and video production. Some workshops are geared toward grant writing and fundraising, whereas others deal with camera basics. Because Women Make Movies wants to see more women working professionally in the motion picture industry, one frequently offered workshop teaches the basics of being a camera assistant—the first rung on the professional (and union) ladder toward camera operator and cinematographer.

Government funding cutbacks are a concern for Woman Make Movies, both because it means fewer projects by independent women filmmakers will be funded and because Women Make Movies itself, which is partially funded by government grants, may lose crucial funding for its workshops. At one point, the organization experimented with its own film production wing, but closed it down after realizing it wasn't cost effective and that Women Make Movies would be competing with the filmmakers it distributes for a slice of the already-thin funding pie.

Zimmerman herself is no stranger to the vicissitudes of filmmaking. In 1980, Zimmerman and Jacqueline Shortell-McSweeney directed the half-hour, low-budget video *Why Women Stay*, about the complex issue of women who choose to stay in violent relationships. Close to twenty years later, the video still racks up rentals and is considered to be a classic by many in the domestic violence field.

Looking through the Women Make Movies catalogue is a trip through the work of many cutting-edge women filmmakers. The organization distributes the work of Su Friedrich, Pratibha Parmar, Michelle Parkerson,

Sally Potter, Julie Dash, Allie Light, Ellen Spiro, Tami Gold, Michelle Mohabeer, Trinh T. Minh-ha, Cheryl Dunye, Sadie Benning, Barbara Hammer, Ayoka Chenzira and Lourdes Portillo.

"At this point," Zimmerman said, "I think festivals and distributors have the most difficult relationship with women filmmakers: Just look at lesbian filmmakers who won't have their films shown in lesbian and gay film festivals because they're afraid of having their films ghettoized; the same thing happens with women [filmmakers] not having their films shown in women's film festivals. As a distributor, we're really right in the middle of that, because I understand their decisions, and I can even support them from a business perspective. For example, Trinh T. Minh-ha: If there was the choice between having her film show at New Directors [a prestigious, mainstream New York City film festival] and having it show in the New York Women's Film Festival—if there were a New York Women's Film Festival, which Women Make Movies might even be hosting [in the future]—it would be a very, very hard choice, because New Directors has that prestige value, which is extremely important for her."

Zimmerman noted that many experimental and cutting-edge filmmakers are dismissed by the film critics, who don't seem to understand what the filmmakers are trying to do. "I think that's the biggest problem that women film- and videomakers have right now: When they go through all the struggle to make films that really represent their vision, they are not received by the general public. Many lesbian filmmakers' films are not received by lesbian audiences, especially the experimental films. I was moderating a panel of lesbian filmmakers in San Francisco, and the audience was saying, 'We want *Desert Hearts*. We want stories. We want the old formula with girls in it. And we want sex, we want love.' And the filmmakers were talking about how they were trying to do something different with the style of the films, and the audience just did not want to deal with that.

"We have a series called New Directions in Video, and not a single one of those tapes was programmed on *New Television*, which was the premier public television series for new video art. The style these women are working in, the fact that the content is more important than using special effects—it's real male and female kind of stuff—the fact that they're political through very personal kinds of things, makes it not *New Television*." Zimmerman also added, "I think this is true across the board—it's a small

Debra Zimmerman

example, but it's probably more true for women who are making films in Hollywood than it is for independent women filmmakers. So the real problem is not how do we get more women working in Hollywood, but how do we get films that represent women's visions out. It's not our job per se to make Hollywood an environment that is more sympathetic to women. We specifically have a mandate to work with independent women filmmakers, filmmakers who are not working within the television system or the Hollywood system."

Part of that mandate is to promote the work of filmmakers like Trinh T. Minh-ha, Su Friedrich and Sally Potter, who are, Zimmerman said, "really trying to expand the language of cinema. I think that they've had an incredible effect on film studies and cinema studies. Because of the confluence of what's been happening in cinema studies, because of Laura Mulvey's article ["Visual Pleasure and Narrative Cinema," which posits a female gaze that is radically different from the male gaze of standard Hollywood films] and everything that followed from it, feminist film theory has become absolutely—to use a very male term—seminal in the formulation of theories about visual construction. These filmmakers are incredibly important because they are influencing the way that students are being taught about film. In terms of whether they have an impact, that their films get to the general public—that's a whole other story. They don't."

Zimmerman is just as passionate when it comes to talking about films that Women Make Movies doesn't distribute. "I think that [Dutch director] Marleen Gorris's film *A Question of Silence* [1982] is probably the best feminist film I've ever seen," Zimmerman noted. "You have to watch that film in an audience of men and women to really understand how remarkable it is. The men just don't get it. There are women working in Europe whose work I think is incredibly important, for different reasons. Chantal Akerman's work [*ju tu il elle*, 1974; *Jeanne Dielman, 23 Quai du Commerce, 1080 Bruxelles*, 1975] is very important. Margarethe von Trotta's work [*The Second Awakening of Christa Klages*, 1978; *Love and Fear*, 1988; *The Promise*, 1994], although I don't really like it, is very important. I saw a film made by a Turkish woman called *The Marriage Chamber* and that was incredibly feminist. Ann Hui from Hong Kong who made a wonderful film called *Romance of the Book and Sword* [1987]—it's better than *The Last Emperor* [Bernardo Bertolucci, 1987]. Ann Hui has never made 'feminist' films, but sometimes to me what's most feminist is the thing that doesn't stand up and shout feminism. By Hui's just having this woman character be part of the action, be right out there on the battlefield, it's just so incredibly, subtly feminist, and it's a women's movie. When you talk about films for women, you have to remember that the filmmakers don't just live in the world of production, they also live in the real world, which is the world of the audience."

A major problem, even today, is convincing men that films by and about women are important. At a screening of Trinh T. Minh-ha's *Surname Viet Given Name Nam* (1989), a man in the audience asked the filmmaker, "There are so many important things to make a film about, why did you make a film about women?" The question didn't surprise Zimmerman.

"That, to me, is exactly what goes through men's minds," she said. "People who have seen this film don't get it. They don't understand—why is she focusing on women? Why is she focusing on details? Why is she focusing on the look on a woman's face? That is incredibly feminist, to look at all the small things, all the parts that make up the whole. I know that there are lots of men who are not going to like this film. When we go around trying to get people to show it, I can guarantee you that eighty percent of the people we'll be talking to are men, not women, and they're the ones who are the gatekeepers, they're the ones who decide whether the film [shows for] two nights or three nights or a week."

But Zimmerman has seen changes in distribution across the board and more opportunities for women filmmakers to get their work before the general public: "The development of multi-media technologies, including the Internet, and the growth of new cable channels have opened new doors. But," she noted, "funding cutbacks in the government's support of the arts and mergers of print and electronic media companies threaten the ground we've gained."

Debra Zimmerman

265

Christine Vachon

Poison, Swoon, Safe

Even if Christine Vachon never produces another movie, her place in film history is secure. Her genius lies in producing expensive-looking films for very little money. Vachon first made her mark as a co-founder of Apparatus Productions, a nonprofit film organization that funded short films by new filmmakers, but the film world really sat up and took notice when Vachon produced Todd Haynes's *Poison* (1991) for $250,000. Tom Kalin's *Swoon* (1992), the story of 1920s' child killers Leopold and Loeb, cost even less than *Poison* and brought Vachon still more acclaim. Today her name is synonymous with low-budget art films, or, more importantly, with low-budget *gay* art films, films that push at the confines of the silver screen.

Vachon first met Todd Haynes and Barry Ellsworth, who shot *Poison*'s acclaimed black-and-white AIDS allegory sequences, while studying semiotics at Brown University. The trio later founded Apparatus Productions and, still later, collaborated on *Poison*.

After college graduation in 1983, Vachon moved to New York City and worked as a proofreader so that she could work on no-budget independent movies like Sheila McLaughlin's *She Must Be Seeing Things* (1988) for little or no pay. This independent film apprenticeship allowed her to move on to paid work with small mainstream movies like the horror film *Demon Lover*.

Apparatus Productions, founded in 1987 and funded by the New York State Council for the Arts and private donations, brought Vachon fame and name recognition in no-budget independent film circles. But her big payoff came with *Poison*. Writer-director Haynes—creator of the cult-classic short *Superstar: The Karen Carpenter Story* (1987)—had conceived of a shorter, cheaper venture, but Vachon convinced him that money could be raised for a feature production and, if the budget was low enough, *Poison* could recoup its costs. The film went on to win the 1991 Grand Jury Prize at the influential Sundance Film Festival and receive critical acclaim. With its study of homoeroticism, homophobia and AIDS phobia, *Poison* became a central exhibit in the controversy over National Endowment for Arts funding.

Writer-director Tom Kalin originally came to Vachon for advice, and she convinced him, as she had Haynes, that he could use his material to make a low-budget feature. Vachon picked up funding for *Swoon* from *American Playhouse* and a distribution deal from Fine Line Features. Like *Poison*, *Swoon* was highly controversial. The film was a sympathetic look at Leopold and Loeb's gay relationship and their crime, and with it, Vachon solidified her role as a producer unafraid to take on controversy, including a film looking at the underside of gay life.

"What has to happen," said Vachon, "is there have to be lots of different kinds of representation, then there won't be this emphasis and weight placed upon how to construct an image that is positive to the entire gay and lesbian community, which is a fairly preposterous enterprise to begin with. Take films that are touted as being bastions of so-called positive imagery, films like *Longtime Companion* (1990). Another example is *Claire of the Moon* (1993)—if that's a positive lesbian image, then I don't want to be a lesbian. To me, *Swoon* isn't negative images, and neither is *Poison*."

Vachon followed *Swoon*'s success with *Postcards from America* (1994), inspired by the work of New York artist and writer David Wojnarowicz, who died of AIDS in 1992. Directed by Canadian Steve McLean, *Postcards*

Films Produced by Christine Vachon

Poison

Swoon

Postcards from America

Go Fish

Safe

Christine Vachon

James Lyons in Todd Haynes's *Poison,* produced by Christine Vachon

from America follows a young man's journey through a mythical America, a landscape haunted by his past experiences as an abused child and later as a New York City street hustler, and his present attraction to dangerous and potentially violent men.

Vachon noted that in *Postcards,* "you see a lot of men having a lot of sex and occasionally treating each other very violently. But it's about something that happened. It's about a time and a texture of a time, and the last thing I would want to do is impose any kind of politically correct gridwork on it."

Vachon has been accused by the lesbian community of political incorrectness for producing films that are about gay men. When asked when she will produce a lesbian film, Vachon facetiously commented, "My official statement on that is, 'Never.' I'm only doing white, gay films." Vachon explains that she bases her choice of films to produce on the subject matter and the rapport she feels with a film's director. That does not exclude lesbian projects. In fact, Vachon was instrumental in bringing the independent lesbian film *Go Fish* (1994) to a mainstream distributor and national acclaim. *Go Fish* was submitted to Vachon by its creative team, Rose Troche and Guinevere Turner, and was picked up for release by the Samuel Goldwyn Company, the theatrical distributor of Donna Deitch's *Desert Hearts* (1985).

"[*Go Fish*] came across my desk, and I stuck it in my VCR," noted Vachon. "It was doing something I'd never really seen a film do before, which was assume a completely lesbian space from the beginning, and it was really funny, really well written, and really sexy. No one came out or anything. It was like a real slice of life. It was surprisingly accomplished and commercial for the amount of money I knew that they must have spent. When I go to film festivals and I go to the dyke hour, there tends to be a lot of experimental stuff or people looking at their vaginas in the mirror. When there's something more conventional, the crowd goes wild, because they never see that.

"It all comes down to economics, because there really isn't any money for gay men's films either," Vachon stated. "I get asked a lot if Hollywood is homophobic. But the issue really is, is money homophobic? If a gay film does really great box office, then another gay film will be released—the same with a lesbian film. That's just the way it works. Lesbians will go to see films like *The Living End* [Gregg Araki, 1992], *Poison* and *Swoon*, which are films that I don't think should be identified as completely gay films, but I don't think gay men will go to see lesbian films. So an even smaller section of the gay community has to be targeted."

Is the queer film coming of age? Are more heterosexuals interested in seeing queer movies? "Yes," said Vachon, "they are coming of age, but I'm not sure how much these films cross over. Todd Haynes, when asked if it is easier to get money now that films like *Poison, Swoon* and *Paris Is Burning* [Jennie Livingston's 1990 documentary about drag balls] are doing well, said 'No, I think it's easier for Jonathan Demme to get money to do a film about AIDS.' And I think that's very true. The so-called more easy acceptance of queer images comes down to letting people like Demme make their queer movies. I have nothing against Demme making *Philadelphia* [1993], it's just that I wish it were easier for me to get money to make my films."

Money is also the reason that Apparatus Productions no longer exists as a regranting entity for short films: "Basically," Vachon said, "Apparatus has been shot down as arts funding has leaked out of the metropolitan area. We don't have any money; we haven't received any funding from the New York State Council for the Arts. If I had some tremendous amount of energy or if I had a twin, I could probably pound the grant pavement and get some more money for it, but I can't. Ideally, I'd like to hand it over to somebody else who could do that, because Apparatus has a name and a reputation, but it would have to be somebody dedicated not only to the nonprofit world, but somebody who also had a handle on arts administration, and that person has not materialized."

Vachon has herself directed several short films, including 1987's *The Way of the Wicked*, a tongue-in-cheek look at a girl's first communion, which can still be seen at small festivals. But Vachon does not want to go back to directing. "Part of being a producer has to do with volume," she explained, "being able to do lots of different projects and being able to put my stamp on a lot of different kinds of films, which I don't think I could do if I were only directing. I don't feel unfulfilled in my role as a producer. I've conceived and have a very creative relationship to many of the projects that I'm working on now."

Vachon also produced Haynes's film *Safe* (1995), about a southern California woman who comes down with an environmental illness. *Safe* represents a financial milestone for Vachon: Its budget weighed in at $1 million, still low by industry standards, but a far cry from *Poison*'s $250,000 budget. Funding sources for *Safe* included *American Playhouse*, Great Britain's Channel 4 TV and some of *Poison*'s original investors.

In 1994 Vachon was presented with the Frameline Award, awarded by the organization that produces the San Francisco International Lesbian and Gay Film Festival for outstanding contributions by lesbian and gay film- and videomakers. Past Frameline Award recipients include directors Pratibha Parmar, Barbara Hammer and the late Marlon Riggs, and the late film historian Vito Russo.

Ada Gay Griffin

Third World Newsreel

Ada Gay Griffin is the executive
director of Third World Newsreel, an independent distributor
of films and videos by and about
people of color and people from
developing countries. But Griffin is more than just an administrator—she is also a director
and producer. In 1987, she
teamed up with veteran documentarian Michelle Parkerson

Ada Gay Griffin (photo by Leigh H. Mosely)

to co-direct *A Litany for Survival: The Life and Work of Audre
Lorde*, the award-winning study of the late poet, released in
1995.

"I'm one of a number of women filmmakers, especially
documentary filmmakers, who did not get formally trained in
film school, in part because I come to filmmaking and the
media arts community from a more activist perspective,

seeing media as a tool for social change," said Griffin. "I was very much influenced by a lot of the work that came out in the seventies, particularly the documentaries, the work of people like [American] Barbara Kopple and [Ethiopian] Haile Gerima—realist dramatic work. I was very much taken with the explosion of third world cinema, which used a dramatic context to re-present the history and the conditions of unheard voices, people who had been left out of the historical interpretations of identity and were participants in world cultures. I began working [at Third World Newsreel] in the area of distribution, then realized the opportunity—almost the responsibility—for creating projects that wouldn't otherwise get done. And being in a place like Third World Newsreel really enabled me to meet the

Audre Lorde in *A Litany for Survival: The Life and Work of Audre Lorde,* directed by Ada Gay Griffin and Michelle Parkerson (still by Salimah Ali)

craftspersons, people representing groups and cultures and identities that had been not represented *behind* the camera as well. I met cinematographers, location sound people, camera assistants and editors who *were* of color and who had a real passion as well, but had been trained in very specific areas. So I knew that once I had an idea of what kind of film I wanted to make, there were alliances I could make and be able to work with people who were highly skilled but who were otherwise waiting for the next project."

The film that Griffin decided she wanted to make was a profile of Audre Lorde, one of the most influential voices in black poetry today. "I was a student of black feminist writing and thought. I made myself very familiar with Audre's work, but also with that of other people, like Toni Cade Bambara and Barbara Smith [co-founder with Lorde of Kitchen Table: Women of Color Press] and a whole number of writers who may not at various times call themselves feminist, but there certainly was a flowering and a clarifying of black, female points of view that were breaking out of second-class citizenship within the black movement and the women's movement. There was a very definite breaking away. I got to be a fly on the wall watching that happen and trying to figure out what my role was going to be, how I would use this awareness, because I had come from a much more provincial upbringing and life, coming from a very small town in western Pennsylvania.

Films by Ada Gay Griffin

A Litany for Survival:
    The Life and Work of Audre Lorde

"Later, when I was working for Third World Newsreel, by now as a sort of administrator, I found out that Audre had become ill again with cancer, and decided, after several months of agonizing over it, to muster up the courage to ask her to take on what I knew would be a Herculean task [the documentary]. There hadn't been an example of anyone doing that at that point—there was no *Tongues Untied* [the landmark 1989 film on black gay poetry by the late Marlon Riggs] yet. I had not made a film per se prior to that time; I wasn't even really sure I could do it, but somehow I got Third World Newsreel to give me their support—moral and institutional support to move forward on the project.

"I was lucky enough to invite Michelle Parkerson into the mix, and she agreed to come on board. That was 1986, 1987. What I liked about working with Michelle was that, first of all, we have different strengths; put together, we represented a very strong team that had the right kind of skills to approach this project. What I brought to the project was a real sense of commitment to empowering the subject and creating a vehicle through which the subject could responsibly influence the film—I wanted Audre Lorde to have a sense of ownership of the finished film."

Litany took several years to make, in part because the directors had to stop filming to raise the $500,000 needed to make it. Griffin noted, "It took years for the funding community to realize that this film wasn't going to go away, this was definitely going to be made." Early sources were the New York State Council on the Arts, the Open Meadows Fund, the Astraea Foundation and the Chicago Resource Center. "We found we were getting support exclusively from foundations where the program officer was either a woman of color or a lesbian. They represented a very much marginalized group. When you are, in Audre's case, a black lesbian and a feminist, that combination of identities is a major set of obstacles. The problems that any black woman is going to encounter in society to become a filmmaker or to

Ada Gay Griffin

make a film are not something that should be taken lightly at all, especially with a black lesbian project." Major funding for the film finally came in the form of a commission by the Independent Television Service (ITVS), which aired the film on its public television series *P.O.V.* Other funding came from the Corporation for Public Broadcasting and the National Black Programming Consortium.

The time it took to get funding allowed Griffin and Parkerson more opportunities to film Lorde—*Litany* follows a continuum in Lorde's life, rather than just presenting a moment in that life. "I doubt I will be able to do another project like *Litany* anytime soon," mused Griffin. "It just felt to us that we needed to make a bigger film while we had the opportunity to do that, given the changing funding picture, given the relative stability we had, which included a very close relationship to Audre. We knew we could take our time and make a film that we could be satisfied with. And that extended even to the point of making a film we couldn't complete in her lifetime and all of us reconciling to that fact. The last footage we shot with Audre, we shot six weeks before she passed away. That was a blessing, that was incredibly gracious of her to allow us to do that.

"We used what we had," said Griffin of the funding constraints and lengthy shooting period. "We took the weaknesses of the project and made them strengths. And that is part of the beauty of what the film has to say."

Taking weaknesses and turning them into strengths is also part of the mission of Third World Newsreel. The organization runs a low-cost, year-long production workshop in film and video for twelve people of color. "It's quite a successful program," noted Griffin. Workshop graduates include Dawn Suggs, the Not Channel Zero Collective, Bridgett Davis, members of the Borderlands Collective—"emerging artists working primarily in or originating from New York City who are pursuing careers in independent film and video," said Griffin. The workshop program is funded by foundation grants. "We see ourselves as a holistic organization," added Griffin, "so as long as we fund distribution, we're also going to fund training. We also fund our own productions, the most recent being *Litany* and *The Women Outside: Korean Women and the U.S. Military*, directed by J. T. Takagi and Hye Jung Park, which was also shown on *P.O.V.*" Third World Newsreel also distributes works that it did not fund, but which were made by independent filmmakers. "In all," said Griffin, "we distribute works by over two hundred artists."

Griffin noted, "Third World Newsreel places its primary emphasis on diversity. It has a commitment to understanding the interconnected relationships between the learning process, the development of film and video practices, and the genres that are being interlinked. It doesn't put a priority on documentary or dramatic or experimental forms, but looks at all of them as being important. It really seeks out the margins of culture and of society. The fact that there are more black people and other people of color, women and gay people depicted in cinema and making films can't take precedence over the fact that there are still many voices that are not heard and are not represented. Third World Newsreel tries to find a way to function as an advocate for those perspectives."

In addition to its distribution and training programs, Third World Newsreel acts as a fiscal sponsor for filmmakers applying for grants from nonprofit foundations and provides equipment access and technical assistance to emerging media artists. "One of our functions is to push work and artists who are at the margins of the larger independent film and media community away from the margins and into the consciousness of the larger community," noted Griffin, "and to help advance the careers of those people who otherwise might take longer to be seen as valid and talented and essential contributors to the field. There aren't just ten major artists,there are hundreds of them, and we feel a commitment to nuturing their existence."

Griffin is now developing a project that focuses on small-town America from a black perspective. "I think of it as being a documentary," Griffin said. "The black experience in America has most recently been looked at through urban eyes, and it's time to ask questions of the suburban and the rural experiences for black Americans now, and find out what life is like there."

**Ada Gay
Griffin**

275

Barbara Grier

Mail-Order Movie Mogul

Barbara Grier

Barbara Grier is best known as the publisher of Naiad Press in Tallahassee, Florida, the world's largest publisher of lesbian books. But she has also gained a reputation as a force behind low-budget lesbian films—and rightfully so. In 1985, Jeff Lipsky of the Samuel Goldwyn Company, which had bought the distribution rights to Donna Deitch's film *Desert Hearts* (1985), called up Grier to ask for marketing advice. Grier was an obvious choice for Lipsky, because Naiad published Jane Rule's novel *The Desert of the Heart*, upon which Deitch's film is based.

Goldwyn had planned to open *Desert Hearts* in approximately twenty cities. After consulting with Grier, the number of cities was increased to two hundred. Grier sent out flyers to everyone on her mailing list. "I told him," Grier said, "if you will put this movie in a tiny city somewhere, away from all your big fat markets, women will rent buses from all around to come and see it. And they did." Not only was the film's run successful, but Naiad sold

36,000 copies of the Rule novel in the fourteen months after *Desert Hearts* was released. Later, when Lipsky moved to distributor Skouras Pictures, he again called on Grier's acumen for the marketing of Jill Godmilow's 1987 film about Gertrude Stein and Alice B. Toklas, *Waiting for the Moon.*

Naiad Press runs a healthy mail-order business, and at one point Grier decided to expand by adding lesbian videos to her catalogue. Now, with publishing taking a financial nosedive across the board, it is video sales that keep Naiad viable.

In 1990, Grier saw an article in an Oregon newspaper about filmmaker Nicole Conn's still-unfinished lesbian feature *Claire of the Moon*, and seized the opportunity. Conn had invested the majority of her production funding in 35mm film stock and 35mm camera rentals—a departure from the less expensive 16mm or Super 16mm many independent filmmakers use—and had run out of money. Grier called Conn with an offer: She would give Conn an advance to make a video about making the film [*Moments: The Making of Claire of the Moon* (1992)], and Conn could use the advance to finish her feature. Grier also convinced Conn to write a novel version of her screenplay, which Naiad published, to help pay off production debts. Grier noted that, "*Claire* cost Nicole about $180,000 to make, and that didn't include any money for publicity or advertising. Naiad did all the publicity and advertising." Conn tried to sell the finished *Claire* to all the independent distributors, but, Grier noted, "They all refused. So suddenly we were in the business of self-distribution." Grier also added that the Samuel Goldwyn Company picked up distribution rights to the independent lesbian film *Go Fish* (1994) because it saw how successful *Claire* had been.

Although *Claire* was a critical flop, lesbian audiences loved it, and when the film was released on video, it quickly became a Naiad bestseller. "I know many women," Grier said, "who are already on their second copy of *Claire*." Grier added that, in terms of Naiad's sales, *Claire* has done much better than *Desert Hearts* because of ancillary sales: Naiad sells *Claire* posters, still photos and soundtrack albums in addition to the video, the novel and *Moments*. "We could have made a killing if we had had photos of Helen Shaver and Patricia Charbonneau [the stars of *Desert Hearts*]," mused Grier.

Moments, Grier said, cost very little to make: "Nicole went up to a lab in Oregon for a week and cut together leftover footage from *Claire*. She self-edited it and had a master struck. It only cost a few hundred dollars to do, but it was very successful and sold very well. It is, in fact, an excellent documentary, a really good movie about making a movie."

But Grier wasn't content with simply selling lesbian videos. She saw a lot of short lesbian films at film festivals and wanted to find a way to get them out of the festivals and into the videocassette players of lesbians worldwide. So she joined forces with Northern Arts Entertainment, a Massachusetts distributor of art films, to start Northern Arts/Naiad Press Video. "We had done self-distribution with *Claire*," said Grier, "and we didn't want to do that again. We wanted a seasoned partner." Grier was influenced by First Run Features' *Women from Down Under*, a compilation video of lesbian short films from Australia and a strong seller for Naiad. Northern Arts/ Naiad Press Video chose to follow First Run's lead with its first offering *I Became a Lesbian and Others Too!*, a compilation of four short lesbian films, in 1996. Grier chose the four shorts because they were all witty and intelligent, her two key criteria for video selections. Other Northern Arts/ Naiad Press videos include Marta Balletbò-Coll's *Costa Brava* (1995) and Marilyn Freeman's *Meeting Magdalene* (1996), both of which received critical raves and audience awards during their festival runs.

Another aspect of the Northern Arts/Naiad Press partnership was the creation of the Athena Awards, given to recognize excellence in lesbian film, video and television. The concept behind the Athena Awards was threefold: to provide critical recognition to outstanding lesbian projects; to provide financial prizes to the filmmakers in the form of services donated from major suppliers; and to distribute the winning works via the Northern Arts/ Naiad Press Video label. Award categories include experimental film, short film, animation, best documentary, best music video and best feature film.

Grier has been a champion at finding alternative sources of revenue for lesbian films. As with *Claire of the Moon*, Naiad has published book versions of *Costa Brava*, *Meeting Magdalene* and the comedy *Devotion* (1995), which Northern Arts/Naiad Press Video also distributes.

Grier has also been optioning the rights to Naiad Press novels, although none have actually made it to the screen. The book that has come closest is mystery novelist Katherine V. Forrest's *Murder at the Nightwood Bar*, which was optioned by Tim Hunter, who directed *River's Edge* (1986). The screenplay and casting are ready, but Hunter is still trying to find investors for the film. At one point Hunter expected to shoot the film in 1994, but financing fell through and *Nightwood Bar* remains unmade.

In 1994, Grier helped filmmaker Mindy Kaplan find $250,000 for the production costs of *Devotion*, which was shot in Vancouver, Canada, with a professional cast. Not wanting *Devotion* to end up in postproduction limbo like *Claire of the Moon*, Grier made sure that Kaplan had a well thought-out budget and production plans. Grier decided to help Kaplan after reading the screenplay, which she said was "hilarious. And it has a happy ending, which frankly I think lesbian films could use."

Grier continues to network with emerging lesbian filmmakers, especially those who are working on short projects. Her primary quest is to find works of quality that are appealing to a lesbian market. She wants to release a compilation video of lesbian shorts every year, in addition to the Athena Awards compilation. The sixtysomething Grier said, "I may be a dinosaur, but I'm having too much fun to stop now."

**Barbara
Grier**

Selected Filmography

Distributor Key: TWN: Third World Newsreel; VDB: Video Data Bank;
WMM: Women Make Movies

Anders, Allison

Gas Food Lodging 1992 101 min (available on home video)

Mi Vida Loca 1994 92 min (available on home video)

Four Rooms [first segment of anthology film] 1995 (available on home video)

Grace of My Heart 1996 100 min (available on home video)

Balletbò-Coll, Marta

Harlequin Exterminator 1991 14 min, 16mm (Frameline)

Intrepidissima 1992 7 min, 35mm (Frameline)

Costa Brava 1995 92 min (Northern Arts/Naiad Press Video)

Benning, Sadie

A New Year 1989 4 min (VDB, WMM)

Living Inside 1989 4 min (VDB, WMM)

Me and Rubyfruit 1989 4 min (VDB, WMM)

Jollies 1990 11 min (VDB, WMM)

Welcome to Normal 1990 19 min (VDB, WMM)

If Every Girl Had a Diary 1990 6 min (VDB, WMM)

A Place Called Lovely 1991 14 min (VDB, WMM)

It Wasn't Love 1992 20 min (VDB)

Bharadwaj, Radha

Closet Land 1991 81 min (available on home video)

Borden, Lizzie

Regrouping 1976 77 min

Born in Flames 1983 90 min (available on home video)

Working Girls 1986 90 min (available on home video)

Love Crimes 1992 85 min (available on home video)

Let's Talk About Sex 1994 35 min director's cut

Campion, Jane

Peel 1982 9 min, 16mm color (WMM)

Passionless Moments 1983 13 min, 16mm B&W (WMM)

A Girl's Own Story 1983 27 min, 16mm B&W (WMM)

After Hours 1984 26 min, 16mm color (WMM)

Two Friends 1986 76 min, 16mm color

Sweetie 1989 97 min (available on home video)

An Angel at My Table 1990 158 min (available on home video)

The Piano 1993 121 min (available on home video)

Portrait of a Lady 1996 135 min (available on home video)

Chenzira, Ayoka

Syvilla: They Dance to Her Drum 1979 25 min, 16mm (TWN, WMM)

Hair Piece: A Film for Nappy-Headed People 1985 10 min, 16mm color (TWN, WMM)

Secret Sounds Screaming: The Sexual Abuse of Children 1986 30 min, color video (TWN, WMM)

Five Out of Five 1987 7 min, color video (WMM)

The Lure and the Lore 1988 15 min, color video (TWN)

Zajota and the Boogie Spirit 1988 18 min, 16mm

Dash, Julie

Four Women 1977 4 min, 16mm color (TWN)

Diary of an African Nun 1978

Illusions 1983 34 min, 16mm B&W (TWN, WMM)

Praise House 1991 25 min, color video (TWN, WMM)

Daughters of the Dust 1991 114 min (available on home video)

Davis, Zeinabu irene

Crocodile Conspiracy 1986 13 min, 16mm (TWN)

Cycles 1989 17 min, 16mm B&W (WMM)

A Period Piece 1991 4 min, color video (WMM)

A Powerful Thang 1991 57 min, 16mm color (WMM)

Mother of the River 1995 28 min, 16mm B&W (WMM)

Deitch, Donna

Desert Hearts 1985 93 min (available on home video)

The Women of Brewster Place 1989 200 min (available on home video)

"Esperanza" [segment of *Prison Stories: Women on the Inside*] 1991 (available on home video)

Friedrich, Su

Cool Hands, Warm Heart 1979 16mm B&W (WMM)

Gently Down the Stream 1981 14 min, 16mm B&W (WMM)

The Ties That Bind 1984 55 min, 16mm B&W (WMM)

Damned If You Don't 1987 42 min, 16mm B&W (WMM)

Sink or Swim 1990 48 min, 16mm B&W (WMM)

First Comes Love 1991 22 min, 16mm B&W (WMM)

Rules of the Road 1993 31 min, 16mm color (WMM)

Lesbian Avengers Eat Fire Too [with Janet Baus] 1993 55 min color video

Hide and Seek 1996 65 min, 16mm B&W (WMM)

Gorris, Marleen

A Question of Silence 1982 92 min (available on home video)

Broken Mirrors 1984 110 min

The Last Island 1990 101 min

Antonia's Line 1995 93 min (available on home video)

Griffin, Ada Gay

A Litany for Survival: The Life and Work of Audre Lorde [with Michelle Parkerson] 1995 90 min, 16mm (TWN)

Hammer, Barbara

Schizy 1968 8mm

A Gay Day 1973 3 min, 16mm (Canyon)

I Was/I Am 1973 7.5 min, 16mm (Canyon)

Menses 1973 4 min, 16mm (Canyon)

Sisters! 1973 8 min, 16mm (Canyon)

Dyketactics 1974 4 min, 16mm (Canyon, WMM)

Jane Brakhage 1974 10 min, 16mm (Canyon)

Women's Rites or Truth Is the Daughter of Time 1974 8 min, 16mm (Canyon)

"X" 1974 8 min, 16mm (Canyon)

Superdyke 1975 22 min, 16mm (Canyon)

Psychosynthesis 1975 8 min, 16mm (Canyon)

Multiple Orgasm 1976 6 min, 16mm (Canyon)

Moon Goddess 1976 15 min, 16mm (Canyon)

Available Space 1977 20 min, 16mm (Canyon)

The Great Goddess 1977 25 min, 16mm (Canyon)

Sappho 1978 7 min, 16mm (Canyon)

Double Strength 1978 20 min, 16mm (Canyon, WMM)

Eggs 1978 10 min, 16mm (Canyon)

Haircut 1978 6 min, 16mm (Canyon)

Home 1978 12 min, 16mm (Canyon)

Dream Age 1979 12 min, 16mm (Canyon)

Women I Love 1979 27 min, 16mm (Canyon, WMM)

Our Trip 1980 4 min, 16mm (Canyon)

Arequipa 1981 10 min, 16mm (Canyon)

Machu Piccu 1981 15 min, 16mm (Canyon)

Sync Touch 1981 12 min, 16mm (Canyon, WMM)

Pools [with Barbara Klutinis] 1981 6 min, 16mm (Canyon)

Picture for Barbara 1981 10 min, 16mm (Canyon)

Pond and Waterfall 1982 15 min, 16mm (Canyon)

Audience 1982 33 min, 16mm (Canyon)

Stone Circles 1983 10 min, 16mm

Bent Time 1984 22 min, 16mm

Doll House 1984 4 min, 16mm

Parisian Blinds 1984 7 min, 16mm

Tourist 1984 7 min, 16mm

Optic Nerve 1985 16 min, 16mm

Place Mattes 1987 8 min, 16mm

No No Nooky TV 1987 12 min, 16mm

Endangered 1988 18 min, 16mm

Two Bad Daughters [with Paula Levine] 1988 12 min, video

Still Point 1989 8 min, 16mm

Sanctus 1990 19 min, 16mm

Vital Signs 1991 9 min, 16mm

Nitrate Kisses 1992 63 min (available on home video)

Eight in Eight 1995 video and mixed media installation

Out in South Africa 1995 51 min, color video (WMM)

Tender Fictions 1996 58 min, color video

Many of Hammer's shorter works are available on home video on the compilation tapes *Lesbian Sexuality*, *Lesbian Humor*, *Optical Nerves* and *Perceptual Landscapes*.

Light, Allie

Mitsuye and Nellie: Asian American Poets [with Irving Saraf] 1981 58 min, color video (WMM)

In the Shadow of the Stars [with Irving Saraf] 1991 93 min (available on home video)

Dialogues with Madwomen 1993 90 min, 16mm color (WMM)

Rachel's Daughter's 1997 106 min

Lupino, Ida

Not Wanted [uncredited] 1949 94 min (available on home video)

Never Fear 1950 82 min (available on home video)

Outrage 1950 75 min

Hard, Fast and Beautiful 1951 79 min

The Hitchhiker 1953 71 min

The Bigamist 1953 80 min (available on home video)

The Trouble with Angels 1966 112 min (available on home video)

Mehta, Vijaya

Smiriti Chitre (Memory Pictures) 1983

Rao Saheb 1985

Pestonjee 1988 114 min

Mohabeer, Michelle

Exposure 1990 8 min (WMM)

Coconut/Cane & Cutlass 1994 30 min, 16mm color (WMM)

Two/Doh 1996 5 min, 16mm color

Child-play 1997 30 min, 16mm color

Nair, Mira

Jama Masjid Street Journal 1979

So Far from India 1982

India Cabaret 1985

Children of a Desired Sex 1987

Salaam Bombay! 1988 113 min (available on home video)

Mississippi Masala 1992 118 min (available on home video)

The Perez Family 1995 112 min (available on home video)

Kama Sutra: A Tale of Love 1997

Negrón-Muntaner, Frances

AIDS in the Barrio [with Peter Biella] 1989

Puerto Rican ID [segment of PBS series *Signal to Noise*] 1994

Brincando El Charco: Portrait of a Puerto Rican 1994 55 min, 16mm color/
B&W (WMM)

Oxenberg, Jan
Home Movie 1972 12 min
I'm Not One of Them 1974 3 min
A Comedy in Six Unnatural Acts 1975 26 min
Thank You and Good Night 1991 77 min (available on home video)

Parkerson, Michelle
. . . But Then, She's Betty Carter 1980 53 min, 16mm color (WMM)
Gotta Make This Journey: Sweet Honey in the Rock [producer] 1983 58 min,
  color video (WMM)
Storme: The Lady of the Jewel Box 1987 21 min, 16mm color (WMM)
Odds and Ends (A New Age Amazon Fable) 1993 28 min, video
A Litany for Survival: The Life and Work of Audre Lorde [with Ada Gay Grif-
  fin] 1995 90 min (TWN)

Parmar, Pratibha
Emergence 1986 18 min, color video (WMM)
Sari Red 1988 12 min, color video (WMM)
ReFraming AIDS 1988 36 min
Memory Pictures 1989 24 min
Bhangra Jig 1990 4 min
Flesh and Paper 1990 26 min, 16mm color (WMM)
Khush 1991 24 min, 16mm color (WMM)
A Place of Rage 1991 52 min, 16mm color (WMM)
Double the Trouble, Twice the Fun 1992 25 min, color video (WMM)
Warrior Marks 1993 54 min, 16mm color (WMM)
Memsahib Rita [segment of the anthology film *Siren Spirits*] 1994 16mm
  color (WMM)
The Colour of Britain 1994 50 min
Jodie: An Icon 1996 24 min, 16mm color (WMM)

Portillo, Lourdes
After the Earthquake 1979 23 min, 16mm B&W (TWN, WMM)
Las Madres: The Mothers of Plaza de Mayo [with Susana Muñoz] 1985 64 min,
  16mm color (WMM)
La Ofrenda [with Susana Muñoz] 1989 55 min

Columbus on Trial 1993 18 min, color video (WMM)
The Devil Never Sleeps 1995 57 min

Rozema, Patricia

I've Heard the Mermaids Singing 1987 81 min (available on home video)
White Room 1990 91 min
When Night Is Falling 1994 96 min (available on home video)

Saalfield, Catherine

Bleach, Teach, and Outreach [with Ray Navarro] 1989 25 min, video
Ends and Means [with DeeDee Halleck] 1990 30 min, video
Keep Your Laws Off My Body [with Zoe Leonard] 1990 12 min, video (WMM)
Among Good Christian Peoples [with Jacqueline Woodson] 1991 30 min, video
  (TWN)
Bird in the Hand [with Melanie Hope] 1992 30 min, video
I'm You, You're Me: Women Surviving Prison Living with AIDS [with Debra
  Levine] 1993 26 min, color video (WMM)
Sacred Lies, Civil Truths 1993 60 min, video
B.U.C.K.L.E. [with Julie Tolentino] 1993 11 min, video
Cuz It's Boy 1994 13 min, video
Outta the Blue 1995 4 min, video
Positive: Life with HIV [co-producer] 1995 public television series
When Democracy Works 1996 30 min, video

Seidelman, Susan

Smithereens 1982 90 min (available on home video)
Desperately Seeking Susan 1985 104 min (available on home video)
Making Mr. Right 1987 95 min (available on home video)
Cookie 1989 93 min (available on home video)
She-Devil 1989 99 min (available on home video)
Confessions of a Suburban Girl 1991 60 min
The Dutch Master 1994 30 min

Tait, Margaret

Portrait of Ga 1952 4 min
Orquil Burn 1955 35 min
The Drift Back 1956
Where I Am Is Here 1964 35 min
Hugh MacDiarmid—A Portrait 1964 9 min

The Big Sheep 1966 40 min

A Pleasant Place 1969

On the Mountain 1974 34 min

Aerial 1974 4 min

Colour Poems 1974 12 min

Place of Work/tailpiece 1976 40 min

Some Changes 1981 22 min

The Look of the Place 1981 18 min

Land Makar 1981 32 min

Blue Black Permanent 1993

Trinh, Minh-ha T.

Reassemblage 1982 40 min, 16mm color (WMM)

Naked Spaces: Living Is Round 1985 135 min, 16mm color (WMM)

Surname Viet Given Name Nam 1989 108 min, 16mm color (WMM)

Shoot for the Contents 1991 101 min, 16mm color (WMM)

A Tale of Love 1995 108 min, 35mm color (WMM)

Vachon, Christine

The Way of the Wicked 1987 15 min, 16mm color

Poison [producer] 1991 85 min (available on home video)

Swoon [producer] 1992 95 min (available on home video)

Postcards From America [producer] 1994 93 min (available on home video)

Go Fish [executive producer] 1994 85 min (available on home video)

Safe [producer] 1995 105 min (available on home video)

Welbon, Yvonne

Monique 1991 3 min, 16mm B&W (TWN)

The Cinematic Jazz of Julie Dash 1992 27 min, color video (TWN, WMM)

Sisters in the Life: First Love 1993 30 min, video (TWN)

Missing Relations 1994 12 min, B&W video (TWN)

Remembering Wei Yi-fang, Remembering Myself: An Autobiography 1995 29
min, 16mm color (WMM)

Zimmerman, Debra

Why Women Stay [with Jacqueline Shortell-McSweeney] 1980 30 min, B&W
video (WMM)

Distributors	*Home Video Sales by Mail*
Canyon Cinema	Facets Multimedia
2325 Third Street #338	1517 West Fullerton Avenue
San Francisco, CA 94107	Chicago, IL 60614
telephone (415) 626-2255	1-800-331-6197
Frameline	Naiad Press (lesbian videos)
346 Ninth Street	P. O. Box 10543
San Francisco, CA 94103	Tallahassee, FL 32302
telephone (415) 703-8650	1-800-533-1973
fax (415) 861-1404	
	TLA Video
Video Data Bank	1520 Locust Street, Suite 200
School of the Art Institute of Chicago	Philadelphia, PA 19102
37 South Wabash Avenue	1-800-333-8521
Chicago, IL 60603	
telephone (312) 345-3550	Wolfe Video (lesbian and gay videos)
	P. O. Box 64
Third World Newsreel	New Almaden, CA 95042
335 West 38th Street, 5th floor	1-800-438-9653
New York, NY 10018	
telephone (212) 947-9277	
fax (212) 594-6417	
Women Make Movies	
462 Broadway, Suite 500	
New York, NY 10013	
telephone (212) 925-0606	
fax (212) 925-2052	

**Selected
Filmography**

Bibliography

Acker, Ally. *Reel Women: Pioneers of the Cinema, 1896 to the Present.* New York: Continuum, 1991.

Cole, Janis, and Holly Dale. *Calling the Shots: Profiles of Women Filmmakers.* Kingston, Ontario: Quarry Press, 1993.

Cook, Pam, and Philip Dodd, eds. *Women and Film: A Sight and Sound Reader.* Philadelphia: Temple University Press, 1993.

De Lauretis, Teresa. *Alice Doesn't: Feminism, Semiotics, and Cinema.* New York: Macmillan, 1985.

Fischer, Lucy. *Shot/Countershot: Film Tradition and Women's Cinema.* Princeton, New Jersey: Princeton University Press, 1989.

Flitterman-Lewis, Sandy. *To Desire Differently: Feminism and the French Cinema.* Chicago: University of Illinois Press, 1990.

Fregoso, Rosa Linda. *The Bronze Screen: Chicana and Chicano Film Culture.* Minneapolis: University of Minnesota Press, 1993.

Gamman, Lorraine, and Margaret Marshment, eds. *The Female Gaze: Women as Viewers of Popular Culture.* London: The Women's Press, 1988.

Gish, Lillian, with Ann Pinchot. *The Movies, Mr. Griffith and Me.* New York: Avon Books, 1969.

Haskell, Molly. *From Reverence to Rape: The Treatment of Women in the Movies,* 2nd ed. Chicago: The University of Chicago Press, 1987.

Holmlund, Chris, and Cynthia Fuchs, eds. *Between the Sheets, In the Streets: Queer, Lesbian, and Gay Documentary.* Minneapolis: University of Minnesota Press, 1997.

Kaplan, E. Ann, ed. *Psychoanalysis and Cinema.* New York: Routledge, 1990.

Kaplan, E. Ann. *Women and Film: Both Sides of the Camera.* New York: Methuen, 1983.

Kaplan, E. Ann, ed. *Women and Film Noir.* London: British Film Institute, 1980.

Kuhn, Annette, ed. *The Power of the Image: Essays on Representation and Sexuality.* New York: Routledge, 1985.

Kuhn, Annette. *Women's Pictures: Feminism and Cinema.* New York: Routledge, 1982.

Kuhn, Annette, with Susannah Radstone, eds. *Women in Film: An International Guide.* New York: Fawcett Columbine, 1990.

Lent, John A. *The Asian Film Industry.* Austin: University of Texas Press, 1990.

Mayne, Judith. *Directed by Dorothy Arzner.* Indianapolis: Indiana University Press, 1994.

Mayne, Judith. *The Woman at the Keyhole: Feminism and Women's Cinema.* Indianapolis: Indiana University Press, 1990.

Mellen, Joan. *Women and Their Sexuality in the New Film.* New York: Dell, 1973.

Murray, Raymond. *Images in the Dark: An Encyclopedia of Gay and Lesbian Film and Video.* New York: Plume/Penguin, 1996.

Olson, Jenni, ed. *The Ultimate Guide to Lesbian and Gay Film and Video.* New York: Serpent's Tail, 1996.

Penley, Constance, ed. *Feminism and Film Theory.* New York: Routledge/BFI Publishing, 1988.

Quart, Barbara Koenig. *Women Directors: The Emergence of a New Cinema.* New York: Praeger, 1988.

Rosen, Marjorie. *Popcorn Venus: Women, Movies, and the American Dream.* New York: Coward, McCann and Geoghegan, 1973.

Russo, John. *Making Movies: The Inside Guide to Independent Movie Production.* New York: Dell, 1989.

Russo, Vito. *The Celluloid Closet: Homosexuality in the Movies.* New York: HarperCollins, 1987.

Straayer, Chris. *Deviant Eyes, Deviant Bodies: Sexual Re-Orientation in Film and Video.* New York: Columbia University Press, 1996.

Vermilye, Jerry. *Ida Lupino.* New York: Pyramid, 1977.

Film Fatales

About the Authors

Judith M. Redding is a Philadelphia-based independent filmmaker. A graduate of the London International Film School, her films and videos include *Mondays,* winner of third prize/experimental in the 1994 Visions of U.S. Video Contest, and *but would you take her back?,* which won the 1996 Athena Award for outstanding experimental film. She is the film and video editor of *Curve* magazine, former associate editor of *Video Insider* magazine and her writing on film has appeared nationally in many magazines. She teaches video production and lives in Philadelphia.

Victoria A. Brownworth is a columnist for *Curve* magazine. Her *Philadelphia Daily News* column was nominated for a 1993 Pulitzer Prize and her writing appears in numerous publications including the *Philadelphia Inquirer,* the *New York Times,* the *Village Voice,* the *Nation,* the *Baltimore Sun,* the *Los Angeles Times* and *Spin.* She is the author of *Too Queer* (Firebrand, 1996) and the editor of *Night Bites* (Seal, 1996). She lives in Philadelphia.

Popular Culture Titles from Seal Press

Listen Up: *Voices from the Next Feminist Generation,* edited by Barbara Findlen. $14.95, 1-878067-61-3. For the first time, the voices of today's young feminists, the "Third Wave," are brought together to explore and reveal their lives. Topics include racism, sexuality, identity, AIDS, revolution, abortion and much more.

Dharma Girl: *A Road Trip Across the American Generations* by Chelsea Cain. $12.00, 1-878067-84-2. Written to the unmistakable beat of the road, this memoir chronicles the twenty-four-year-old author's homecoming to the Iowa commune where she grew up with her counterculture parents.

SurferGrrrls: *Look, Ethel! An Internet Guide for Us!* by Laurel Gilbert and Crystal Kile, with illustrations by Ellen Forney. $15.00, 1-878067-79-6. Calling all cyberchicks, wired women and girl geek wannabes as well as any woman ready to merge onto the digital freeway! This book will free you from the shackles of technophobia, reveal the secret history of women in computing, provide fabulous online resources for women and girls, and enhance your cyborg culture repertoire.

Night Bites: *Vampire Stories by Women,* edited by Victoria A. Brownworth. $12.95, 1-878067-71-0. Featuring sixteen original works, this subversive collection offers gothic atmosphere with a contemporary twist, scintillating writing and enough blood and lust to satisfy even the most discriminating connoisseurs.

She's a Rebel: *The History of Women in Rock & Roll* by Gillian G. Gaar. $16.95, 1-878067-08-7. Packed with interviews, facts, photos and personal anecdotes from women performers, writers and producers, *She's a Rebel* tells the fascinating story of the women who have shaped rock and pop music for the last five decades.

Wired Women: *Gender and New Realities in Cyberspace* edited by Lynn Cherny and Elizabeth Reba Weise. $16.00, 1-878067-73-7. A provocative and impassioned look at what woman are doing on the net—topics include handy hints for women who wish to avoid flames, women in media fandom, women's experiences in the gender-bending world of MUDs and online censorship.

Ordering Information: If you are unable to obtain a Seal Press title from a bookstore, please order from us directly. Checks, MasterCard and Visa are accepted. Enclose payment with your order and 16.5% of the book total for shipping and handling. Washington residents should add 8.6% sales tax. Send to: Orders Dept., Seal Press, 3131 Western Avenue, Suite 410, Seattle, Washington 98121. (800) 754-0271 orders only; (206) 283-7844 phone; (206) 285-9410 fax; sealprss@scn.org. Visit our website at www.sealpress.com.